VOCABULARY
FOR A NEW
WORLD

. . . .

VOCABULARY FOR A NEW WORLD

· · · ·

LINDA J. PALUMBO
Cerritos College

FRANK J. GAIK
Cerritos College

Macmillan Publishing Company
New York

Editor: Eben W. Ludlow
Production Supervisor: Jane O'Neill
Production Manager: Pamela Kennedy Oborski
Text and Cover Designer: Blake Logan
Cover illustration: Map image Copyright © 1990, Northern Cartographic, Inc., Burlington, Vermont. Used with permission.

This book was set in Meridien by Waldman Graphics, Inc., and was printed and bound by R. R. Donnelley & Sons. The cover was printed by Phoenix Color Corp.

Macmillan Publishing Company
866 Third Avenue, New York, New York 10022

Macmillan Publishing Company is part of
the Maxwell Communication Group of Companies.

Library of Congress Cataloging-in-Publication Data

Palumbo, Linda J.
    Vocabulary for a new world / Linda J. Palumbo, Frank J. Gaik.
        p.   cm.
    Includes index.
    ISBN 0-02-390567-0
    1. Vocabulary.   2. Learning and scholarship—Terminology.
    3. Universities and colleges—Curricula—Terminology.   I. Gaik,
    Frank J.   II. Title.
    PE1449.P28   1992
    428.1—dc20   91-19333
                            CIP

Printing: 4 5 6 7   Year: 7 8

PREFACE

. . . .

Vocabulary for a New World takes advantage of new advances in theories of learning and study skills, making extensive use of context cues, affective associations, and inference. We have included open-ended questions for critical reflection, classroom activities, and writing. More important, we have tried to integrate students' own interests and ideas into the text. Today's students, many of whom are now classified as "non-traditional," deserve the opportunity to use language to form and express their views. Students also have the right to demand that a vocabulary text enhance their cultural and cross-cultural literacy so that language can be explored as a means to bridge private experience and public issues. Respect for students—for their capacity to think, for their sense of humor, for their richly varied lives—is the informing principle of this volume.

Vocabulary for a New World carefully leads students from easier to harder exercises, questions, and readings, both within chapters and throughout the text as a whole. Even the easiest material, however, invites students to make judgments and amuse themselves. Chapters are consistent, so students will know what to expect, but supplementary material varies from chapter to chapter. Cartoons, illustrations, and anecdotes enliven even the most abstract discourse. We believe that the volume encourages browsing and that the students will be excited about what they learn. The material for this book has received extensive testing in college classrooms, having been compiled with the assistance of fellow educators across the disciplines as well as with advice from business people, technicians, and professionals in a variety of fields. Words were selected according to the following criteria: their frequency of use in textbooks, major periodicals, and "educated talk"; their conceptual depth; and their contribution to cultural or cross-cultural literacy.

Several special features characterize *Vocabulary for a New World*:

The Book

- Teaches students up to 1,000 words. Over 300 words are given entries, contexts, and exercises. Introductions to the readings present students with definitions of an additional 150 words, which they then encounter in context. Two chapters on word parts introduce students to 100 essential roots and over 500 words derived from them. Word-form exercises allow students to turn one new word into many.

- The *More Words* supplements for advanced learners include 300 additional words and 100 additional word parts and a hefty supplement from each of the academic disciplines.
- Words are grouped into domains to foster cognitive development as well as cultural and cross-cultural literacy.
- The chapter on name derivatives opens the book on a human note, drawing students into a language that is not simply an abstract system but also one infused with people and ideas.
- Separate chapters on using context and using the dictionary/thesaurus teach strategies for building active vocabulary outside the classroom.
- The chapters on word parts classify roots by topic rather than by language to build retention and reduce confusion.
- English is presented as an international, cross-cultural language.
- Attention is given to myth, arts, sciences, and history to enhance success in general education courses and to introduce concepts current in those fields.
- Politics, business, economics, law, and computers are treated so as to build practical competence in the real world.

Chapter Material

- Chapters may be used in or out of sequence; chapters are broken into sections that may be taught independently.
- Alphabetical master lists give instructors and students a quick overview of each chapter.
- Anecdotes and cartoons enliven the text while reinforcing key concepts.
- In addition to pronunciations and definitions, background information is provided on each word to spark interest and highlight relevant issues.
- Lighthearted narratives appear at intervals throughout each chapter. The narratives weave words from the section into more extended contexts. To encourage reading, some of the stories have surprise endings or unexpected themes.
- Each chapter includes a reading that is characteristic of college experience:

    1. selections from primary texts, such as Machiavelli's *The Prince*
    2. essays reprinted from journals such as the *Atlantic Monthly*
    3. extracts from recent books that are widely used in college, such as Richard Rodriguez's *Hunger of Memory*
    4. lecture notes from a typical college class
    5. extracts from college textbooks
    6. essays by prominent professionals

- Cultural and linguistic diversity adds interest to the readings.

Student Exercises

- Exercises are varied, from traditional true–false and matching to open-ended questions that involve the students in critical reflection while providing an affect-link, which educational research suggests is crucial to learning.
- *Yes–No–because* questions following entries provide immediate feedback and use inference to help deep processing.
- Exercises in word forms teach students to turn one word into many words.
- Substantial chapter reviews reinforce learning.
- Collaborative learning activities, questions for thought and discussion, and introductions to the readings provide for a lively classroom experience of vocabulary growth.
- Three writing assignments for each chapter are for a paragraph, a page, and a full essay, respectively, allowing maximum flexibility.
- Answer keys, at the back of each chapter, are easy to use and provide rationales for right answers.

Instructor's Manual

- A substantial *Instructor's Manual* provides chapter tests, a midterm and a final, answer keys, further suggestions for classroom activities and teaching strategies, practice with word forms and sentence completion, sample handouts, and sample answers to discussion and writing questions.

Acknowledgments

Many thanks are due to the talented writers, editors, and educators whose guidance helped shape this book: Dr. Naomi Barnett, Lorain County Community College; Fred S. Kai, El Camino College; Cindy Thompson, Northeast Louisiana University; Dr. Sebastian J. Vasta, Camden County Community College; and Linda Wong, Lane Community College. It was a privilege to work at Macmillan with Eben Ludlow, whose expertise is not only comprehensive but good-humored. We particularly appreciate the care taken by Wendy Conn, Jane O'Neill, and Kathy Pruno to ensure a readable, workable, and attractive text. We owe special thanks to colleagues at Cerritos: to Michael Ochoa and John Boyle for their expert guidance and to Lacreta Scott and Robert Chester for their enthusiastic support.

CONTENTS

• • • •

CHAPTER 6   Words of Emotion and Power   157

CHAPTER 7   Yes, It Is Your Business   183

Chapter 1

WHAT'S IN A NAME?

Quick Reference Word List

berserk	dunce	lynch	philistine
bloomers	fink	Machiavellian	puritanical
bowdlerize	galvanize	masochist	sadist
boycott	gerrymander	maudlin	tawdry
braille	guillotine	mausoleum	valentine
chauvinist	jim crow laws	maverick	vandalism
draconian	laconic	mesmerize	

Introduction: What Is an Eponym?

The first thing we learn is our name. As children we name a new pet, a toy, or an imaginary friend. As we grow older, we may help to name younger siblings. We never stop naming: we assign nicknames to loved ones, and sometimes we engage in that less pleasant practice of name-calling. If we choose names for our own children, we carefully select names that send the right message. Political parties and religions also appreciate the power of naming and choose names carefully. All the vocabulary words in this chapter started out as names of real people or groups. They are called eponyms. Sometimes the people were pleased to have their names take on new meanings. English is a living language, and names continue to form words. Perhaps some day students of vocabulary will be surprised to learn that the word *Reaganomics* had its origin in a real person.

I. Private Behavior

Some individuals and groups have given their names to expressions of emotion.

1. berserk [bir ZIRK]: frenzied, raging.

Berserk was the name of an ancient Scandinavian warrior famed for ferocious and wild bravery. Berserkers, warriors in this tradition, committed acts of raging destruction. To "go berserk" today is to become frenzied, usually in uncontrollable rage.

If you faced bad news calmly, would you go berserk?

Yes   No   because _____

. . . .

Have You Heard?
Who Is Adam?

In the Hebrew Bible, God formed the first person out of the dust of the ground. The first person had the right to name plants and animals. It was God who named the first person 'adham, from which we get the modern names Adam and Adie. The names mean "from the earth." Many people assume that 'adham was always a man's name. It was not: in the Bible the name is generic (neutral) until the first person is split into the first man and the first woman. What is the origin of your name? Consult reference books in the library or check baby-naming books at a local bookstore.

2. maudlin [MAUD lin]: tearfully sentimental.

The word *maudlin* is an old-fashioned pronunciation of (Mary) Magdalene, a woman whom painters often show weeping at the crucifixion of Jesus. Her sentimental grief often is contrasted with the quiet grief of Jesus' mother.

If you wept uncontrollably over a romantic movie, would you be maudlin?

Yes   No   because _____

3. laconic [luh KON ik]: brief, terse, concise, pithy.

The Laconians never wasted words. When invaded by the Persians and asked to surrender their weapons, the Laconians replied, "Come and get them." When told what would happen if they lost a battle, the Laconians responded with one word: "If."

If you took ten minutes to explain why you were two minutes late to dinner, would you be laconic?

Yes   No   because _____

4. valentine [VAL en tine]: a sweetheart chosen on Saint Valentine's Day, or a card sent to a love interest on that day.

Valentines may be laconic or maudlin, but let us hope they make no one berserk. Saint Valentine's Day is celebrated on February 14 in honor of a third-century Catholic martyr, but it started in older pagan love festivals. Valentine's name is found in love stories, such as the charming legend that he fell in love with his jailer's daughter and signed his farewell message to her, "From your Valentine."

If you sent your tax forms to the IRS on February 14, would they be valentines?

Yes   No   because _____

5. sadist [SAY dist]: one who gets pleasure, especially sexual pleasure, from hurting or mistreating others.

The Marquis de Sade was jailed for torturing a prostitute in eighteenth-century France. He lived riotously and died in an insane asylum. His philosophical novels describe violent sexual acts and have inspired controversy for two hundred years.

If your neighbors enjoyed torturing their pets, would they be sadists?

Yes   No   because _____

6. masochist [MASS oh kist]: one who gets pleasure, especially sexual pleasure, from being dominated or hurt by another person.

The old joke has it that a sadist is someone who is kind to a masochist. Leopold von Sacher-Masoch depicted lurid sexual scenes in his novels, which always featured a woman who liked to victimize her male "slaves." Sacher-Masoch himself signed contracts with women who agreed to behave like his characters.

If you left a relationship after your partner hurt you, would you be a masochist?

Yes   No   because _____

Matching: Match the definition with the vocabulary word.

A. ___ Brief, to the point.   (a) maudlin

B. ___ One who enjoys receiving pain.   (b) sadist

C. ___ Raging, frenzied.   (c) laconic

D. ___ One who enjoys giving pain.   (d) berserk

E. ___ Sadly sentimental.   (e) masochist

                                               (f) Adamic

True-False: Write "T" for true and "F" for false.

F. ____ The Laconians probably talked themselves to death.

G. ____ A maudlin valentine would make you cry.

H. ____ A prisoner would enjoy having a sadist for a jailer.

I. ____ It would be easy for a berserk person to be laconic.

J. ____ People who insist on working at jobs they hate might be called masochists.

Using Context: Fill in each blank with the vocabulary word that best suits the context.

Who Liked the Movie?

The ending of that movie was so sad and sentimental that it made my companions _____. Usually I can take anything without caring too much, but this time I got so angry at everyone's pointless tears that I nearly went _____. "Do you enjoy suffering?" I asked. "Does pain give you pleasure, like some kind of _____?" They told me that my response sounded cruel and that if I enjoyed abusing them so much I had to be a _____. My sweetheart, who was one of the group, mentioned that on February 14 I might have no _____. That brief statement might have been a _____ way to tell me that next time we all went to the movies I should be more tolerant of their emotional displays.

For Your Critical Reflection: Of the following types of people, who is tolerated in our present society, and who is not tolerated: maudlin, sadists, laconic, berserk, masochists? Why or why not?

_____

_____

II. Public Behavior

Other people have inspired the names of public actions.

7. maverick [MAV rick]: a person who acts independently by refusing to belong to any one group.

Samuel Maverick was a Texas cattle rancher who refused to brand his herd. When his cattle stampeded and mixed with neighboring herds, Maverick rounded them up and claimed all unbranded cattle as his own. So he gained by breaking a rule.

If you voted for a candidate just because everyone else voted that way, would you be a maverick?

Yes   No   because _____

8. bowdlerize [BAHD lir ize]: to remove supposedly offensive passages from a book, to expurgate.

Maverick refused to be bound by the rules of others; Thomas Bowdler wanted to bind others by his rules. In 1818 he published an edition of Shakespeare from which he removed all sexually explicit and religiously irreverent passages. Surprised but not daunted by critics, he went on to bowdlerize Gibbon's *Decline and Fall of the Roman Empire*. Bowdlerized editions of classic texts continue to be produced today.

If you read a "complete and unexpurgated" edition of a smutty story, would you have read a bowdlerized text?

Yes   No   because _____

9. boycott [BOY kot]: a joining together of people in refusal to transact business, usually as an act of protest.

Landlord Charles C. Boycott was suddenly left alone one day when he refused to lessen the hardships suffered by his Irish tenants. After his employees walked out, local farmers, shopkeepers, and even the postal carrier stopped dealing with the Boycott family, making it difficult to obtain food and services. Eventually the Boycotts had to leave Ireland. Now people boycott products or firms by doing the same thing—leaving them alone.

If you and your friends refused to buy a product because the company polluted the air, would you be participating in a boycott?

Yes   No   because _____

10. vandalism [VAN duhl izm]: willful, often malicious, destruction of property.

In the fifth century, the Vandals, an East Germanic tribe, invaded parts of Europe and northern Africa. They were notorious for demolishing works of art and precious monuments. In modern uses of the term, vandalism often refers to actions of mobs, gangs, or young pranksters who destroy property.

If your office windows were broken by strong winds in a hurricane, would your school have been vandalized?

Yes   No   because _____

11. lynch [LINCH]: the execution (usually hanging) of a person without a lawful trial.

Shortly after the American Revolution, Colonel William Lynch established a procedure whereby criminals who evaded the law were punished by a group of neighborhood men. The process quickly became abused: captives would be interrogated and beaten until they confessed, at which point punishment, often severe, would begin. Eventually, lynching came to be associated with the pursuit and killing of anyone who became the unlucky focal point of group hatred.

If you were sent to death row after your trial, would you have been lynched?

Yes   No   because _____

Matching: Match the definition with the vocabulary word.

K. ____ Execute without trial.   (a) vandalism

L. ____ Leave alone in protest.   (b) boycott

M. ____ Willful destruction of property.   (c) lynch

N. ____ One who refuses to act with the group.   (d) bowdlerize

O. ____ Remove offensive passages.   (e) maverick

                                                  (f) gibbonize

True-False: Write "T" for true and "F" for false.

P. ____ A lynch mob would be a welcome sight to any maverick.

Q. ____ A bowdlerized text contains all the words of the original.

R. ____ Most store owners would welcome people who wanted to vandalize their property.

S. ____ Mr. Maverick refused to brand his cows.

T. ____ If you wanted to boycott a company, you would purchase all its products.

Using Context: Fill in each blank with the vocabulary word that best suits the context.

Protest

I run the only bookstore left in the town of Centerville. All the other bookstores have become video rental shops, but I've always been something of a _____, so I still sell books. A group of protesters came in to say that *Romeo and Juliet* contains dirty passages and that I shouldn't sell it to children except in a _____ edition. I refused. They told me I'd eventually go broke if the whole town decided to _____ my store. A few people knocked some books onto the floor, which made me worry that they would commit some serious _____. One protester even had a rope, and for a moment I actually wondered if they planned to _____ me. However, they left peacefully, only saying that they would tell everyone not to read *Romeo and Juliet*. Funny thing, though—in two days I sold my entire stock of Shakespeare's books.

For Your Critical Reflection: Would you lead a boycott to protest a bowdlerized college textbook? Why or why not?

_____

_____

Doonesbury © 1988 G. B. Trudeau. Reprinted with permission of Universal Press Syndicate. All rights reserved.

III. Law and Politics

Sometimes the public actions to which people have given their names have had an impact on law or politics.

12. chauvinist [SHOH vin ist]: one who is fanatically devoted to one's nation, race, or sex, usually with contempt for others.

Nicholas Chauvin was a soldier in the army of the French Napoleon I. Chauvin became famous for his boisterous and unreasoning attachment to the lost cause of Napoleon's dreams of empire. Chauvin attracted ridicule for his fanaticism. The term *chauvinism* now seems to be used chiefly against men who insist on believing in male superiority.

If your brother pays his female employees the same wages as his male employees who do the same work, is he acting like a chauvinist?

Yes No because _____

13. jim crow laws [jim CROH lawz]: laws discriminating against or segregating black Americans.

Jim Crow was the stage name taken by Thomas Dartmouth Rice, a white actor who performed his song "Jump Jim Crow" in blackface. "Jim Crow" soon became a derisive term for black Americans. The various discriminatory and segregationalist laws created after 1890 were not abolished until the 1964 Civil Rights Act.

Are laws that permit busing for integration jim crow laws?

Yes   No   because _____

14. draconian [drah KOHN ee yuhn]: cruel and severe, usually inhumanly so. The word usually refers to laws or rules.

Jim crow laws often were draconian. Draco, an Athenian lawgiver who lived in the seventh century B.C., gave the death penalty for so many crimes that his name became a byword for severe but legal repression. The orator Demades said that Draco's code was written in blood.

If your friend were condemned to death for stealing a loaf of bread, would you be right in complaining about such draconian justice?

Yes   No   because _____

15. Machiavellian [MAK ee ah VELL ee yin]: favoring political cunning and dishonesty to foster arbitrary power.

Draconian laws might appeal to a Machiavellian ruler who wanted to remain in charge. Machiavelli was an Italian statesman in the sixteenth century who wrote *The Prince.* Many readers believed him to have been inspired by the devil, because Machiavelli tried to demonstrate that duplicity and cruelty could serve a ruler's interests better than straightforward kindness. Now the term often describes anyone willing to be ruthless to get ahead.

If your coworker told you personal secrets that could get him fired if others knew, would he be behaving like a Machiavellian?

Yes   No   because _____

16. gerrymander [GAIR ee man dir]: voting district(s) arranged to favor one party or candidate.

Machiavellian political leaders might welcome gerrymandering. Elbridge Gerry wanted to make sure that as many Jeffersonians as possible were elected from Massachusetts in the late eighteenth century. After he helped draw his Essex County district into an oddly long shape, one critic exclaimed, "Why, it's a salamander." Another responded, "No, it's a gerrymander." Because districts

. . . .

Guess What!
The Pygmalion Effect

Your name can influence the way people think about you.

In California, teachers who read essays written by Lisas, Karens, Davids, and Michaels assigned higher grades than they did to similar essays supposedly written by Berthas, Adeles, Elmers, and Huberts. If a taste for unusual names were to filter through the population, perhaps these expectations would be reversed.

This phenomenon itself has a name—"the Pygmalion effect"— named after a legendary Greek sculptor who fell in love with a statue he created. Pygmalion insisted that the statue be made human by the gods.

Robert Rosenthal discovered the Pygmalion effect. He found that children actually do better in school if their teachers have been told that the class is "bright," regardless of the real previous records of the students. And students actually do worse if teachers expect them to be slow. The Pygmalion story reminds us of how our images of others can affect their lives and our own.

need to have approximately the same number of people but may have any size or shape, we still hear accusations of gerrymandering.

If the Democrats, the Republicans, and the smaller parties all are satisfied with the outline of your district, has there been a gerrymander?

Yes   No   because _____

Matching: Match the definition with the vocabulary word.

U. ____ Crafty in order to get power.   (a) mandarin

V. ____ Inhumanly cruel or severe.   (b) Machiavellian

W. ____ Laws that segregated.   (c) draconian

X. ____ Fanatical lover of one's group.   (d) chauvinist

Y. ____ Unfair voting district.   (e) gerrymander

                                                         (f) jim crow laws

True-False: Write "T" for true and "F" for false.

Z. ____ Male chauvinists would be the first people to vote for a woman for president.

a. ____ Gerrymandered districts often do not fairly express the wishes of the voters.

b. ____ People who are loyal to their friends even if they suffer for it probably are Machiavellian.

c. ____ Jim crow laws promote integration.

d. ____ Those who favor draconian justice would impose overly harsh penalties even for minor crimes.

Using Context: Fill in each blank with the vocabulary word that best suits the context.

Nightmare

Last night I dreamt I'd been transported to a terrible society. The governor had been unfairly elected and got in only because the district was a

_____. He was not trustworthy, either, probably because

in order to get ahead he had behaved in _____ ways. For

example, he hired mostly women to work for him and then passed a law

that prevented women from being paid to work in politics. I guess he

needed money to pay a lot of bribes. None of the men protested. I won-

dered whether they really were _____, or whether they

were just scared. After all, free speech was no longer tolerated, and punish-

ments for breaking any of the new laws were _____.

Everyone was subject to segregation based on the old

_____, and crossing the wrong boundaries could mean a

charge of treason. I was very glad to wake up.

For Your Critical Reflection: Which would be the most unjust society in which to live—one with gerrymandering, jim crow laws, or draconian laws? Why? Can all three exist in one society? How?

_____

_____

IV. New Technology

People who create, discover, or popularize objects (or methods) often see their names endure as well. Sometimes, as with the guillotine, the person wishes the object could have been called something—anything—else.

17. bloomers [BLOOM irz]: loose, baggy underpants or trousers gathered at the bottom, worn by girls or women.

In nineteenth-century America women wore large, long skirts that made it difficult to walk through the streets. Amelia Bloomer used her influence as a magazine editor to popularize a pantaloon costume that came to be associated with her name. "Those who have tried it will very likely soon end their career in a lunatic asylum, or, perchance, in the State prison," wrote one critic. Today women often wear slacks, bloomers being one variety.

Would swimming be easier in a bathing suit than in bloomers?

Yes   No   because _____

18. guillotine [GIL uh teen]: an instrument for beheading people with the fall of a heavy blade.

Joseph Guillotin only wanted to help the causes of democracy and humanity when he advocated the use of the blade for executions: in eighteenth-century France, aristocrats used to die by the sword and peasants by hanging. Decapitation for all would be swift and merciful, he argued. He struggled to avoid the association of his name with the machine. After his death, his children changed their names legally.

If you called Joseph Guillotin a sadist, would he agree?

Yes   No   because _____

19. braille [BRALE]: a system of writing in which letters are encoded as raised dots to be felt by the fingertips of the blind.

Another Frenchman, Louis Braille, invented a system in 1824 that would change lives. Braille, blinded at the age of three, was only fifteen when he developed the code of raised dots that simplified writing and reading for the blind.

If you were blind, would road signs in braille help you to drive?

Yes   No   because _____

20. mesmerize [MEZ mir ize]: to hypnotize or put into a trancelike state.

Franz Anton Mesmer studied medicine, philosophy, and law in eighteenth-century Vienna. When he used rhythmic movements of body and objects to induce trances in his patients, the world was intrigued and scandalized. Was he a fake? Patients thronged around him, but the scientific community refused to accept his theories. After his death, one of his pupils identified and named *mesmerism*. Today one can be "mesmerized" if attention is held in a nearly hypnotic state.

If a stranger were so busy staring at you that she or he did not notice a major earthquake, might you think you had mesmerized that person?

Yes   No   because _____

21. galvanize [GAL vun ize]: to shock, excite, or stimulate, as if by electric shock.

Luigi Galvani was a professor of anatomy in eighteenth-century Italy. One story has it that he was preparing a frogs' legs dinner for his wife when he accidentally shocked a dead frog with electricity. The muscles of the frog jumped, making Galvani wonder what effect electricity could have on the body. Others went so far as to wonder if electric shock could restore life to the dead. Mary Shelley's *Frankenstein* is about a corpse galvanized into life. Now people are galvanized whenever they are suddenly excited into action.

If you had always been laconic but were shocked into lengthy speech by a marriage proposal, would that proposal have galvanized you?

Yes   No   because _____

22. mausoleum [MAW zuh lee um]: a lavish tomb.

Both before and after galvanism offered the hope that the dead could be restored to life, living people have had to both honor and dispose of the deceased. King Mausolus of Caria died in the fourth century B.C. His wife Artemisia, who inherited the throne, had sculptors compete for the design of her husband's tomb. The resulting mausoleum was one of the Seven Wonders of the ancient world. Today people respectfully refer to a real tomb as a mausoleum, but a humorous use of the word *mausoleum* also exists to describe any ornate but tediously decorated room.

Would you call the average hamburger stand a mausoleum?

Yes   No   because _____

Matching: Match the definition with the vocabulary word.

e. ____ Loose pants gathered at the bottom.   (a) braille

f. ____ Raised dots for the blind to read.   (b) guillotine

g. ____ To excite as if by shock.   (c) bloomers

h. ____ To hypnotize or put into a trance.   (d) mausoleum

i. ____ A lavish tomb.   (e) galvanize

j. ____ An instrument for beheading.   (f) mesmerize

                                                     (g) hypnotize

True-False: Write "T" for true and "F" for false.

k. ____ Most people like to go to the guillotine for their birthdays.

l. ____ The invention of braille made reading easier for many blind people.

m. ____ Bloomers were worn by conservative dressers in the nine-teenth century.

n. ____ If you were mesmerized until something galvanized you, you suddenly stopped being mesmerized.

o. ____ If you see a real mausoleum, you can be sure that someone wanted to honor a person who had died.

Using Context: Fill in each blank with the vocabulary word that best suits the context.

Chopping Heads

"How many heads are we chopping today?" my mother asked. "I'd better sharpen that blade if we have more than ten." I knew we had at least fifteen, so a perfect blade would be needed. The rhythmic sound of my mother's sharpening lulled me, making me cease my work as if _____. I could just imagine the smashing of that killing machine I'd heard so much about, the _____. Suddenly I

was shocked by the entrance of a little girl wearing _____,
whose appearance _____ me into action. I knew I had a
lot to do. I took the little girl's hand and led her into a room that had not
been used for years. It was cold, dark, and loaded with curious objects from
a dreadful past. "Do I have to wait in this _____?" she
asked. "It is so dark in here that the only books I could read would have to
be in _____." I assured her that, fortunately, the wait
would be very short. I slowly returned to my mother to see if the sharpening had been completed. It had been. "We are behind," she said, "and you
had better hurry, or you will never chop all that lettuce in time for the
school picnic."

For Your Critical Reflection: The guillotine was developed during the French
Revolution in response to J. I. Guillotin's call for "humane execution." Last
used in France in 1791, it was abolished along with the death penalty in
1981. Can (or should) there be a humane execution? What are the qualities
of a humane execution?

_____

_____

V. Insults

Plenty of perfectly fine people have suffered the fate of having their names
associated with evil, stupidity, intolerance, or tastelessness. Let us hope that
you fare better than the people listed below.

23. dunce [DUNS]: a stupid person, one who cannot learn.

Friar Elias Duns, known as Duns Scotus, was one of the most well-known
scholars of the Middle Ages. It was Duns Scotus who created the doctrine of
the Immaculate Conception of Mary. He was even known as the "Subtle Doctor." After his death his followers stuck narrowly to his hair-splitting old arguments, refusing to change with the times. Thus "dunce" came to mean someone who *would* not, then someone who *could* not, learn new ideas.

If you got the best grade in the class, would you be a dunce?

Yes   No   because _____

24. fink [FIHNGK]: an informer or a strikebreaker.

Some authorities say that Fink was the last name of a notorious strikebreaker. Others say that the word derived from "Pinks," as the Pinkerton detectives were called. The Pinks helped control and inform on strikers during the American union movement of the 1890s. Today anyone is a fink who sides with authority figures rather than with coworkers, other children, or members of any group to which the person belongs. In 1974 residents of Fink, Texas, hosted National Fink Week. People named Fink came from all over the country to help rescue the name from its bad reputation.

If your son gets angry at your daughter for eating the last cookie, would he be correct to call her a fink?

Yes   No   because _____

25. philistine [FILL us teen]: someone who smugly lacks culture and taste.

The original Philistines lived in Palestine from 1000 B.C. and frequently battled Israelites for control of the land. Israelites looked down on the Philistines, and the feeling probably was mutual. The Victorian English writer Matthew Arnold adapted the term to characterize middle-class people who were narrowly conventional in their tastes. Such attitudes, Arnold believed, hampered the development of culture.

If you learn as much as you can about art and music, are you a philistine?

Yes   No   because _____

26. tawdry [TAW dree]: cheap and showy, usually used to describe finery.

Saint Audrey did dress up in her younger days as Princess Ethelreda of East Anglia, but her taste did not give us this word. Leaving her husband, Ethelreda founded a monastery, where she was abbess until her death. Saint Audrey's fair was held annually for many centuries in England. The gaudy lace neckpieces and trinkets that were sold as souvenirs were named after the saint, whose name often was pronounced "tawdry."

Is that simple strand of real pearls you bought last year tawdry?

Yes   No   because _____

27. puritanical [pyir ih TAN ih kul]: overly strict in morals, usually with a religious overtone.

The Puritans wanted to purify the Church of England in the sixteenth and seventeenth centuries. Their intolerance made them difficult to live with, so they came to America. Although the Puritans were strict in morals, they did not dislike sex. As long as sexual pleasure took place within the confines of marriage, Puritans happily supported it. Nevertheless, the term is most often used today to describe people who are overly strict in sexual morals.

Would someone call you a puritanical person for attending a lot of wild parties?

Yes   No   because _____

Matching: Match the definition with the vocabulary word.

p. ____ Cheap and showy.   (a) fink

q. ____ Overly strict in morals.   (b) philistine

r. ____ A stupid person.   (c) dunce

s. ____ An informer.   (d) tawdry

t. ____ Someone lacking in taste.   (e) puritanical

                                             (f) Pinkerton

True-False: Write "T" for true and "F" for false.

u. ____ Most puritanical people wear a lot of tawdry jewelry—and nothing else.

v. ____ A philistine might object to an unusual work of art even though the work itself was excellent.

w. ____ People who cross picket lines to take the jobs of striking workers often are called finks by strikers.

x. ____ Although he was a fine scholar, Duns Scotus has given us the word *dunce,* used to indicate stupidity.

y. ____ A philistine and a puritan probably would agree that art should inspire, not confuse.

Using Context: Fill in each blank with the vocabulary word that best suits the context.

Happy Birthday

"Isn't that jewelry beautiful? And there's so much of it!" exclaimed my sister, when she opened her first birthday present. I thought it was wonderfully polite of her to hide her disappointment when she received such

_____ finery instead of the sheet music she requested.

But some of our relatives are _____ compared with my

elegant sister. One uncle, who is very strict and _____ ,

gave a donation to charity in my sister's name instead of giving her a gift.

My sister was gracious, as always, even when our uncle said, "I knew you

wouldn't want a gift for yourself, because your brother told me so." What?

Me? Surely my sister knows I'd never be such a _____ as

to try to win over our uncle at her expense. After the party I asked her the

secret of her politeness. She said, "In the long run I get more presents by

being polite than I would get by being rude. Because I like presents, I

would have to be a _____ not to be nice." And I had al-

ways thought it was the kindness of her heart.

For Your Critical Reflection: What strategies would you give a person who was in danger of becoming one of the following: fink, philistine, dunce, or puritan?

_____

_____

Chapter Review

I. Yes-No Questions

1. Carl Sandburg said, "The greatest cunning is to have none at all." Would Machiavellians be interested in this information?

   Yes   No   because _____

2. Françoise Sagan says, "I like men to behave like men—strong and childish." Is Sagan making fun of men who are chauvinistic?

   Yes   No   because _____

3. Would a society with draconian justice, jim crow laws, and a guillotine be a free society?

    Yes   No   because _____

4. Might a fink call your gift tawdry?

    Yes   No   because _____

5. Would a dunce recognize Machiavellian tricks?

    Yes   No   because _____

6. Would most people prefer to be galvanized or mesmerized rather than vandalized?

    Yes   No   because _____

7. Would a person who went crazy after breaking a pencil be berserk?

    Yes   No   because _____

8. Would a philistine like sado-masochistic art?

    Yes   No   because _____

9. Would most sadists prefer a lynching to a valentine?

    Yes   No   because _____

10. Would a Machiavellian praise a gerrymander?

    Yes   No   because _____

11. Are you more likely to have maudlin emotions at a funeral than during a math test?

    Yes   No   because _____

12. Would someone who wanted to bowdlerize the Bible be a maverick?

    Yes   No   because _____

13. Would a laconic person be talkative?

    Yes   No   because _____

14. Is braille designed only for the puritanical?

    Yes   No   because _____

15. Are lynch mobs and jim crow laws draconian?

    Yes   No   because _____

16. Would a vandal protect mausoleums?

    Yes   No   because _____

17. Would a masochist fall in love with a sadist?

Yes   No   because _____

18. Would a puritanical person rather see bloomers than bikinis on the beach?

Yes   No   because _____

II. Using Context: Use the word list at the beginning of the chapter to fill in the blanks. You might not use all the words, or you might use one word more than once.

Valentine's Day

It was February 14. I knew that my beloved never wanted to see me again,

but I wanted to send a _____ anyway. You may think

I am stupid. You may think I like to suffer. But even if I am a

_____ or a _____, as you think, and as

my beloved seems to think, I still was determined to express my undying

love on that special day. You see, I cherish a kind of ideal love in my heart:

I could dream for hours over a snapshot I'd taken of my beloved last April

Fool's Day. I could stare at that picture for hours, _____

by every feature on that dear face. Yes, I just had to get the perfect card.

I gazed at the hundreds of cards in the row before me. That lacy one

with the fake gold trim and plastic beadwork looked too

_____ for my taste. But there were plenty more.

There were sexist cards for male _____,

_____ cards with only a few choice words on them,

_____ cards for weepy and sentimental types, cards in

_____ for the blind, and even very unusual cards for

_____ who wouldn't run with any crowds. In a corner I

saw stiff, moral, dull cards for the _____ at heart. But

where was the card for me? What would my beloved think if I remained

silent on this day? Finally, I found it. It said, "I may be a philistine, but I

would love to spend eternity in a mausoleum with you." How beautiful!

III. **Practice with Word Forms:** Fill in each blank with the proper form of the word.

A. *chauvinist, chauvinistic, chauvinism:* Patriotism, defined as a love of one's country for its good points, is a time-honored virtue, but _____, which makes a person blind to a country's faults or problems, does a nation little good. The _____ citizen refuses to hear any criticism of the country and therefore takes no part in improving it; the _____ will not tolerate a slight to a nation's name, flag, or history.

B. *philistine, philistinism:* Just as a chauvinist only wants to hear the best about a country or group, the _____ appreciates art only if it comforts the afflicted, honors tradition, and uplifts the best of humanity. The daring artist who explores the more unseemly side of life will always be rejected, if not downright abused, when a culture is dominated by _____.

C. *masochist, masochistic, masochism:* Philosophers and psychologists have always been fascinated by the phenomenon of _____. Why would a person deliberately suffer pain? What benefit does the _____ derive from suffering? Can the horrors and cruelty of the world be partially blamed on the _____ tendencies of people?

Reading for Chapter 1

NICCOLO MACHIAVELLI

The Prince

The first people who read Niccolo Machiavelli's The Prince *thought he was inspired by the devil. But Machiavelli did not set out to be evil. Nor did he recommend evil behavior unless it was used to promote a stable state. Machiavelli simply wanted to change the foundation of political ethics from ''What should be'' to ''What is''—in other words, from idealism to realism. Sixteenth-century Italy was organized (or disorganized) into city-states often torn by strife from within and without. Machiavelli, like many Europeans of his day, saw France as the ideal state: Francis I had created unity and stability. From Machiavelli's viewpoint, his success came from being clever, not from being good. Machiavelli is the first to admit that the power of rulers is based less on whether they are good than whether people* thought *they were good. In this passage, Machiavelli explains the advantage to rulers who know ''how to play the fox.''*

Words to Notice

Prepare for the reading by reviewing the following key words:

candor: honesty

regard: care

pledges: promises

to resort to: to rely on

antiquity: ancient history (here Homer and Virgil)

allegorically: by means of fables and symbols

nurtured: reared

snares: traps

bearing of the lion: acting courageously

operative: useful

precept: advice

dissembler: one who lies

IN WHAT WAY PRINCES SHOULD KEEP THEIR WORD

1   How praiseworthy it is that a prince keeps his word and governs by candor instead of craft, everyone knows. Yet the experience of our own time shows that those princes who had little regard for their word and had the craftiness to turn men's minds have accomplished great things and, in the end, have overcome those who governed their actions by their pledges.

2   You must recognize that there are two ways of fighting: by means of law, and by means of force. The first belongs properly to man, the second to animals; but since the first is often insufficient, it is necessary to resort to the second. Therefore, a prince must know how to use both what is proper to man and what is proper to beasts. The writers of antiquity taught rulers this lesson allegorically when they told how Achilles and many other ancient princes were sent to be nurtured by Chiron the centaur, so that he would train them in his discipline. Their having a creature half-man and half-beast as tutor only means that a prince must know how to use both the one and the other nature, and that the one without the other cannot endure.

3   Since a prince, then, is required to know how to assume a beastlike nature, he must adopt that of the fox and that of the lion; for a lion is defenseless against snares, and a fox is defenseless against wolves. Hence a prince ought to

be a fox in recognizing snares and a lion in driving off wolves. Those who assume the bearing of the lion alone lack understanding. It follows, then, that a wise prince cannot and should not keep his pledge when it is against his interest to do so and when his reasons for making the pledge are no longer operative. If all men were good, this would be a bad precept, but since they are evil and would not keep a pledge to you, then you need not keep yours to them. Nor did a prince ever lack legitimate reasons by which to color his bad faith. One could cite a host of modern examples and list the many peace treaties, the many promises that were made null and void by princes who broke faith, with the advantage going to the one who best knew how to play the fox. But one must know how to mask this nature skillfully and be a great dissembler. Men are so simple and so much inclined to obey immediate needs that a deceiver will never lack victims for his deception. Of recent examples proving this, there is one I will not omit. Pope Alexander VI never gave thought to anything but deception and never lacked someone on whom to practice it. There never was a man who made promises more persuasively or swore to them more solemnly and kept so few of them as he. Yet his tricks always brought the results he desired, for he knew this side of the world well.

Questions for Class Discussion

1. Are there people you know who still practice Machiavellian principles?
2. Under what conditions should a leader break a pledge?
3. What is the best way for a people to respond to a Machiavellian leader?

Making a New World

For Class Discussion

1. Which of the discoveries or actions named in this chapter has most benefited the world? Why? Which do you believe the world could live without? Why?
2. If you were hiring people for your organization, which kinds of people would you hire? Why?
3. If you could have your name remembered for any accomplishment you can dream of, what would it be? (Lisa Cole might dream of discovering a Cole vaccine to prevent cancer.)

Collaborative Learning

1. What's in your name?
   Purpose: To understand the various reasons for our names.

    A. Introduce yourself to members of your group by sharing how you got your name or anecdotes about your name ("I am Candace, named after an Ethiopian queen in the Bible").

    B. Make a list of the three most common ways that people get their names.

    C. Report to the class, letting your scribe introduce team members and their stories.

2. Who am I?

Purpose: To be able to identify the features of people described in the vocabulary words.

    A. Write a brief description of a person or object that embodies or expresses one of the words from the chapter. The word itself should not be mentioned. The description ends with "Who am I?" or "What am I?" (For example: "I do not smoke, drink, or dance. I believe the body is sacred and should be covered, not exposed. The world is sinful, and my job is to live purely and to insist that others live as I do." Who am I?[1])

    B. Select a reporter to read your riddle to the class.

    C. Ask the class to guess the answer.

Ideas for Writing

1. In a paragraph, describe someone you know who is a maverick, a sadist, a masochist, a dunce, or a philistine.

2. In a page, write a letter to someone you know who tends to behave in ways that are maudlin, Machiavellian, or puritanical. Explain what the word means and give advice to help the person reform.

3. At home, look up in an encyclopedia the person who most interests you from this chapter. Write one paragraph giving more detailed information and explaining why you find the person interesting.

More Words for Chapter 1

bowie knife: a type of large knife with a heavy guard (invented by James Bowie)

Bunsen burner: a laboratory burner (invented by Robert Wilhelm Bunsen)

Casanova: an unprincipled and profligate male lover (the memoirs of Giovanni Giacomo Casanova)

Cyrillic alphabet: the alphabet used in the USSR and other countries (named for Saint Cyril, Greek missionary)

[1] *Answer:* a puritan.

decibel: a unit of sound measurement (after Alexander Graham Bell)

derrick: part of a support structure of an oil rig (derived from a kind of gallows named after a sixteenth-century executioner named Derrick)

doily: small lace or cut paper mat (from a textile merchant named Dolly)

epicure: one who believes that pleasure is life's highest good (from the Greek philosopher Epicurus, whose theory was somewhat different)

Ferris wheel: a large upright wheel with cars for passengers (invented by George Washington Gale Ferris)

Frisbee: a plastic disk tossed between players (named for the Frisbe Pie Company)

guy: slang and informal for a person (after Guy Fawkes, who tried to blow up Parliament in London in 1605)

macadam: road paving made of layered stones (after John Loudon McAdam)

Molotov cocktail: a bottle filled with flammable liquid with cloth to serve as the fuse (after Vyacheslav Molotov, a minister of the USSR in the 1940s)

nicotine: the active drug in tobacco (after Jean Nicot, who first brought tobacco to France)

pasteurization: the heating of milk or other beverages to kill microbes (discovered by Louis Pasteur)

Pyrrhic victory: a win—but at a great cost (after King Pyrrhus of Epirus)

ritzy: luxurious (after the hotel magnate, Cesar Ritz)

saxophone: a musical instrument (invented by Antoine Joseph Sax)

zeppelin: an airship (developed by Count Ferdinand von Zeppelin)

Answer Key to Chapter 1

I. PRIVATE BEHAVIOR

Yes-No Questions

1. No; you would be calm.
2. Yes; maudlin people weep.
3. No; your speech was lengthy.
4. No; you cannot be a lover to the IRS.
5. Yes; they enjoyed the pain of others.
6. No; you would be fleeing from pain.

Matching

A. (c) B. (e) C. (d) D. (b) E. (a)

True-False

F. F G. T H. F I. F J. T

**Using Context: Who Liked
the Movie?**

maudlin, berserk, masochist, sadist,
valentine, laconic

II. PUBLIC BEHAVIOR

Yes-No Questions

7. No; you now run with the
   crowd.
8. No; a complete text is now
   bowdlerized.
9. Yes; boycotters do not patronize.
10. No; natural forces are not willful.
11. No; you had a trial.

Matching

K. (c) L. (b) M. (a) N. (e)
O. (d)

True-False

P. F Q. F R. F S. T T. F

Using Context: Protest

maverick, bowdlerized, boycott, vandalism, lynch

III. LAW AND POLITICS

Yes-No Questions

12. No; he is paying them equally.
13. No; they do not segregate.

14. Yes; it is severe punishment for a
    minor crime.
15. No; she is trusting you.
16. No; no one party is favored.

Matching

U. (b) V. (c) W. (f) X. (d)
Y. (e)

True-False

Z. F a. T b. F c. F d. T

Using Context: Nightmare

gerrymander, Machiavellian, chauvinists, draconian, jim crow laws

IV. NEW TECHNOLOGY

Yes-No Questions

17. Yes; bloomers are loose and
    baggy.
18. No; the guillotine was designed
    to be painless.
19. No; you could not touch them
    while driving.
20. Yes; the person was frozen.
21. Yes; it energized you out of
    silence.
22. No; it is not lavishly decorated.

Matching

e. (c) f. (a) g. (e) h. (f) i. (d)
j. (b)

True-False

k. F l. T m. F n. T o. T

Using Context: Chopping Heads

mesmerized, guillotine, bloomers, galvanized, mausoleum, braille

V. INSULTS

Yes-No Questions

23. No; you would not be stupid.
24. No; she had not sided with authority.
25. No; you had learned much about art.
26. No; it is not cheap and showy.
27. No; a puritanical person would not attend.

Matching

p. (d) q. (e) r. (c) s. (a) t. (b)

True-False

u. F v. T w. T x. T y. T

Using Context: Happy Birthday

tawdry, philistines, puritanical, fink, dunce

REVIEW

I. Yes-No Questions

1. Yes; cunning is important to Machiavellians.
2. Yes; chauvinistic men want to be manly.
3. No; these items suggest a harsh society.
4. Yes; a fink might be willing to hurt you.
5. No; dunces are stupid.
6. Yes; vandalism damages things.
7. Yes; a broken pencil should be no big deal.
8. No; philistines do not take risks with art.
9. Yes; sadists enjoy seeing others suffer.
10. Yes; Machiavellians manipulate rules to get ahead.
11. Yes; funerals are sad.
12. Yes; most people see no need to do this.
13. No; laconic people use few words.
14. No; braille is for the blind.
15. Yes; both are harsh and unjust.
16. No; vandals destroy property.
17. Yes; one enjoys feeling pain and the other enjoys causing or seeing pain.
18. Yes; bloomers are more modest.

II. Using Context: Valentine's Day

valentine, dunce, masochist, mesmerized, tawdry, chauvinists, laconic, maudlin, braille, mavericks, puritanical

III. Practice with Word Forms

A. chauvinism, chauvinistic, chauvinist
B. philistine, philistinism
C. masochism, masochist, masochistic

Chapter 2

USING CONTEXT

Quick Reference Word List

acquisition	cultural literacy	mnemonic	punctuation cues
active	deep processing	devices	root word
vocabulary	definition cues	parallelism	association
affect	discourse	parenthetical	rote memorization
association	example cues	remarks	success hypothesis
context	input hypothesis	passive	visual association
context cues	italics cues	vocabulary	"W" markers
contrast cues	learning	pronoun cues	word association

Introduction: Using Context

By the time you were ten years old you already knew over twenty thousand words. That means you learned over two thousand words a year! How did you learn them? Did you use a dictionary? Did you use flash cards? Did your parents stick name tags to household objects? No, you learned these words by paying attention to how they were used. You learned the words from *context*. Using context remains the best way to learn new words. Most adults learn only about two hundred to five hundred new words a year. But people who learn to use context continue to learn thousands of words a year. In this chapter, you will learn to reawaken your childhood strategies for learning from context. You will also learn several ways to study and learn vocabulary.

1. To Acquire or Learn?

What's the best way to learn vocabulary? There is no right answer. Each person is different. In this section, we provide you with a variety of techniques for adding to your vocabulary.

1. **success hypothesis** [suk SESS heye POTH uh SISS]: the idea that vocabulary is the key to success.

"Your boss knows more words than you. That's why she's your boss." Vocabulary is more important to the success of executives than education, intelligence, or social class, according to a famous study by Johnson O'Connor (see the reading for this chapter). People still debate about O'Connor's ideas: does vocabulary help success, or does success help vocabulary?

. . . .

Have You Heard?
Mnemosyne, the Goddess of Memory

The ancient Greeks respected memory so much that they personified memory as a goddess. Her name was Mnemosyne [nee MAHS uh nee]—the mother of all the arts. We now refer to devices or tricks to aid the memory as mnemonics [nee MON iks]. The ancients had several tricks for remembering, especially when they had to give long speeches without notes. One favorite trick for memory was called "place mnemonics." Teachers of oratory such as Aristotle and Cicero taught their students to imagine their long speeches as a journey through their house. Thus, each room becomes a major argument or section and each table, chair, or painting becomes a subpoint or example. To remember your speech, you took yourself through a mental tour of your own house, just as a museum guide might lead you through a museum.

The modern theories of memory came from the seventeenth-century philosopher John Locke. Locke believed that we are born ignorant. He called our minds a *tabula rasa,* or blank slate. What we know is a collection of bits of knowledge. To remember, you must associate, or link, ideas together. To improve your memory, then, you must establish a conscious habit of improving what the mind does "naturally," associating one idea with another.

If you believed in the success hypothesis, would you probably study vocabulary seriously?

Yes   No   because _____

2. passive vocabulary [PASS iv voh KAB yoo LAIR ee]: the words you can recognize when you listen or read.

We all have four vocabularies: (1) listening, (2) reading, (3) speaking, and (4) writing. Your passive vocabulary consists of words you understand when others use them, even though you are not likely to use them yourself.

Does your passive vocabulary allow you to use all the words you can read?

Yes   No   because _____

3. active vocabulary [AK tiv voh KAB yoo LAIR ee]: the words you use frequently when you speak or write.

Your active vocabulary depends on the situation. You use different words when you talk to friends, teachers, ministers, or judges. Most active vocabulary is learned by imitation. Your active vocabulary is always smaller than your passive one.

Would you need a large and precise active vocabulary if you never spoke or wrote?

Yes   No   because _____

4. acquisition [ACK wih ZIH shun]: the natural, unconscious way to learn.

Most ten-year-olds know twenty thousand words. They did not learn them by conscious effort. They "acquired" them. Linguists believe that "acquisition" occurs naturally when you pay attention to the meanings of words that you read and hear. You can acquire words all your life. One method is to select a field of interest and immerse yourself in it: take classes, read articles, attend lectures, join a club or organization, or rent videos.

If you do not acquire words by a certain age, can you ever acquire them?

Yes   No   because _____

5. input hypothesis [IN put heye POTH uh SISS]: linguist Stephen Krashen's theory that you get most of your language skills—including vocabulary—from reading or listening, not from study and practice.

According to Professor Krashen, when you listen and read—especially when you do it for pleasure—you learn almost everything you need to know about language, from spelling and punctuation rules to how to explain ideas. Improving vocabulary means improving your input (reading and listening).

According to the input hypothesis, do you have to practice your writing to acquire vocabulary?

Yes   No   because _____

6. deep processing [DEEP PRAHS ehss ng]: a deep intellectual or emotional understanding of a concept.

We memorize some things for a moment, others for a test, and others for a lifetime. Long-term memory requires deep processing—an intellectual or emotional commitment to a word or concept. Deep processing comes mostly from deliberate study or passionate debate about a concept.

Will flash cards help you with deep processing?

Yes   No   because _____

7. cultural literacy [KULT er ul LITT er uh see]: knowledge shared by members of a community or culture.

In 1983, E. D. Hirsch introduced the idea of "cultural literacy." Hirsch said that reading requires more than a large vocabulary; you also need to know history and culture. Hirsch's idea is controversial because we all inhabit different cultures and perhaps "cross-cultural literacy"—knowledge of cultures different from our own—is equally valuable. In college, both types of cultural literacy are needed. If you lack historical background, sometimes a desk encyclopedia can be as useful as a dictionary.

Test your cultural literacy in the following passage. (Your teacher may ask you to use a dictionary or encyclopedia.)

> In the early or mid-seventies—with OPEC and with President Nixon's "floating" of the dollar—the world economy changed from being international to transnational.
>
> [Peter Drucker, *The New Realities*]

Would knowing what OPEC or Nixon's "floating dollar" means help you to understand what transnational means?

Yes   No   because _____

Matching: Match the definition with the vocabulary word.

A. ____The natural and unconscious mode of increasing vocabulary.

(a) success hypothesis

B. ____The words you can use precisely when writing or speaking.

(b) passive vocabulary

C. ____The theory that you learn most from reading and listening.

(c) active vocabulary

D. ____The words you can recognize when reading or listening.

(d) acquisition

E. ____The theory that vocabulary is the key to success.

(e) cultural literacy

F. ____The way that you understand a word or concept for life.

(f) deep processing

G. ____The background knowledge you need to learn new words.

(g) input hypothesis

(h) shallow processing

True-False: Write "T" for true and "F" for false.

H. ___ The theory that vocabulary is the key to success is undisputed.

I. ___ The words you know when reading are the same ones you know when listening.

J. ___ According to Stephen Krashen, you learn more when you read than when you talk.

K. ___ Active vocabulary can be improved through practice in speaking and writing.

L. ___ A good way of acquiring vocabulary is to consciously make long lists of words.

M. ___ Meaningful writing, such as writing a term paper, is a good method of deep processing.

For Your Critical Reflection: What is the most important knowledge for you as a student, cultural or cross-cultural literacy? Why? Which is more important for the world today?

_____

_____

II. Learning Realities and Strategies

Here you will learn some strategies for studying vocabulary in class and at home.

8. learning [LERN ng]: the conscious, deliberate, and strategic method of knowing new things.

Just as acquisition is natural and unconscious, learning is deliberate and planned. Here are some strategies: (1) take a vocabulary class; (2) work through the exercises in a popular book on vocabulary; (3) make a list in the back of books or in a notebook of any new words you learned; (4) check the glossary (word list) in the back of your textbooks; (5) make up flash cards for words you do not know; (6) look up important new words in the dictionary; (7) underline new words when you read.

Would a person interested in learning vocabulary buy vocabulary books?

Yes   No   because _____

**"I think you'll find my test results are a
pretty good indication of your abilities
as a teacher."**

Herman © 1989 Jim Unger. Reprinted with permission of
Universal Press Syndicate.

9. **mnemonic devices** [nee MON ik de VICE iz]: a formula or rhyme to help
   you remember.

Thirty days has September,
April, June, and November.

I before E
except after C,
or sounded like A,
as in neighbor and weigh.

These little verses are mnemonic devices; they help us remember. Making up
your own mnemonics can help you remember. Mnemonics can sometimes be
idiosyncratic or even off-color. Murray Suid refers to "demon mnemonics" for
spelling, partially because *demon* helps him to spell mn*emon*ic and partially because mnemonics can be wicked: "Pedants step on the *peds* of children who
make grammar mistakes and crush them like *ants.*"

If you wanted to use mnemonics to remember, is it better to make up your
own?

Yes No because _____

10. word association [WERD uh SOHS ee AY shun]: learning a word
   by associating its form or sound with one you know.

Learn a new word by connecting it with words you already know. This is one
form of mnemonic device. "A re*join*der *join*s my answer to a question." "A
re*splend*ent person is *splend*idly bright." "An i*nnocu*ous person would *n*ever
k*nock* yo*u* over."

A milliner is a hat maker. Would you use word association if you remembered
that a milliner is "the man from Milan with a million hats"?

Yes   No   because _____

11. visual association [VISZ oo ul uh SOHS ee AY shun]: learning a word
   by associating it with a picture in your mind.

Learn a new word by visualizing (imagining) people you know. Think of your
friendly nephew Greg when you learn that *gregarious means friendly*. When you
learn *hypochondriac,* imagine your sickly uncle who always demands *hypo*dermic
injections every time he gets a sniffle.

A martinet is a rigid disciplinarian. Would visualizing your dictatorial tennis
coach marching on the net be a good visual association for martinet?

Yes   No   because _____

12. root word association [ROOT werd uh SOHS ee AY shun]: learning
   a word by learning its etymology, or word history.

Learn a new word by learning the word history. Every word has a story. For
example, the dictionary defines *cosmopolitan* as "world citizen." It was coined
by the ancient Greek philosopher Diogenes when he was asked about what
city-state he belonged to. He answered: "I am a citizen of the world."

The root of eccentric is the Greek *ekkentros,* "not having the earth as the center."
Would imagining an eccentric person being "out of this world" be a root word
association?

Yes   No   because _____

13. affect association [A fekt uh SOHS ee AY shun]: learning a word
   by connecting it to affect (feelings).

Learn a new word by connecting its meaning to your strongest emotions. Learning vocabulary takes more than logic. Learn a new list of words, perhaps from

the thesaurus, to describe (1) people you love, (2) people you hate, (3) people you admire and want to imitate, (4) your ideal self, and (5) your worst self.

Will affect association be useful to you if you neither loved nor hated nor felt strongly about anything?

Yes   No   because _____

14. rote memorization [ROHT MEM or ih ZAY shun]: memorizing through routine, drill, and conscious repetition.

Learn a new word by repeating it. Repetition can help you remember, but repetition in context is best. For instance, a biology major will hear "mitosis" more times in college than an English major, and a biology major might care more about learning it. Here are some tools of rote memorization: (1) copying words over, (2) flash cards, (3) recitation, and (4) self-testing.

Fresco means painting on wet plaster. Would an art major hear the word *fresco* repeated more times than most other students?

Yes   No   because _____

Matching: Match the method with the vocabulary word.

N. ___ Connect the meaning of a word to people you love or hate.

(a) Word Lover Association

O. ___ Connect *gregarious* with its root *greg*, meaning "flock."

(b) mnemonic devices

P. ___ Take a vocabulary class, make glossaries, and use flash cards.

(c) word association

Q. ___ Recite a new word and definition to yourself over and over.

(d) visual association

R. ___ Imagine a person you know whom the new word describes.

(e) root word association

S. ___ Create rhymes or slogans to help you remember.

(f) affect association

T. ___ Connect *resplendent* to a word you know, *splendid.*

(g) rote memorization

(h) vocabulary learning

For Your Critical Reflection: According to the followers of John Locke, association was a natural method of learning. Is this true? Do you naturally associate, or do you have to train yourself?

_____

_____

III. Context Cues

You once learned from context naturally, but now you must develop the conscious habit. This section introduces you to the most important context cues.

15. context [KON text]: the words and sentences that surround a new vocabulary word.

The context is the "co-text," that is, all the print that surrounds a word. The best context for a new word is sometimes more than one sentence. An experienced reader always reads around difficult words and sentences to figure things out.

If you read two sentences around a word to get its meaning, are you using context?

Yes   No   because _____

16. context cues [KON text KYOOS]: key words and phrases that give a clue to the meaning of a word.

Pay attention to cues that suggest meaning. Sometimes you must read beyond the sentence. For example, the sentence "He spoke with alacrity" does not tell you what "alacrity" means. Now consider the following cues:

contrast	He spoke with alacrity. His friend, _by contrast_, mumbled _sadly_ and _without enthusiasm_. He had alacrity all right—_nothing bored him or drained his energy._
example	We were nearly exhausted by the young boy's alacrity—_he jumped up to meet us, cheerfully ate his breakfast, whatever it was, and eagerly leaped into his chores._
parallelism	His alacrity for the daily chores inspired us, _just as_ his energy for endless games of checkers delighted us, and _just as_ his enthusiasm for improvement excited us.
series	He jumped to the telephone, gestured passionately, and spoke with alacrity.
definition	He spoke with alacrity, _that is_, eagerness.

If people admired your alacrity, would they find you boring and without energy?

Yes No because _____

17. **discourse** [DISS kors]: more than one sentence spoken or written together.

Discourse is language in use. Learn new words by paying attention to discourse rules. Modern American writing, for instance, is organized around the paragraph. Sometimes a new word is introduced in the first sentence, but you must read the whole paragraph to get the meaning.
    Use your ability to use context cues to read the following passage:

I spent a startling and *enthralling* couple of hours not long ago with two computer scientists in Canada who said, "Yes, it can do that," every time I asked if the software they had developed was capable of answering one of the questions I wanted to tease it with."

[Cullen Murphy, "Caught in the Web of Bytes"]

Would you likely be bored and tormented during an "enthralling couple of hours"?

Yes No because _____

18. **definition cues** [DEFF uh NISH n KYOOS]: words that deliberately define a word in the context of its use.

Most writers define their terms right in the text. Pay attention to clues such as *that is to say, that is, i.e., in other words,* or *namely.* The following sentence uses *it is*:

The cult of wabi has entered deeply into the cultural life of the Japanese people. *It is* in truth the worshipping of poverty. . . .

[Daisetz Suzuki]

Practice: Practice your ability to use definition cues by answering the following question. The answer is printed below.
Question: *Wabi* means (a) praise of money, (b) worshipping of poverty, (c) cultural life.[1]
Practice using definition cues in the following passage:

Can it use the dictionary as what is called a reverse dictionary—*that is,* can it locate a word if you only know the definition . . .?

[Cullen Murphy, "Caught in the Web of Bytes"]

_____
[1] *Answer:* (b) worshipping of poverty.

Question: When do you need a reverse dictionary? (a) you know a definition only, (b) you read backwards.[2]

Sometimes authors provide a definition cue in a different sentence. As in the following:

> There is an even newer *transnational* ecology. The environment no more knows national boundaries than does money or information.
>
> [Peter Drucker, *The New Realities*]

Practice: Does *transnational* mean "having strict national boundaries"? (a) Yes (b) No[3]

Sometimes writers include a definition but do not signal it with *that is*. For example: "Ivan the Terrible, the famous evil Russian czar, was born in 1530." Because the second phrase tells us who Ivan was, we could insert *that is* before it: "Ivan the Terrible, *that is*, the famous evil Russian czar, was born in 1530."

Question: Where might you place *that is* in the following sentence?[4]

> The transnational economy has now become dominant, controlling in large measure the domestic economies of the national states.
>
> [Peter Drucker, *The New Realities*]

Question: What does Drucker's use of *dominant* imply? (a) the largest, (b) declining, (c) in major control.[5]

Exercise your ability to find a definition in the following passage:

> More important, a computerized dictionary is no longer just a dictionary. It becomes a *data base*, a source of new kinds of knowledge not only for those interested in language but for specialists of all kinds.
>
> [Cullen Murphy, "Caught in the Web of Bytes"]

Could you rewrite the above to say "It becomes a *data base*, that is, a source of new kinds of knowledge?"

Yes   No   because _____

19. example cues [ex AM pel KYOOS]: words that provide an example of a
    word's meaning.

Some words are not explained precisely, but writers tell you what they mean by mentioning examples. Look for words such as *for example, for instance, in particular*, and *namely*. Or pay attention to parenthetical comments that provide examples.

---

[2] *Answer:* (a) you know the definition.
[3] *Answer:* (b) No. The environment, money, and information know no boundaries.
[4] *Answer:* before "controlling in large measure."
[5] *Answer:* (c) in major control: "controlling in large measure."

Exercise your ability to use example cues to understand *patrimonial*:

A medieval manor is the most obvious example of a *patrimonial* society, but not the most interesting one. Modern Japan is. Until a few years ago, the patterns of deference and age-grading which ruled the Japanese family were expected to rule in industry as well. Often the younger generation inherited the position of elders in shops, factories, and corporations, at all levels of the hierarchy.

[Richard Sennet, *Authority*]

If you lived in a patrimonial society, could you expect to inherit your father's position at work?

Yes   No   because _____

Matching: Match the example with the kind of cue. You will use some answers more than once.

U. ____ His rude questions were egregious, that is, against what the group stands for.

    (a) context

V. ____ Her deeds were laudatory—for example, saving the lost child brought cheers.

    (b) context cues

W. ____ All the words that precede and follow a difficult word.

    (c) discourse

X. ____ She didn't sleep; she hibernated. One time she slept through a birthday party.

    (d) definition cues

Y. ____ He was rapacious, grasping and clawing his way to success.

    (e) example cues

Z. ____ These words help us to understand the meanings of word.

Multiple Choice: Use context cues to guess the meaning of the word.

a. ____ The *affable* soldier surprised me, cracking jokes about civil war and sharing wild adventures.
Affable means (a) serious, (b) talkative, (c) wicked.

Cue type: _____

b. ____ I did my best to *evade* the teacher; for example, I wore my Halloween mask all day.
Evade means (a) to praise, (b) to postpone, (c) to hide from.

Cue type: _____

c. ____ We were nearly ruined by her *perfidy*—what a double-crossing traitor!
Perfidy means (a) courage, (b) deceitfulness, (c) generosity.

Cue type: _____

d. ____ She ate two steaks, three potatoes, and a pie—indeed, such a *voracious* appetite I have never seen.
Voracious means (a) hungry, (b) fulfilled, (c) unstoppable.

Cue type: _____

e. ____ The *ubiquitous* graffiti followed us everywhere; even the faculty room was sprayed.
Ubiquitous means (a) obscene, (b) in all places, (c) badly painted.

Cue type: _____

For Your Critical Reflection: Do you ever use context cues in your own writing—such as definition or example—to help your readers understand the meanings of your words? Why or why not?

_____

_____

IV. Textual Cues

This section helps you notice those small textual cues (punctuation marks and key words) that writers use to cue their meanings.

20. punctuation cues [PUNK choo AY shun KYOOS]: standard marks of meaning—including period, comma, colon, semicolon, parentheses, dash, bracket—that help you identify the meaning of a word.

Learn a new word by paying attention to punctuation.

Words in a *series* often are synonymous (they mean the same thing). They are punctuated with commas: "He ate oranges, bananas, pineapple, and guava." (You can presume a guava is a fruit.)

Definitions and examples are usually preceded by a *colon*: "There are several ways to think of a colon: (1) as a preview to the example, (2) as a formal introduction, or (3) as a means of introducing a list."

Dashes (or parentheses) introduce parenthetical comments—as in this sentence—to define or explain.

Would it be easy to find punctuation cues in a sentence that was punctuated incorrectly?

Yes   No   because _____

21. parenthetical remarks [PEAR en THET uh kuhl reh MARKS]:
comments that explain, define, or qualify the meanings of words.

Parenthetical remarks are like the actor's "asides" to the audience. Parenthetical remarks are punctuated by two parentheses (. . .), two dashes— . . . —, two brackets [. . .], or two commas, . . . ,. A dash sometimes comes at the end of the sentence—like this.
  Use parenthetical clues to understand the following passage:

> The opposite direction, moving toward the midline, is called *medial* (*medius* is Latin for "middle"). Thus, the little finger is medial to the thumb. (Remember, all terms refer to the anatomical position and thus the palms are forward.)
>
> [Boyle, "Anatomical Terminology"]

Based on the passage above, is the little finger of the hand closest to the middle of the body?

Yes   No   because _____

22. italics cues [eye TAL iks KYOOS]: the standard punctuation for
highlighting a foreign word or word used as a word.

Learn new words in italics. Foreign words and phrases are in italics. Words needing special emphasis sometimes appear in italics. Words in italics slant to remind you of Renaissance Italian script: *Italics* and *Italian* have the same root. Note the following example:

> Now, how shall we denote the "top" or "head" of a human body and its opposite? For the direction toward the head we use "superior" because the Latin word *super* means "above." And for its opposite we use "inferior" (*inferus* is Latin for "below").
>
> [Boyle, "Anatomical Terminology"]

Is *super* italicized both because it is foreign and because it is used as a word?

Yes   No   because _____

23. "W" markers [DUHB el YOU MARK erz]: relative pronouns that show the meanings of words—who, what, when, where, why.

The "W" markers (relative pronouns) can suggest the meaning of descriptions. Note the following example:

> The *quarantine* ward is <u>where</u> we keep people with dangerous communicable diseases.

Question: Would a person in quarantine see many visitors? (a) Yes (b) No[6]

Practice using "W" markers to figure out the meanings of the italicized words:

> A *pedant* is one <u>who</u> brags about knowledge by criticizing others.
> *Depilatories* are <u>what</u> people use to remove unwanted hair from their bodies.
> You will reach *nirvana* <u>when</u> you enter a state of divine bliss.
> Rapid *inflation* is the reason <u>why</u> your salary cannot keep up with prices.
> A *metronome* is a device <u>which</u> helps musicians keep time.

Would you likely reach nirvana in a room of pedants tapping their feet to metronomes?

Yes   No   because _____

24. pronoun cues [PROH nown KYOOS]: words that refer to other words: it, they, that, these, those.

Writers use pronouns to avoid repetition. Pronouns stand for other nouns. To read pronouns you must make a mental connection with their referents. Words to which pronouns refer are called *antecedents*.
Practice: Test your ability to use pronoun cues in the following by identifying pronouns and their referents:

> Scientific terminology is a precise tool. *It* allows people of different times and languages to conduct complex discussions in a small number of words. Conciseness is necessary in scientific discussion, for *it* actually saves time and ensures clarity of understanding.
>
> [Boyle, "Anatomical Terminology"]

Question: What does the first *it* refer to? _____[7]

Question: What does the second *it* refer to? _____[8]

---

[6] *Answer:* (b) no.
[7] *Answer:* scientific terminology.
[8] *Answer:* conciseness.

Question: Based on the preceding passage, what does *conciseness* mean?

_____[9]

Based on the preceding passage, does scientific terminology ensure clarity of understanding?

Yes   No   because _____

Finish the Sentence: Practice using ''W'' cues by completing the following sentences:

   f. A penitentiary is a place *where* _____

   g. A referee is one *who* _____

   h. You become an adolescent *when* _____

   i. Aspirin is *what* some people take *when* _____

   j. The kennel is the place *where* _____

   k. Her magnificent talent is the reason *why* _____

Context Cues: Guess at the meanings of the italicized words by using context cues. Answer the multiple choice questions that follow. You may refer back to the text.

Punctuation Cues

(1)   Do you want to learn to read, study, and *comprehend* better? The best
(2) method is to *scrutinize* your texts for special context cues. Every writer
(3) has a *panoply* of context cues *to imply* the meaning of unfamiliar words.
(4) Writers want to communicate, and this intention makes them careful to
(5) provide a cue, clue, or *signal* to the reader. One such cue can be found
(6) in punctuation. Writers use semicolons (;) to show the *parallelism* be-
(7) tween two or more clauses; each clause is equally important to the over-
(8) all meaning of the sentence. The semicolon functions as a *caesura* be-
(9) tween the two clauses. This *caesura*, or pause, provides a mental rest;
(10) you can *contemplate* the meaning of the one clause and build expecta-
(11) tions for the second. A colon (:) suggests that a definition or example
(12) will follow: it works like a small spotlight that signals to the reader to
(13) keep reading for more information. An English professor who harps on
(14) punctuation is usually called a *pedant* (too concerned with the trifles of
(15) correctness). But once you see punctuation as a signal system to guide
(16) you through discourse, you will never again find learning it to be an
(17) *arduous* task.

[9] *Answer:* to say a great deal with a minimum of words.

l. ＿ In line (1) *comprehend* means (a) forget, (b) memorize, (c) understand deeply.

m. ＿ In line (2) *scrutinize* means (a) study carefully, (b) scan briefly, (c) ignore completely.

n. ＿ In line (3) *panoply* means (a) a few, (b) a variety, (c) a habit.

o. ＿ In line (3) *to imply* means (a) to mask, (b) to define, (c) to suggest.

p. ＿ In line (5) a *signal* is (a) a cue, (b) a clue, (c) both *a* and *b*.

q. ＿ In line (6) *parallelism* means (a) similar in meaning, (b) geometrical, (c) boxlike.

r. ＿ In line (8) *caesura* is (a) a cut, (b) a pause, (c) a salad.

s. ＿ In line (10) *contemplate* means (a) reflect on, (b) memorize, (c) sleep deeply.

t. ＿ In line (12) the colon after *follow* (a) introduces an example, (b) provides a pause, (c) is not needed.

u. ＿ In line (14) a *pedant* is explained (a) by "trifles," (b) by "harp," (c) parenthetically, (d) *a*, *b*, and *c*.

v. ＿ In line (17) *arduous* means (a) boring, (b) difficult, (c) artful.

For Your Critical Reflection: If experienced readers are familiar with context cues, and using context cues helps vocabulary, does it automatically follow that experienced readers have a better vocabulary?

_____

_____

V. Grammatical and Stylistic Cues

25. parallelism [PEAR uh LELL izm]: the deliberate balancing of sentence parts.

Many writers use parallel (or balanced) sentences. Parallel sentences, written to be read with great formal dignity, cue the meanings of words. Sometimes the words are balanced to be similar; sometimes they are balanced to be opposites. Parallel phrases include *either . . . or, neither . . . nor,* and *not only . . . but also.* Note the following examples:

I came, I saw, I conquered!

Give me liberty or *give me* death!

Neither run *nor* walk away, my dear, before I *both* return *and* triumph.

Some people *not only* act bellicose, *but also* pretend to be great warriors.

Practice your ability to read parallelism cues in the following passage:

How can I describe my emotions at this catastrophe, or *how* delineate the wretch whom with such infinite pains and care I had endeavored to form?

[Mary Shelley, *Frankenstein*]

Question: *Delineate* means (a) dissect, (b) disinherit, (c) draw, sketch, define.[10]

Other writers repeat phrases. Test your ability on the following passage from Machiavelli:

One could *cite* a host of modern examples and *list* the many peace treaties, the many promises that were made null and void by princes who broke faith with the advantage going to one who best *knew how* to play the fox. But one must *know how* to mask this nature skillfully and be a great dissembler.

[Machiavelli, *The Prince*]

Question: Are "cite" and "list" opposites? (a) Yes (b) No, because

_____ [11]

Is a "great dissembler" somebody who can hide his ability to "play the fox"?

Yes   No   because _____

26. contrast cues [KON trast KYOOS]: words that cue the meaning of the word because they signal its opposite.

A good writer will tell you what a word means by carefully signaling its opposite meaning. Writers often include the following phrases:

by contrast: She likes apples; he, *by contrast,* abhors them.

never: She will always be true and *never* practice infidelity.

instead of: *Instead of* acting calmly, he ran around frantic.

however: He listened carefully; *however,* his mind was not swayed.

on the other hand: She wanted peace; *on the other hand,* she demanded justice.

nevertheless: He was old and tired; *nevertheless,* he worked indefatigably.

although: *Although* she demurred at first, she finally agreed to sail.

---

[10] *Answer:* (c) the parallel "hows" suggest a parallel meaning between *describe* and *delineate.*

[11] *Answer:* (b) no, because they are parallel in syntax "could cite . . . and list."

Practice your ability to read contrast cues in the following passages:

> More important, a computerized dictionary is *no longer* just a dictionary. It becomes a data base, a source of new kinds of knowledge *not only* for those interested in language *but* for specialists of all kinds.
>
> [Cullen Murphy, "Caught in the Web of Bytes"]

Question: "No longer just a dictionary" suggests something (a) more than (b) less than a dictionary?[12]

> How praiseworthy it is that a prince keeps his word and governs by candor *instead of* craft, everyone knows.
>
> [Machiavelli, *The Prince*]

Question: Are "candor" and "craft" the same or opposite? (a) Same (b) Opposite, because _____ [13]

Exercise your ability to read contrast cues in the following:

> Scrolling through the primary topic window you find an article assigned by your professor. Since you *don't* feel much like talking, you use the mouse instead to choose and open the article for reading, viewing, and listening.
>
> [Richard Paske, "Hypermedia: A Brief History and Report"]

Whatever a "mouse" is, do you need to talk to make it operate?

Yes   No   because _____

Multiple Choice: Use context cues to guess the meaning of the word.

> Gaston Gonnet and Frank Tompa . . . are authors of several programs that promise not only to facilitate the task of retrieving large bodies of text—often an ungainly procedure—but also to help ensure that *The Oxford English Dictionary* continues to enjoy pre-eminence as the English language's dictionary of record.
>
> [Cullen Murphy, "Caught in the Web of Bytes"]

w. ____ *Facilitate* means to (a) make tasks easier, (b) make tasks more complicated.

x. ____ *Ungainly* means (a) something that is easy to do, (b) something that is difficult to do.

y. ____ *Ensure* means (a) pay for damage, (b) make sure, (c) postpone.

---

[12] *Answer:* (a) more than.
[13] *Answer:* (b) opposite, because the cue is "instead of."

z. ___ *Pre-eminence* means (a) a position of great respect, (b) a pleasurable status.

Here we have an appreciation of transcendental aloofness in the midst of multiplicities—which is known as *wabi* in the dictionary of Japanese cultural terms.

[D. T. Suzuki, "Aspects of Japanese Culture—*Wabi*"]

A. ___ The word *which* refers to (a) multiplicities, (b) appreciation, (c) aloofness.

B. ___ The word *wabi* is italicized (a) because it is Japanese, (b) because it is emphasized as a word.

C. ___ *Transcendental aloofness* means you are (a) deep in multiplicities, (b) separate from multiplicities.

D. ___ The word *wabi* describes (a) being transcendent, (b) being aloof, (c) an appreciation.

His jaws opened, and he muttered some inarticulate sounds, while a grin wrinkled his cheeks. He might have spoken, but I did not hear; one hand was stretched out, seemingly to detain me, but I escaped, and rushed down stairs. I took refuge in the courtyard belonging to the house which I inhabited. . . .

[Mary Shelley, *Frankenstein*]

E. ___ The word *muttered* means (a) shouted, (b) cried, (c) mumbled.

F. ___ *Inarticulate sounds* are (a) hard to understand, (b) loud and roaring, (c) groaned and moaned.

G. ___ *Detain* means (a) to hold, (b) to touch, (c) to bless.

H. ___ *Refuge* means (a) a medicine, (b) solace or peace, (c) a hiding place.

I. ___ *Inhabited* means (a) rented, (b) lived in, (c) research in.

Chapter Review

I. Using Cues: Use cues to help you understand vocabulary words and answer questions about the following passages:

We hold these truths to be self-evident; that all men are created equal; that they are endowed by their creator with certain unalienable rights; that among these are life, liberty, and the pursuit of happiness; that to secure these rights, governments are instituted among men, deriving their just powers from the consent of the governed; that whenever any form of government becomes destructive of these ends, it is the right of the people to alter or abolish it, and to institute new government, laying its foundation on such principles and organizing its powers in such form, as to them shall seem most likely to effect their safety and happiness. Prudence indeed will dictate that governments long established should not be changed for light and transient causes, and accordingly all experience hath shewn that mankind are more disposed to suffer while evils are sufferable, than to right themselves by abolishing the forms to which they are accustomed.

[Thomas Jefferson, The Declaration of Independence]

We hold these truths to be self-evident;

1. ____ *Self-evident* means (a) essential, (b) needing evidence, (c) believed without proof needed.

that all men are created equal; that they are endowed by their creator with certain unalienable rights; that among these are life, liberty, and the pursuit of happiness;

2. ____ *Endowed* implies not only *provided* but also (a) blessed, (b) burdened, (c) changed.

3. ____ *Unalienable* means (a) not foreign, (b) unable to be removed, (c) hard to move.

that to secure these rights, governments are instituted among men, deriving their just powers from the consent of the governed;

4. ____ *Secure* means (a) reach for, (b) guard from danger, (c) create.

5. ____ *Instituted* means (a) designed, (b) voted on, (c) arrested.

6. ____ *Deriving* means (a) coming from, (b) given to, (c) causing.

7. ____ *Consent* means (a) blessing, (b) agreement, (c) control.

that whenever any form of government becomes destructive of these ends, it is the right of the people to alter or abolish it, and to institute new government, laying its foundation on such principles and organizing its powers in such form, as to them shall seem most likely to effect their safety and happiness.

8. ____ *Alter* means (a) abolish, (b) change, (c) reconsider.

9. ____ *Abolish* means (a) alter, (b) change, (c) destroy.

10. ____ *To effect* means (a) to guarantee, (b) to bring about, (c) to abolish.

Prudence indeed will dictate that governments long established should not be changed for light and transient causes,

11. ____ *Prudence* means (a) sexual chastity, (b) common wisdom, (c) without care.

12. ____ *Dictate* means (a) order or command, (b) explain, (c) allow.

13. ____ *Transient* means (a) emotional, (b) foreign, (c) quickly passing.

> and accordingly all experience hath shewn that mankind are more disposed to suffer while evils are sufferable, than to right themselves by abolishing the forms to which they are accustomed.

14. ____ *Disposed to* means (a) pleased to, (b) inclined to, (c) designed to.

15. ____ *Accustomed* means (a) used to, (b) pleased by, (c) oppressed by.

> My grandmother! . . . A mysterious woman to me, my only living grandparent. A woman of Mexico. The woman in long black dresses that reached down to her shoes. My one relative who spoke no word of English. She had no interest in *gringo* society. She remained completely aloof from the public. Protected by her daughters. Protected even by me when we went to Safeway together and I acted as her translator. Eccentric woman. Soft. Hard.
>
> [Richard Rodriguez, *The Hunger of Memory*]

16. ____ "My only living grandparent" (a) is a parenthetical remark, (b) is a definition, (c) refers to grandmother.

17. ____ The two sentences beginning "Protected" are (a) in opposition, (b) parallel, (c) in a series.

18. ____ *Gringo* means (a) rich, (b) English speaking, (c) civilized.

19. ____ *Aloof* means (a) distant, (b) segregated, (c) protected.

20. ____ *Eccentric* means (a) proud, (b) outside of normal, (c) confused.

II. Using Context: Use context cues to help you understand vocabulary words and answer questions about the following passage.

The "one-corner" style is psychologically associated with the Japanese painters' "thrifty brush" tradition of retaining the least possible number of lines or strokes which go to represent forms on silk or paper. . . . A simple fishing boat in the midst of the rippling waters is enough to awaken in the mind of the beholder a sense of the vastness of the sea and at the same time of peace and contentment—the Zen sense of the Alone. Apparently the boat floats helplessly. It is a primitive structure with no mechanical device for stability and for audacious steering over the turbulent waves, with no scientific apparatus for braving all kinds of weather—quite a contrast to the modern ocean liner. But this very helplessness is the virtue of the fishing canoe. . . .

[D. T. Suzuki, "Aspects of Japanese Culture—Wabi"]

1. ___ The *"one-corner"* style and the *"thrifty brush"* tradition are (a) associated in the emotions, (b) associated by their names, (c) associated in the mind.

2. ___ The *"thrifty brush"* tradition is called "thrifty" because (a) it is inexpensive, (b) it can be bought at drug stores, (c) it uses a small number of brush strokes.

3. ___ The *simple fishing boat* and the *vastness of the sea* are (a) parallel, (b) in contrast, (c) similar.

4. ___ The *Zen sense of the Alone* is a feeling of (a) being lost at sea, (b) being one with nature, (c) being at peace.

5. ___ *Apparently* means (a) seems to be but is not really, (b) unfortunately, (c) ideally.

6. ___ The boat is *primitive* because (a) it was painted long ago, (b) it is the opposite of a modern ocean liner, (c) it is helpless.

7. ___ *With no mechanical device* and *with no scientific apparatus* are parallel phrases suggesting that (a) apparatus and device are opposites, (b) apparatus is a kind of device, (c) the words *mechanical* and *scientific* are highly valued in *wabi*.

8. ___ *Audacious steering over the turbulent waves* is explained in the phrase (a) "braving all kinds of weather," (b) "modern ocean liner," (c) "very helplessness."

9. ___ The word *But* in the last sentence suggests that (a) the *Apparently* sentence is now explained, (b) the boat is not really helpless, (c) the helplessness is a virtue, (d) all of the above.

10. ___ The word *virtue* means (a) problem, (b) strength, (c) mystery.

Reading for Chapter 2

JOHNSON O'CONNOR

Vocabulary and Success

In 1934, Johnson O'Connor wrote a famous article, "Vocabulary and Success." Some people believe that it started the whole industry of vo-

*cabulary books. In a study of the characteristics of successful executives,
the Human Engineering Laboratory discovered that vocabulary—not
education, intelligence, or breeding—was the key to success. Before this
article, most people acquired their vocabulary from their reading, or
perhaps in school. But O'Connor's research suggested that with diligent
pursuit of a larger vocabulary, success was in everyone's grasp.*

Words to Notice

Optional Exercise: Use context cues to guess the meanings of the boldfaced
words; then, check your answers.

A. Many causes of success **elude** our understanding and remain **intangibly** beyond a clear definition.

   elude means _____

   intangibly means _____

B. Nevertheless, some **concrete constituents** of success have been **isolated** and studied in the laboratory.

   concrete constituents are _____

   isolated means _____

C. An **extensive** knowledge of the exact meanings of English words **accompanies** outstanding success.

   extensive _____

   accompanies means _____

D. Successful men and women are **designated** by a special **appellation,** "executive."

   designated means _____

   appellation means _____

E. Normally, vocabulary is **acquired** early in life, before we have made **appreciable** progress in life.

   acquired means _____

   appreciable means _____

F. In general, school success **preludes** executive success. Schooling may be the **vital** factor.

   preludes means _____

   vital means _____

G. A high score may reveal an underlying **aptitude** for language. It may be some **flair** for words.

aptitude means _____

flair means _____ [14]

1   What is success? And how is it gained? Whether one thinks of success as financial reward, or as assured social position, or as satisfaction in able work accomplished and recognized, or as a combination of the three and something more, many factors contribute. Most of them elude our understanding and remain intangibly beyond definition. A vital force drives some persons over every obstacle. With others that great generalization, character, adds strength of a different sort. Neither may ever be restricted to a hard and fast formula; certainly, at the moment, neither can be measured. But other more concrete constituents of success have been isolated and studied in the laboratory. One of these is a large English vocabulary.

2   An extensive knowledge of the exact meanings of English words accompanies outstanding success in this country more often than any other single characteristic which the Human Engineering Laboratory and the Johnson O'Connor Research Foundation have been able to isolate and measure.

3   Although it is impossible to define success rigidly, a large vocabulary seems to be typical, not exclusively of executives, but of successful persons. It happens that in the business world successful men and women are designated by this special appellation, *executive*. The successful lawyer or doctor is marked by no such name. But if, to the best of one's ability, one selects successful persons in the professions, they also score high in vocabulary.

4   Was it luck? Or was it significant of something not recognized? The Laboratory listed the vocabulary scores of one hundred executives and, parallel with them, the scores of one hundred miscellaneous college graduates. The difference between the two arrays was striking. Only nine per cent of the college graduates scored as high as the average major executive.

5   Why do large vocabularies characterize executives and possibly outstanding men and women in other fields? The final answer seems to be that words are the instruments by means of which men and women grasp the thoughts of others and with which they do much of their own thinking. They are the tools of thought.

6   Before accepting so far-reaching a conclusion several more obvious explanations must be examined and excluded. The first and most natural supposition is that successful persons acquire words with age and with the experiences of

[14] *Answers:* A. **elude** means escape; **intangibly** means abstractly. B. **concrete constituents** are real parts; **isolated** means separated. C. **extensive** means wide; **accompanies** means follows. D. **designated** means identified; **appellation** means title. E. **acquired** means learned naturally; **appreciable** means noticeable. F. **preludes** means comes before; **vital** means necessary. G. **aptitude** means talent; **flair** means style.

life. Success does not usually occur early. The successful group were necessarily older in both years and experience than the general run of college graduates with whom they were compared; and their large vocabularies might be the inevitable result of age.

7   To probe this point a study of the growth of vocabulary with age was undertaken. From nine, the earliest age for which the Laboratory has a large number of measurements, to twenty-two or twenty-three, vocabulary expands steadily and at a uniform rate. Through this school period the score on the vocabulary test of one hundred and fifty items improves five items a year. From twenty-five to fifty vocabulary continues to increase, but changes no more in these twenty-five years than in two school years, not enough to explain the high scores of executives. Normally, vocabulary is acquired early in life, before most men have made appreciable progress toward a responsible position. The large vocabularies of successful persons come before success rather than after. Age and the experiences of life may contribute new words, but certainly do not explain in full the high vocabulary scores of business executives.

8   The next thought is that effective schooling may be the source both of a wide vocabulary and of executive success. It is known, from the work which the American Telephone and Telegraph Company has undertaken, that there is a relationship between school success and business success later in life. Although not everyone who leads his class becomes a brilliant executive, and although not everyone who fails in school fails in life, in general school success preludes executive success. Schooling may be the vital factor of which the large vocabularies which the Laboratory is measuring are but by-products.

9   To obtain evidence bearing on this point, the Laboratory measured the vocabularies of twenty men who had left school at the age of fifteen and who had worked their way into major positions. They also averaged only seven errors. Their scores equaled those of the college-graduate executives. In the case of these twenty men it is their vocabularies which are important rather than their formal school education. Their large vocabularies are not the result of schooling and must be significant for some other reason than as a by-product of an educational background.

10   Is, then, a college background of no importance? Has the non-college man the same chance of becoming an executive as has the college graduate? This fact seemed worth determining. Of the major executives in a large industrial organization, sixty per cent are college graduates, forty per cent non-college. At first glance, college would seem to have done little, for almost half are not college men. But, to be fair to education, there is another angle from which to view this result. Of the college graduates with this same company more than three quarters are in executive positions, whereas, of the non-college men, well under a tenth are in similar positions. College graduates, in general, average measurably higher in vocabulary than do non-college persons. Furthermore, of the college group a significantly larger percentage are executives.

11   One would like to conclude without further preamble that the vocabularies of the college group are large because of directed effort and that these purposefully gained vocabularies have contributed to executive success. Non-

college executives, then, are those rare individuals who pick up words so easily that their vocabularies are large without effort. But there is one other possibility to investigate.

12   Although the vocabulary test was designed to measure knowledge which must have come through books or by word of mouth, a high score may reveal an underlying aptitude for language. It may be some flair for the meanings of words which is the contributing factor in both vocabulary and success later in life. The primary purpose of the Human Engineering Laboratory is the isolation and measurement of aptitudes in an attempt to aid each boy and girl in finding a type of work in which he or she has the best chance of success. The Laboratories, now located in ten different cities, are open to any boy or girl, from the age of five on, interested in spending two or more periods of three hours or three hours and a half in going through a set of so-called sample jobs or work-samples and discussing his or her educational or vocational problems. Seventeen aptitudes have been isolated in this study, fourteen of which can be measured with some accuracy, and three others approximated. Yet that particular characteristic which contributes to a large vocabulary has not been found. For the time, we must leave the conclusion of this part of the research in abeyance and admit that the large English vocabularies of successful executives may reveal an unfound aptitude.

Questions for Class Discussion

1. What does O'Connor mean by calling words "the tools of thought"?
2. O'Connor completed his study in 1934. What has changed that might now challenge his thesis?
3. Does vocabulary lead to success, or does success lead to vocabulary?

Making a New World

For Class Discussion

1. What were the ways that you "acquired" the vocabulary you have?
2. What were the ways you "learned" vocabulary in your life?
3. What do you do when you are reading and you come across a new word?

Collaborative Learning

1. Acquisition/Learning
   Purpose: To understand the difference between acquisition and learning.

A. Make a list of five recommendations to your school to increase the amount of acquisition that occurs for most students. You can use your elementary or high school, or your present college.
B. Justify your choices.
C. Report to the class.

2. Context Cues
Purpose: To identify context cues to guess at meanings.
A. Make a list of the italicized words in the passage.

> Unable to *endure* the *aspect* of the being I had created, I rushed out of the room, and continued a long time *traversing* my bedchamber, unable to *compose* my mind to sleep. At length *lassitude succeeded* to the *tumult* I had before *endured*; and I threw myself on the bed in my clothes, *endeavoring* to seek a few moments of forgetfulness. But it was *in vain*; I slept, indeed, but I was disturbed by the wildest dreams.
>
> [Mary Shelley, *Frankenstein*]

B. Examine the passage to find context cues to their meanings (even if you already know them).
C. Make a list of the different context strategies you tried.
D. Rewrite the passage using more familiar words.
E. Report to the class.

Ideas for Writing

1. In a paragraph, write a mnemonic device to help you remember the meaning of the following: *mnemonic devices, deep processing,* and *context cue.*
2. In a page, write a story using five different context cues.
3. At home, write to Johnson O'Connor, agreeing or disagreeing with his thesis about success and vocabulary.

Answer Key to Chapter 2

I. TO ACQUIRE OR LEARN?

Yes-No Questions

1. Yes; it would lead to success.
2. No; you understand but do not use.
3. No; active vocabulary must be used.
4. Yes; unconscious learning continues.
5. No; you must read and listen.
6. No; they are best for rote memory.
7. Yes; they exemplify the change.

Matching

A. (d) B. (c) C. (g) D. (b) E. (a)
F. (f) G. (e)

True-False

H. F I. F J. T K. T L. F
M. T

II. LEARNING REALITIES AND STRATEGIES

Yes-No Questions

8. Yes; they require conscious learning.
9. Yes; the creation helps memory.
10. Yes; milliner and Milan sound alike.
11. Yes; it is a vivid picture.
12. Yes; it is based on the word history.
13. No; you need emotions for this method.
14. Yes; art majors study painting.

Matching

N. (f) O. (e) P. (h) Q. (g)
R. (d) S. (b) T. (c)

III. CONTEXT CUES

Yes-No Questions

15. Yes; context surrounds a key word.
16. No; alacrity means energized.
17. No; you would be interested.
18. Yes; it is a definition.
19. Yes; "younger generation inherited" is the example.

Matching

U. (d) V. (e) W. (a) or (c) X. (e)
Y. (e) Z. (b)

Multiple Choice

a. (b); example   b. (c); example
c. (b); definition d. (c); example
e. (b); example

IV. TEXTUAL CUES

Yes-No Questions

20. No; the punctuation marks would miscue.
21. Yes; medial means middle; palms are forward.
22. Yes; "Latin word *super* means."
23. No; it is a place of irritation and discomfort.
24. Yes; it is concise.

Finish the Sentence

f. where prisoners are kept.
g. who calls fouls.
h. when you begin to mature.
i. when they have minor pains.
j. where we keep pets temporarily.
k. why she is admired.
(Many other answers are possible.)

Context Cues

l. (c) m. (a) n. (b) o. (c) p. (c)
q. (a) r. (b) s. (a) t. (a) u. (d)
v. (b)

V. GRAMMATICAL AND STYLISTIC CUES

Yes-No Questions

25. Yes; *knew* and *must know* are parallel.
26. No; it is used instead of interacting.

Multiple Choice

w. (a) x. (b) y. (b) z. (a) A. (b)
B. (a) C. (b) D. (c) E. (c) F. (a)
G. (a) H. (c) I. (b)

6. (a) 7. (b) 8. (b) 9. (c) 10. (b)
11. (b) 12. (a) 13. (c) 14. (b)
15. (a) 16. (c) 17. (b) 18. (b)
19. (a) 20. (b)

CHAPTER REVIEW

I. Using Cues

1. (c) 2. (a) 3. (b) 4. (b) 5. (a)

II. Using Context

1. (c) 2. (c) 3. (b) 4. (c) 5. (a)
6. (b) 7. (b) 8. (a) 9. (d)
10. (b)

THE DICTIONARY GAME

Quick Reference Word List

abridged/unabridged/
  collegiate
citations
cross-references
definitions
dialect/regional
entry words
etymology
front matter/back
  matter

general/specialized
  dictionaries
guide words
informal/colloquial/
  nonstandard
multiple entries
obsolete/archaic/rare
part of speech
prescriptive/
  descriptive

pronunciation
pronunciation key
slang/vulgar/derogatory
syllabification
thesaurus
usage notes

Introduction: Using the Dictionary

Although the most effective way to learn new words seems to be through context—reading and speaking—many of us turn to the dictionary when we need to know more about a word. Perhaps you cannot figure out the meaning of a word from your reading, but that word strikes you as crucial. Perhaps the language in the passage you are reading seems stuffy, out of date, or falsely learned, and you want to find a better way to convey the message. Perhaps you are reading something highly technical and need precise, specialized definitions. Or perhaps you are reading a passage so full of slang that you wonder whether the usage is faulty or whether the writer is striving for an artistic effect. In these cases, careful use of dictionaries can help you make better sense of the vocabulary at hand. Dictionaries can tell you where a word has come from, what shades of meaning it has today, and sometimes even its social status. Because most college students are acquainted with dictionaries but not expert in making the best use of them, this chapter is designed to help you use dictionaries judiciously and critically as part of developing your vocabulary.

Calvin & Hobbes © 1986 Universal Press Syndicate. Reprinted with permission. All rights reserved.

. . . .

Have You Heard?
Why Do Dictionaries Seem to Disagree?

When a word has different meanings, the dictionary will list definitions in order, not at random. However, the order varies from dictionary to dictionary. *The American Heritage Dictionary of the English Language* starts with the most general definition and proceeds to more and more specialized definitions. *Webster's Ninth New Collegiate Dictionary* begins with the oldest known use of the word and gradually works up to most recent uses. *The Random House Collegiate Dictionary* gives the most commonly used meaning of the word first and then less and less common ones. Be sure to check the front matter of your dictionary (see section I of this chapter) to see the order in which definitions appear.

I. The Book Itself

There is no such thing as "the dictionary." Dictionaries come in many styles and philosophies. They do not always agree with each other about what words to include, how many definitions are needed, or what usage is proper. You may want to use different dictionaries for different purposes.

1. abridged/unabridged/collegiate [uh BRIJD] [UN uh BRIJD] [cuh LEEJ et]: shortened/full length/appropriate for college students.

An *abridged* dictionary is shortened. The smallest dictionaries are pocket abridged dictionaries, usually published as paperbacks. Pocket dictionaries are easy to carry but *are not* always easy to use: words appear in few forms, and multiple definitions are kept to a minimum, forcing the user to do more work.
Unabridged dictionaries are the massive books you see at the library. Some unabridged dictionaries come in one large volume; others come in multiple volumes. Unabridged dictionaries are the most complete dictionaries, useful for anyone who hopes to develop vocabulary. Although you cannot carry around an unabridged dictionary, you might want to have one available when you study.
Collegiate dictionaries, as you may have gathered, are medium-sized dictionaries designed to be as complete as possible without being bigger than a large textbook. Sometimes called desktop dictionaries, these volumes are designed with the needs of the general adult in mind.

If you feel insecure about your skill in English, should you buy the smallest dictionary you can find?

Yes   No   because _____

2. prescriptive/descriptive [preh SKRIP tihv] [deh SKRIP tihv]: saying what should be done/telling about what is done.

Prescriptive dictionaries tell the reader how words *should* be used. Think of doctors writing prescriptions for medication. Prescriptive dictionaries help you correct your language.

Descriptive dictionaries describe how people actually use language, even if that usage is incorrect. Most dictionaries in English are descriptive, so you should not think of them as substitutes for handbooks in grammar or composition.

These terms represent the goals of dictionaries, not their actual achievement. Prescriptive dictionaries would be useless if they did not change as language evolved. On the other hand, editors of descriptive dictionaries have to decide whether to include *delite* or *duhlite* as spellings for *delight*. To leave out common misspellings implies that some spelling is better than others. Section IV of this chapter under "usage" explains how dictionaries grapple with the problem of correctness. To see where your dictionary stands on the continuum from prescriptive to descriptive, check the preface or introduction, which is part of the front matter.

If you agree with Noah Webster, who says that "it is always better to be *vulgarly* right than *politely* wrong," would you be more interested in a descriptive dictionary than in a prescriptive one?

Yes   No   because _____

3. front matter/back matter [FRUNT MATT ir] [BACK MATT ir]: printed before the main book/printed in the back of the book.

Anything printed before the first page under the letter *A* is called the *front matter* of your dictionary. Anything printed after the last entry under *Z* is part of the *back matter*. Most unabridged and collegiate dictionaries provide a wealth of information in these places.

The *front matter* provides a guide to your dictionary. It may include the title page, a copyright page, a preface or introduction that tells you the philosophy of the dictionary, the table of contents, a list of contributors, lists of consultants, special articles, and various guidelines for making the most of the particular dictionary.

Before you buy a dictionary, look over the front matter. Check the date on the copyright: you want a dictionary that is fairly recent, because new words enter the language and old ones shift meanings. The preface or introduction (or both) can tell you how prescriptive the dictionary is, how definitions are arranged, and what kind of help the editors are striving to give you. The table of contents will list extra features provided in the back matter. A glance at lists of contributors and consultants is useful to make sure that science, for example, is adequately represented.

Special articles include essays on the history of the language and proper usage. The specific guidelines will include a pronunciation key, a list of abbreviations, and explanations of how to locate words and read entries. Too many abbreviations might make entries difficult to read. Precise labeling, such as labeling *ain't* as nonstandard, is helpful for college students. After you buy your dictionary, read through the front matter a little more closely.

The *back matter* provides a research library in miniature. Its listings sometimes are called *supplements*. Dictionaries vary greatly in front and back matter, but here are some of the features: nations of the world, populations of major cities, distances between cities, weights and measures, American colleges and universities, biographies, dates, maps, foreign words and phrases, proofreaders' marks, common names, characters from literature, characters from scripture, chemical elements, word elements (roots, prefixes, suffixes), commercial and financial terms, business mathematics, signs and symbols, geographic features of the world, presidents of the United States, the Constitution of the United States, and the Declaration of Independence.

If you are looking up *Hercules* but do not find it listed, should you check the table of contents to see what supplements are in the back matter?

Yes   No   because _____

4. general/specialized dictionaries [JEN ir ul] [SPESH uh lized]: dictionaries for nonspecialists/dictionaries for specialists.

General dictionaries are for ordinary usage. Here are some popular ones:

Webster's New International Dictionary, unabridged. This dictionary is more prescriptive than the Third New International.

Webster's Ninth New Collegiate Dictionary. This collegiate dictionary is based on the Third International.

Webster's Third International Dictionary, unabridged. This dictionary is more descriptive than the New International.

The American Heritage Dictionary of the English Language, unabridged. A fairly conservative usage panel votes on correctness.

The Random House College Dictionary. This collegiate dictionary is descriptive with good labeling.

The Compact Edition of the Oxford English Dictionary (informally called the *OED*), abridged. This two-volume condensed version of the unabridged

OED emphasizes British usage and provides a history of each word. It is useful if you need to know what a word meant to, say, Shakespeare.

Specialized dictionaries give fuller treatment of words from the perspective of different fields of study. They are useful if you are studying a subject in depth or training to work in a profession. Here is a small sampling:

Cinema, A Critical Dictionary

Chambers Biographical Dictionary

Concise Chemical and Technical Dictionary

Dictionary of Computing

Dictionary of Key Words in Psychology

Dictionary of Life Sciences

Dictionary of Philosophy and Religion

Dictionary of Political Thought

The New Harvard Dictionary of Music

Oxford Classical Dictionary

Your reference librarian can point out these sources to you. Or you can check the library's catalog under "dictionaries" or your general subject, such as "computers." If you plan to take several courses in one area, a paperback edition of a specialized dictionary can be a worthwhile purchase.

If you are studying engineering or auto mechanics, would it be wise to assume that there are no specialized dictionaries that can help?

Yes   No   because _____

Matching: Match each question with the best answer. Some answers might be used more than once.

A. ___ What kind of dictionary fits in your pocket? (a) front matter

B. ___ Which dictionary will tell you everything you could possibly need? (b) descriptive dictionary

C. ___ What is the dictionary college students should keep on their desks? (c) collegiate dictionary

D. ___ Which dictionary will tell you how words *should* be used? (d) back matter

E. ____ Which dictionary describes how most people now use words?

(e) general dictionary

F. ____ Where do you go to learn whether a dictionary is prescriptive?

(f) specialized dictionary

G. ____ Where do you go to see how old a dictionary is?

(g) prescriptive dictionary

H. ____ Where might you find Mark Twain's character Huckleberry Finn?

(h) abridged dictionary

I. ____ Where might you find a copy of the Declaration of Independence?

(i) unabridged dictionary

J. ____ What kind of dictionary helps you learn words in nursing?

Using Context: Fill in each blank with the vocabulary word that best suits the context.

Stranded

Here I am, stuck on a desert island with nothing to read but a huge

_____ dictionary in sixteen volumes. Thank goodness it

is not a specialized dictionary, because at least a _____

dictionary like this one will allow me to find all kinds of words. Not that I

need words much. With no one to talk to, the good advice in this

_____ dictionary will teach me all the rules just so I can

talk to myself. So far I have read only the pages in the beginning, the

_____. Now I'm wondering whether to read the whole

thing from beginning to end or to go right to the _____

to see if it contains any interesting readings, such as the Constitution. Hey!

Maybe these maps can get me off this island!

For Your Critical Reflection: When would you need to use a prescriptive dictionary? A descriptive dictionary?

_____

_____

II. The Page

Once you see how the pages of your dictionary are organized, you will find it easier to look up words. See the sample page as well.

5. guide words [GEYED WIRDS]: first and last words on the page of a dictionary.

Two guide words appear at the top of each page in the dictionary. The word on the left is the first word on that page. The word on the right is the last word on that page. Because entries are arranged alphabetically, a glance at the guide words lets you know whether you are on the right page.

If you were looking up *air bag* and your guide words were *ailing* and *airlock,* would you be on the right page?

Yes   No   because _____

6. entry words [EN tree WIRDS]: words that are defined in dictionaries.

Words defined in dictionaries appear in boldface type. These words are the entry words. When you have found the right page, run down the list of entry words until you find the one you need.

If you wanted to know the meaning for *aircraftsman* on the sample dictionary page printed in this chapter, would you need to read the entry *aircraft?*

Yes   No   because _____

7. multiple entries [MUHL tuh puhl EN trees]: more than one entry per spelling.

Sometimes homonyms—words spelled alike that mean different things—merit more than one entry. *Fawn,* for example, can refer to a young deer or to flattering behavior. Because these two types of fawn really are two separate words rather than two definitions of one word, dictionaries list the word twice, using a little number after each entry word to alert the reader that another entry exists.

Does the word *air* have more than one entry in the sample dictionary page printed in this chapter?

Yes   No   because _____

near the trailing edge of a wing, that controls the roll of the airframe or effects maneuvers, as banks and the like. [< F = *ail(e)* (see AISLE) + *-eron* dim. suffix]

ail·ing (ā′liŋ), *adj.* **1.** suffering from ill health, pain, or physical weakness; sickly. **2.** sick; ill. **—Syn.** See **sick**[1].

ail·ment (āl′mənt), *n.* a physical disorder or illness.

aim (ām), *v.t.* **1.** to position (something that shoots a projectile) so that the projectile will strike its target. **2.** to position (something to be thrown or fired) so that it will travel along a certain path. **3.** to direct (a rocket, missile, etc.) toward its target through use of its internal guidance system: *to aim a rocket at the moon.* **4.** to intend or direct for a particular effect or purpose: *to aim a satire at snobbery.* **—*v.i.* 5.** to strive; try (usually fol. by *at* or an infinitive): *We aim to please.* **6.** *Chiefly Dial.* to intend: *She aims to go tomorrow.* **7.** to direct efforts toward an object: *The book aimed at the approval of the intelligentsia.* **8.** *Obs.* to estimate; guess. **—*n.* 9.** act of aiming or directing anything at or toward a particular point or target. **10.** the direction in which a weapon or missile is pointed; the line of sighting. **11.** something intended or desired to be attained by one's efforts; purpose. **12.** *Obs.* conjecture; guess. **13. take aim,** to sight a weapon or missile at a target: *to take aim and fire.* [late ME *aime(n)* < MF *aesmer* < LL *adaestimāre* = L *ad-* AD- + *aestimāre* (see ESTIMATE); r. ME *ame(n)* < OF (dial.) *amer* < L *aestimāre*] **—aim′er,** *n.* **—aim′ful,** *adj.* **—aim′ful·ly,** *adv.* **—aim′less,** *adj.* **—aim′less·ly,** *adv.* **—aim′less·ness,** *n.* **—Syn. 1.** point. **9.** sighting. **11.** goal; intent, design. AIM, END, OBJECT all imply something that is the goal of one's efforts. AIM implies that toward which one makes a direct line, refusing to be diverted from it: *a nobleness of aim; one's aim in life.* END emphasizes the goal as a cause of efforts: *the end for which one strives.* OBJECT emphasizes the goal as that toward which all efforts are directed: *the object of years of study.*

ain (ān), *adj.* *Scot.* own. [OE *ǣgen*]

ai·né (e nā′), *adj.* *French.* elder; eldest. Also, *referring to a woman,* **ai·née′.** [lit., born before]

ain't (ānt), **1.** *Nonstandard in U.S. except in some dialects. Informal in Brit.* am not. **2.** *Nonstandard.* are not, is not, have not, or has not. [var. of AMN'T (contr. of AM NOT) by loss of *m* and raising with compensatory lengthening of *a*]
—Usage. AIN'T is so traditionally and widely regarded as a nonstandard form that it should be shunned by all who prefer to avoid being considered illiterate. AIN'T occurs occasionally in the informal speech of some educated users, esp. in self-consciously folksy, humorous contexts (*Ain't it the truth! She ain't what she used to be!*), but it is completely unacceptable in formal writing and speech.

Ain·tab (*Turk.* īn täb′), *n.* former name of **Gaziantep.** Also, **Antep, Ayntab.**

Ai·nu (ī′no͞o), *n., pl.* **-nus,** (*esp. collectively*) **-nu. 1.** a member of an aboriginal race of the northernmost islands of Japan, having Caucasoid or Australoid features, light skin, and more body hair than Mongoloids. **2.** the language of the Ainus, of uncertain relationship.

air[1] (âr), *n.* **1.** a mixture of oxygen, nitrogen, and other gases that surrounds the earth and forms its atmosphere. **2.** a stir in the atmosphere; a light breeze. **3.** the apparent character assumed by a person, object, act, situation, etc. **4. airs,** affected or haughty conduct or manners. **5.** *Music.* **a.** a tune; melody. **b.** the soprano or treble part. **c.** an aria. **6.** transportation or travel by airplane: *to arrive by air.* **7.** *Obs.* breath. **8. clear the air,** to eliminate dissension, ambiguity, or tension from a discussion, situation, etc. **9. get the air,** *Slang.* **a.** to be rejected, as by a lover. **b.** to be dismissed, as by an employer. **10. give (someone) the air, a.** to reject, as a lover. **b.** to dismiss, as an employee. **11. in the air,** in circulation; current: *a rumor in the air.* **12. into thin air,** completely or entirely out of sight or reach: *He vanished into thin air.* **13. off the air, a.** not broadcasting: *He goes off the air at midnight.* **b.** no longer being broadcast: *The program went off the air years ago.* **14. on the air,** in the act of broadcasting; being broadcast: *The program will be going on the air in a few seconds.* **15. take the air,** to go out of doors, as for a short walk or ride. **16. tread** or **walk on air,** to feel very happy; be elated. **17. up in the air,** undecided or unsettled: *The contract is still up in the air.* **—*v.t.* 18.** to expose to the air; give access to the open air; ventilate. **19.** to bring to public attention, as an opinion or sentiment. **—*v.i.* 20.** to be exposed to the open air, as in order to be cooled, dried, or ventilated (often fol. by *out*). **—*adj.* 21.** operating by means of air pressure: *an air brake.* **22.** acting upon air: *an air pump.* **23.** of or pertaining to airplanes or to aviation. **24.** taking place in the air; aerial: *air war.* [ME *cir* < OF *air* < L *āer-* < Gk *āer-* (s. of *āēr*) the lower atmosphere, akin to *áein* to blow] **—air′less,** *adj.* **—air′like′,** *adj.* **—Syn. 2.** See **wind**[1]. **3.** See **manner.**

air[2] (âʀ), *Scot.* **—*adj.* 1.** early. **—*adv.* 2.** *Obs.* before; previously. [var. of ERE]

A·ïr (ä′ēr), *n.* a region in N Niger, in the Sahara: low massif and oases. ab. 30,000 sq. mi. Also called **Asben.**

air′ bag′, a large plastic bag so mounted in a car that it inflates automatically upon impact in order to protect passengers from injury in a collision. Also called **air cushion.**

air′ base′, an operations center for units of an air force.

air′ blad′der, 1. a vesicle or sac containing air. **2.** Also called **gas bladder, swim bladder.** *Ichthyol.* a gas-filled sac located against the roof of the body cavity of most bony fishes, originally functioning only as a lung, now serving in many higher fishes to regulate hydrostatic pressure.

air·borne (âr′bōrn′, -bôrn′), *adj.* **1.** carried by the air, as pollen or dust. **2.** in flight; aloft. **3.** *Mil.* (of ground forces) carried in airplanes or gliders: *airborne infantry.*

air-bound (âr′bound′), *adj.* stopped up by air.

air′ brake′, 1. a brake or system of brakes operated by compressed air. **2.** *Aeron.* (not used scientifically) a device for reducing the air speed of an aircraft by increasing its drag.

air·brush (âr′brush′), *n.* an atomizer for spraying paint.

air·burst (âr′bûrst′), *n.* the explosion of a bomb or shell in midair.

air′ cav′alry, an infantry or reconnaissance unit transported by air to combat areas. Also called **sky cavalry.**

air′ cham′ber, a chamber containing confined air, as in a pump, a lifeboat, or an organic body.

air′ coach′, *U.S.* coach (def. 4).

air′ command′, *U.S. Air Force.* a unit of command that is higher than an air force.

air-con·di·tion (âr′kən dish′ən), *v.t.* **1.** to furnish with an air-conditioning system. **2.** to treat (air) with such a system.

air′ condi′tioner, an air-conditioning device.

air′ condi′tioning, 1. a system that controls or reduces the temperature and humidity of the air in an office, dwelling, theater, etc. **2.** the act or process of such controlling. **—air′-con·di′tion·ing,** *adj.*

air-cool (âr′ko͞ol′), *v.t.* to cool with circulated air.

Air′ Corps′, *U.S. Army.* **1.** (before July 26, 1947) a branch of the U.S. Army concerned with military aviation. **2.** (before May 1, 1942) the name for the Army Air Forces.

air·craft (âr′kraft′, -kräft′), *n., pl.* **-craft.** any machine supported for flight in the air by buoyancy or by the dynamic action of air on its surfaces, esp. powered airplanes, gliders, and helicopters.

Aircraft carrier

air′craft car′rier, a warship designed mainly with a large deck for the taking off and landing of aircraft and with storage space for aircraft.

air·craft·man (âr′kraft′mən, -kräft′-), *n., pl.* **-men.** *Brit.* aircraftsman.

air·crafts·man (âr′krafts′mən, -kräfts′-), *n., pl.* **-men.** *Brit.* a noncommissioned officer in the RAF.

air·crew (âr′kro͞o′), *n.* *U.S. Air Force.* the crew of an aircraft. Also, **air′ crew′.**

air′ cur′tain, compressed air directed across a doorway to form a shield to exclude drafts, insects, etc.

air′ cush′ion, 1. an inflatable, airtight cushion. **2.** See **air bag.**

air′ cyl′inder, a cylinder containing compressed air, esp. one used as a reservoir or power source.

air′ divi′sion, *U.S. Air Force.* a unit of command, within an air force, usually composed of two or more wings.

Air·drie (âʀ′dʀē), *n.* a city in central Scotland, near Glasgow. 33,620 (1961).

air·drome (âr′drōm′), *n.* a landing field for airplanes; airport. Also, *esp. Brit.,* **aerodrome.** [AIR(PLANE) + -DROME]

air·drop (âr′drop′), *v.,* **-dropped, -drop·ping,** *n.* **—*v.t.* 1.** to drop (persons, equipment, etc.) by parachute from an aircraft in flight. **—*n.* 2.** the act or process of airdropping.

air-dry (âr′drī′), *v.,* **-dried, -dry·ing,** *adj.* **—*v.t.* 1.** to dry by exposure to the air. **—*adj.* 2.** dry beyond further evaporation.

Airedale
(23 in. high at shoulder)

Aire·dale (âr′dāl′), *n.* one of a breed of large terriers having a wiry, black-and-tan coat and a docked tail.

air·field (âr′fēld′), *n.* a level area, usually equipped with hard-surfaced runways, on which airplanes take off and land. [AIR(PLANE) + FIELD]

air·flow (âr′flō′), *n.* air currents caused by a moving aircraft, automobile, etc.

air·foil (âr′foil′), *n.* *Aeron.* any surface, as a wing, aileron, or stabilizer, designed to aid in lifting or controlling an aircraft by making use of the air currents through which it moves.

Air′ Force′, 1. *U.S.* the department consisting of practically all military aviation forces, established July 26, 1947. **2.** (*l.c.*) *U.S.* a unit of Air Force command between an air division and an air command. **3.** (*often l.c.*) the military organization of any nation that is mainly responsible for its military operations in the air.

air·frame (âr′frām′), *n.* the framework and external covering of an airplane, rocket, etc. [AIR(PLANE) + FRAME]

air′ freight′, 1. a system of transporting freight by aircraft. **2.** freight transported by aircraft.

air·glow (âr′glō′), *n.* a nighttime glow from the upper atmosphere, occurring over middle and low latitudes.

air′ gun′, a gun operated by compressed air.

air′ ham′mer, a pneumatic hammer, usually portable.

air′ hole′, 1. an opening to admit or discharge air. **2.** a natural opening in the frozen surface of a river or pond. **3.** See **air pocket.**

air·i·ly (âr′ə lē), *adv.* **1.** in a gay or breezy manner; jauntily. **2.** lightly; delicately.

air·ing (âr′iŋ), *n.* **1.** an exposure to the air, as for drying. **2.** a public discussion, as of ideas, opinions, proposals, etc. **3.** a walk, drive, etc., in the open air.

air′ jack′et, *Brit.* See **life jacket.**

air′ lane′, a route regularly used by airplanes; airway.

air·less (âr′lis), *adj.* **1.** lacking air. **2.** without fresh air; stuffy: *a dark, airless hallway.* **3.** without a breeze.

air′ let′ter, 1. an air-mail letter. **2.** a sheet of extremely lightweight stationery for use in air mail.

air·lift (âr′lift′), *n.* Also, **air′ lift′. 1.** a system for transporting persons or cargo by aircraft, esp. in an emergency. **2.** act or process of transporting such a load. **—*v.t.* 3.** to transport (persons or cargo) by airlift.

air-line (âr′līn′), *adj.* via airplane: *the air-line distance between Detroit and Washington.*

air·line (âr′līn′), *n.* *Aeron.* **1.** a system furnishing air transport, usually scheduled, between specified points. **2.** the airplanes, airports, etc., of such a system. **3.** Often, **airlines.** a company that owns or operates such a system. **4.** a tube or hose used to pipe air to a deep-sea diver, pneumatic drill, etc.

air·lin·er (âr′lī′nər), *n.* *Aeron.* a passenger aircraft operated by an airline. Also, **air′ lin′er.**

air′ lock′, 1. *Civ. Eng.* an airtight chamber permitting passage to or from a space, as in a caisson, in which the air is kept under pressure. **2.** the impedance in the functioning

act, āble, dâre, ärt; ebb, ēqual; if, īce; hot, ōver, ôrder; oil; *bo͝ok; o͞oze;* out; up, ûrge; ə = *a* as in *alone; chief; siŋ; shoe; thin; that;* zh as in *measure;* ᵊ as in *button* (but′ᵊn), *fire* (fīᵊr). See the full key inside the front cover.

8. pronunciation key [pruh NUNS ee ay shun KEE]: guide for pronouncing words.

Dictionaries help you use pronunciation symbols with a quick-reference key printed at the bottom of each page. Symbols are used on words that people commonly know how to pronounce. Keys vary. For example, in the sample page from *The Random House College Dictionary* reprinted here, *a* with a line over it is pronounced like *a* in *able*.

Should the *u* in *Ainu* sound the same as the *oo* in *air cool*?

Yes   No   because _____

True-False: Write "T" for true and "F" for false.

K. ____ The best way to find the correct page of a dictionary is to scan the entry words.

L. ____ A word has multiple entries because it has different spellings.

M. ____ The pronunciation key for all dictionaries is exactly the same.

N. ____ The boldfaced words in the dictionary are known as entry words.

O. ____ The entry word *aleatory* should be found between *albatross* and *alehouse*.

For Your Critical Reflection: Editors of dictionaries have to decide whose pronunciation is "standard," even though pronunciation varies a great deal according to location, social class, and ethnic group. How do you think editors should decide?

_____

_____

III. The Entry

Entries vary slightly from dictionary to dictionary, but all entries help readers with spelling, pronunciation, grammar (by listing the part of speech), and definitions. Good dictionaries give the history of the word and, in cases where the editors think it might be helpful, cross-references, irregular plurals, and notes on how to use the word properly.

• • • • • • • • • • • • • •

Guess What!
What if I Can't Find the Word?

If you have difficulty locating a word, you may be misspelling the word, or your dictionary may list only a different form of the word (such as *happy* but not *happiness*), or the word may not appear in your dictionary.

First, check to make sure that your word is not the name of a specific person, place, or character. If the word is capitalized, you might check listings under nations of the world, biographies, characters from legend, and so on. These words are sometimes printed in alphabetical lists at the back of unabridged or collegiate dictionaries. If the word is in italics, you might check the list of foreign words and phrases, also located at the back.

Second, try other spellings, making your changes in the first five letters. You may be reversing *i* and *e* or using *k* instead of *c*. To help yourself think of more spellings, try spellings used in rhyming words. Most dictionaries do not list *delite* but do list *delight*. Think of "night" or "right" to help you find the correct spelling. If you have some idea what the word means, look up synonyms (words with almost the same meaning). Your word may appear in that entry.

Third, particularly if you are using a small dictionary, make sure you have eliminated prefixes and suffixes, and then look at other forms of the word. If you want to find the word *collegiate*, you might have to look under *college*.

If, in spite of these efforts, you frequently have trouble locating words, or if the definitions do not seem suited to your needs, congratulations! You probably need a bigger, newer, or more advanced dictionary. Believe it or not, big dictionaries are easier to use than small general ones: large dictionaries usually list more forms of words, include more definitions, and use fewer abbreviations. Use specialized dictionaries if you often must find words for a subject you are studying or an area in which you hope to develop expertise.

---

9. syllabification [sih LAB if ih KAY shun]: separation of words into syllables.

Entry words are broken up into pronunciation units, syllables, to help you say the word correctly. Letters grouped together are pronounced in a single sound. Spaces indicate multiple syllables.

Does the entry for *air-condition* in the sample dictionary page show that the term is broken into four syllables?

Yes   No   because _____

10. pronunciation [pruh NUN see ay shun]: how a word is said.

Pronunciation keys at the bottom of the page and in the front of the dictionary can help you to decipher the symbols. Accent marks (´) indicate stressed syllables, which are spoken more loudly than other syllables. If an entry word has more than one pronunciation listed, the one you see first is judged by the editors to be preferred.

According to the sample dictionary page, is the *a* in *Ainu* pronounced like the *a* in *ain't*?

Yes   No   because _____

11. part of speech [PART uv SPEECH]: type of word.

Most words you need to look up will be nouns, adjectives, verbs, or adverbs. The usual abbreviations are (n), (adj), (v), and (adv). Some words can be slightly changed in form to serve as different parts of speech. If you want *to convince* (v) your friend to vote your way, make a *convincing* (adj) argument. Knowledge of parts of speech and forms of words can help you make the most of your vocabulary.

> **noun (n):** person, place, thing, or idea. A *dictionary* is a noun. So is a *syllable*.
>
> **adjective (adj):** a word that modifies or describes a noun. A *collegiate* dictionary may be more *handy* than a *small* dictionary.
>
> **verb (v):** action or state of being. If you *look* in your dictionary, you may *find* some surprises.
>
> **adverb (adv):** modifies a verb. Guide words help you *rapidly* locate the right page.

According to the sample dictionary page, is *ailing* a verb?

Yes   No   because _____

12. etymology [et ih MOL ih jee]: word history.

The etymology provides a brief history of the word. For example, the word *dictionary* comes from the Latin *dicere*, meaning "to speak." *Dictator, dictation,* and *dictaphone* have the same history. The front matter of your dictionary provides a table of abbreviations used in etymologies. The etymology can help you remember the meaning of a word.

According to the sample dictionary page, do *aim* and *estimate* have the same etymology?

Yes   No   because _____

13. definitions [deh fi NIH shuns]: ways the words are used.

Definitions tell you the ways in which your word is used. Be sure to check the front matter of your dictionary to see the order in which definitions are arranged. The first definition in *Webster's Ninth* is the oldest one, which may not be in common use anymore. Also, remember that definitions are denotations (precise meanings). Check labeling, usage notes, and cross-references for connotations (emotional overtones).

Does the word *air* in the sample dictionary page have more than one definition as well as more than one entry?

Yes   No   because _____

14. citations [siye TAY shuns]: quotations.

A citation is a quotation used for support or example. Citations allow you to see the word used in context. Some dictionaries contain many citations; others contain none. *The Oxford English Dictionary* cites Fanny Burney's novel *Evelina* (1778) to illustrate *ain't*: "Those you are engaged to ain't half so near related to you as we are."

James Thurber wrote about his stubborn and malicious Airedale in a famous story, "The Dog that Bit People." Would a citation from this story be relevant to the entry *Airedale* in the sample dictionary page?

Yes   No   because _____

15. cross-references [KROSS REF run siz]: related words that can be checked.

At the end of the entry, your dictionary may list synonyms and antonyms. Synonyms have almost the same meaning as your word; antonyms have nearly the opposite meaning. You can look up these other words, these cross-references, for a fuller understanding of your word. One or more of the synonyms may have more detailed definitions.

Does the sample dictionary page provide *wind* as a cross-reference for more than one definition of the word *air*?

Yes   No   because _____

Matching: Match the query with the part of the entry that answers the question.

P. ____ What tells you how to break the word
alchemy when you use hyphens?

(a) etymology

Q. ____ What tells you how to correctly say the
word *gregarious* ("likes people")?

(b) definitions

R. ____ What tells you if your word is a noun or a
verb?

(c) part of speech

S. ____ What tells you that *alderman* comes from
the Old English *chief*?

(d) citation

T. ____ What tells you the precise meaning of the
word *sage*?

(e) cross-references

U. ____ What tells you that Tennessee Williams said,
"I will not dissemble my life"?

(f) pronunciation

V. ____ What tells you that *multifarious* is a
synonym for *many*?

(g) syllabification

(h) illustration

Using Context: Fill in each blank with the vocabulary word that best suits the context.

Aiming Higher

Maria used to think that the dictionary was the place to go to find out the

one true meaning of a word. She was in for a surprise. When she looked

up *aim* in her new collegiate dictionary, she found eleven separate

_____. Saying the word was easy, as Maria found when

she checked the _____ and the _____.

But Maria did not expect to find that one word could be both a noun and a

verb, two different _____. For such a small word, *aim*

has a complicated history, according to the _____. Maria

found the precise definition she needed, and her new aim is to aim for

learning more words.

For Your Critical Reflection: Dictionary makers often choose the "best" authors and speakers to use in citations. Think of some speakers and writers you would like to see cited. Can you think of some who should not be cited?

_____

_____

IV. Labels and Usage Notes

Makers of dictionaries want to give you as much information as possible. Some words are no longer used; some are used only in certain regions of the United States or Great Britain. Some are used in a derogatory sense, as insults; some are used as slang. Simply providing the denotation of a word might lead the unsuspecting reader or writer to sound wildly inappropriate. A student writing a formal paper for a biology class would not want to refer to mucus as "snot." Labels designate the limits of a word. Usage notes explain the controversy surrounding words that seem to be in flux.

How do editors decide? Careful monitoring of publications in various fields, consultations with experts, and statistical sampling all help editors to decide what usage is appropriate under what circumstances. Labels include "sports," "French," "poetic," "engineering," and so on. Some common labels are listed in the vocabulary words that follow.

16. informal/colloquial/nonstandard [in FORM uhl] [cuhl OH kwee yuhl] [non STAN dird]: conversational/conversational for some groups/incorrect.

The most common labels tell us which words would not ordinarily appear in formal writing and speeches. _Informal_ and _colloquial_ uses of words are similar: they are correct in conversation but not in writing. To say "That guy really is _somebody_," meaning that the man is an important person, is to use informal or colloquial language. The label _nonstandard_ is a polite way to call a particular word or usage incorrect. To say "This conversation is going _nowheres, irregardless_ of my efforts" is to speak nonstandard English. The correct, colloquial form would be "This conversation is going nowhere, regardless of my efforts."

Is it true that _ain't_ ain't in the dictionary?

Yes   No   because _____

17. slang/vulgar/derogatory [SLAYNG] [VUHL gir] [de ROG uh toar ee]: colorful language/impolite language/insulting language.

Slang usually refers to colorful language that remains in use for a short time. The cartoon character Bart Simpson says "Don't have a cow" to mean what people used to mean when they said "Don't flip out." Unlike vulgar and derogatory language, slang can be an endearing feature of informal conversation. Vulgar language might be obscene or offensive. Derogatory language is insulting and offensive. *Spic* is derogatory.

Would you rather hear slang than be called something derogatory?

Yes   No   because _____

18. dialect/regional [DIE uh lekt] [REEJ uh nul]: expressions used by certain groups or in certain places/expressions particular to certain places.

Words or uses common in some places but not in others sometimes carry a label identifying a location. Southwestern United States, Regional British, and Chiefly British are examples of geographical labels.

Is *ain't* more acceptable in Britain than it is in most parts of the United States, according to the sample dictionary page?

Yes   No   because _____

19. obsolete/archaic/rare [ob SOH leet] [ar KAY ik] [RAIR]: no longer used/old-fashioned/hardly ever used.

Obsolete words once were used but are no longer used. *Archaic* words sound old-fashioned but sometimes occur today, such as the word *eve* for evening. *Rare* words are not common and never were. A rare word is not necessarily old.

Does the second entry for *air* in the sample dictionary page contain any obsolete uses of the word?

Yes   No   because _____

20. usage notes [YOO suj NOHTS]: explanations.

Dictionaries may provide phrases, sentences, and even paragraphs intended to help the reader make decisions about usage. The longer the usage note, the more controversial the usage is. Compare the following two notes on *nauseous*. *The American Heritage Dictionary of the English Language* (1978):

> Employment of *nauseous* in the sense of *nauseated* (experiencing nausea) is considered unacceptable by 88 per cent of the Usage Panel.

Webster's Ninth New Collegiate Dictionary (1987):

> Those who insist that *nauseous* can properly be used only in sense 1 are in error. Current evidence shows these facts: *nauseous* is most often used to

mean physically affected with nausea; extended use is quite a bit less frequent. Use of *nauseous* in sense 1 is much more often figurative than literal, but this use appears to be losing ground to *nauseating*. There seems to be little use of *nauseated* except by those who prescribe it in place of *nauseous*.

Both dictionaries indicate that the word means to make [someone] feel queasy, as in "That oatmeal looks nauseous," and both also suggest that the word can refer to someone who is experiencing nausea, as in "I feel nauseous." *The American Heritage Dictionary* urges readers toward the first meaning, *Webster's Ninth* toward the second.

Dictionaries are not rule books. They guide you toward uses, but you must consider your taste and context—are your readers and listeners going to expect a certain level of formality?—as well as the date of your dictionary.

If you said "I am nauseous" to someone expecting very formal use of language, should that person consider you repulsive?

Yes   No   because _____

True-False: Write "T" for true and "F" for false.

W. ____ *Informal* and *colloquial* describe uses of words for conversation but not writing.

X. ____ *Nonstandard* is a polite way of saying using this word is incorrect.

Y. ____ *Vulgar* language can be offensive.

Z. ____ *Slang* refers to colorful language that remains in use for a short time.

a. ____ The dictionary is noble enough to include no *vulgar* words in it.

b. ____ *Derogatory* indicates a word that has insulting or degrading connotations.

c. ____ A *dialect* or *regional* meaning of a word is the most formal usage.

d. ____ " 'Tis the morn for prancing on the lea" includes some archaic words.

e. ____ *Obsolete* words would be excellent for use in a campaign speech.

f. ____ The longer the usage note the more controversial is the usage of the word.

g. ____ The usage notes for all dictionaries are precisely the same.

For Your Critical Reflection: Usage is the most controversial aspect of dictionary making. Some editors say that the "average" person's use should be standard; others say that the "educated" writer sets the standard. Describe the "average" and the "educated" person. How do they speak? Given all the variety in our country today, where should dictionary makers go to find standard usage?

_____

_____

V. The Thesaurus

The word *thesaurus* comes from roots meaning "treasure house." A thesaurus is designed to help writers find better ways of using words in their active vocabularies.

21. thesaurus [thuh SOAR us]: a backward dictionary.

The thesaurus is a "backward dictionary," a book designed to help you when you know the meaning but not the word. A thesaurus lists synonyms and antonyms (see chapter 2). The word lists are meant to help you write more vividly and precisely. Beware of using unfamiliar words from a thesaurus, because words are sometimes listed without information about their connotations or usage. Calling someone "queer" is not the same as calling the person "unique." The thesaurus comes in two types.

Dictionary-type. You look up your word and read down a list of synonyms, some of which have brief definitions in brackets. Often there are a few antonyms. Boldfaced synonyms can work as cross-references: look them up for more words.

Webster's New World Thesaurus, by Charlton Laird, has one entry for *odd,* but the entry contains four definitions:

> **odd,** *a* **1.** [Unusual] queer, unique, strange; see **unusual** 2. **2.** [Miscellaneous] fragmentary, odd-lot, varied; see **various. 3.** [Single] sole, unpaired, unmatched; see **alone. 4.** [Not even] remaining, over and above, leftover; see **irregular** 1, 4.

Roget's. Peter Mark Roget published the first thesaurus in 1852, arranging entries under large concepts such as "space," "matter," and "sensation." To find words, first look up a related word in the alphabetized index at the back of the book. Under your word will be listings referring you to longer entries, listed by number, under the various classes in the thesaurus. In the entry itself, cross-references are boldfaced, sometimes with the numbers of other entries.

Roget's International Thesaurus, fourth edition, revised by Robert L. Chapman, has nine entries for *odd.* Here is one of them:

> **odd, queer, peculiar, absurd** 510.7, **singular, curious, oddball,** kooky [informal], freaky *or* freaked out [both slang], quaint, **eccentric,** funny, rum [Brit slang]; **strange, outlandish,** off the wall [informal], passing strange, "wondrous strange" [Shakespeare]; **weird,** unearthly; off, out.

If you wanted more words for *odd,* could you find them by looking up *unusual* in *Webster's?*

Yes   No   because _____

True-False: Write "T" for true and "F" for false.

h. _____ A thesaurus is a "backward dictionary."

i. _____ If you owned a thesaurus, you would also need a book of antonyms.

j. _____ Using unfamiliar words listed as synonyms is a good idea.

k. _____ A "dictionary-type" thesaurus and "Roget's thesaurus" are used in the same way.

l. _____ An unabridged and massive thesaurus is called a *megathesaurus.*

For Your Critical Reflection: If you wanted to use the thesaurus but were not sure of the difference between *singular* and *outlandish,* where might you go for help?

_____

_____

Chapter Review

I. **Multiple Choice:** Select the word that correctly finishes the sentence.

1. _____ Desktop dictionaries sometimes are called (a) prescriptive, (b) unabridged, (c) collegiate dictionaries.

2. _____ Some dictionaries provide a miniature research library in the (a) abridgment, (b) back matter, (c) front matter.

3. ____ If you need a synonym when writing, check the (a) multiple entries, (b) thesaurus, (c) specialized dictionaries.

4. ____ General dictionaries sometimes place synonyms in the (a) cross-reference, (b) back matter, (c) preface.

5. ____ A history of your word appears in the (a) guide words, (b) etymology, (c) pronunciation key.

II. True-False: Write "T" for true and "F" for false.

6. ____ When you are looking for a word, the guide words tell you if you are on the right page.

7. ____ Multiple entries tell you the same things as multiple definitions.

8. ____ Syllabification helps you to say a word.

9. ____ The pronunciation key indicates a word's part of speech.

10. ____ Colloquial is a polite way of saying that something is incorrect.

11. ____ Informal is a label that applies to words used in conversation more than in writing.

12. ____ Slang will always be appropriate in some contexts.

13. ____ People with different dialects probably come from different places.

14. ____ Rare words once were common but now are uncommon.

15. ____ *Roget's Thesaurus* is a backward dictionary.

16. ____ Usage notes are needed for every word.

17. ____ The easiest dictionary to use is a pocket abridged dictionary.

18. ____ Specialized dictionaries explain technical terms used in professions.

19. ____ Nouns and verbs are both parts of speech.

20. ____ Citations are found mostly in prescriptive dictionaries.

III. Using Context: Consult the word list at the beginning of the chapter to fill in the blanks. You might not use all the words, or you might use one word more than once.

Power and Change

Dictionaries have a great deal of authority. As Morris Bishop once suggested, every law court has its big dictionary; the law settles cases, rates crimes, and awards millions by quoting _____ of words. Yet dictionaries do not agree. The usage notes in _____ dictionaries are quite strict, whereas the _____ in _____ dictionaries might offer little guidance. And dictionaries must be updated all the time, because even the smallest _____ dictionaries need to add new words and new definitions. With a changing population bringing new ways to say words, _____ changes, too. Famous writers provide interesting new _____ for dictionaries to quote as examples of usage, and sometimes old writers find that their ways of using words have become _____. Words that once were colorful _____ terms among the hip crowds often become standard. Speech rules the day. As the great eighteenth-century lexicographer Samuel Johnson said, "The pen must at length comply with the tongue." Thank goodness dictionaries can change, because some definitions are not only inaccurate but offensively _____, such as definitions of *Jesuit* as "deceitful person," and *Jew* as "unscrupulous bargainer," which once actually appeared in dictionaries. In 1977 one dictionary was threatened with a boycott for defining *Palestinian* as one who "seeks to displace Israelis" as a definition listed in the _____ for that word. Dictionary editors say that they are not responsible for the ways people use words; the dictionary's job is to record usage. Some of the uses seem pretty funny. The thesaurus is even funnier. Imagine listing *stabilize* as a synonym for *define* when the definitions of words continually change! Sometimes it is not surprising that Peter Mark Roget, author of the first _____, among his many fascinating activities, served as a doctor for an insane asylum.

Reading for Chapter 3

CULLEN MURPHY

Caught in the Web of Bytes

Dictionaries are getting easier to use all the time, and lovers of words are finding more ways to use them. Here is a story about the computerized version of the biggest dictionary in English.

Words to Notice

Optional Exercise: Use your dictionary if you do not know the meaning of the following words:

A. **enthralling** means

_____

B. **software** is

_____

C. **facilitate** means

_____

D. **ungainly** means

_____

E. **ensure** means

_____

F. **Latinate words** are

_____

G. **prefixes** appear

_____

H. **pre-eminence** is

_____

I. a **computer terminal** is

_____

J. **homonyms** are

_____

K. **palindromes** are

_____

L. a **data base** is

_____

M. **Germanic words** are

_____

N. **suffixes** appear

_____ [1]

[1] *Answers:* A. **enthralling** means fascinating. B. **software** is a computer's instructions. C. **facilitate** means make easy. D. **ungainly** means difficult. E. **ensure** means guarantee. F. **Latinate words** are usually long. G. **prefixes** appear before a root word (pre-). H. **pre-eminence** is respect. I. a **computer terminal** is a device to input instructions. J. **homonyms** are words that mean the same, but are spelled differently. K. **palindromes** are words that mean the same when pronounced forward or backward "madam"). L. a **data base** is a place to store information. M. **Germanic words** are usually short. N. **suffixes** appear at the end of words (-ion).

1   I spent a startling and enthralling couple of hours not long ago with two computer scientists in Canada who said, "Yes, it can do that," every time I asked if the software they had developed was capable of answering one of the questions I wanted to tease it with. Gaston Gonnet and Frank Tompa, who are members of the department of computer science at the University of Waterloo, in Ontario, are the authors of several programs that promise not only to facilitate the task of retrieving information from large bodies of text—often an ungainly procedure—but also to help ensure that *The Oxford English Dictionary* continues to enjoy pre-eminence as the English language's dictionary of record.

2   Gonnet, Tompa, and I all sat at a terminal linked to a Sun-3/160S work station so that I might see for myself what their system could do with the initial 35,000 or so entries—from *A* to *Chaytif*—of the *OED*'s first edition.

3   Can it make a list, I asked, of all the words that are homonyms and all the words that are palindromes? Can it give examples, from the citations, of sentences that have introduced more than one word to the language? Can it make a list of the words ending in *q*, and one of the words in which *q* is not followed by *u*? Can it identify the adverbs that don't end in -*ly*, and the words that contain all the vowels? Can it pick out the words for which there is a citation from Keats, and then determine what percentage of those words are Latinate in character and what percentage Germanic? Can it pick out the common prefixes and suffixes, and then determine which ones have become more popular over the centuries and which ones less? Can it use the dictionary as what is called a reverse dictionary—that is, can it locate a word if you know only the definition, such as the word that means a battle between frogs and mice, or the word that comes from the Greek for "ox-turning" and refers to writing that goes back and forth from right to left and then left to right on the page?

4   The liturgical response was always "Yes, it can do that."

5   I asked Gonnet if he could find all the words for which *The Atlantic Monthly* provided a citation. He keyed in some instructions, and a few seconds later a list appeared, beginning,

> *Adrip*
>
> *Affranchise*
>
> *Angelus*
>
> *Animistic*
>
> *Anti-*
>
> *Aphorism*
>
> *Attitudinize*
>
> *Avoir dupois*
>
> *Bolter*
>
> *Bummer . . .*

6   *Bummer?* The citation was from 1865, and the meaning not entirely malign: "an idler." The electronic *OED* was certainly capable of making an idler out of

me. After only a few minutes with it I began to experience the onset of serious addiction.

7   Computers will never replace the "harmless drudge" Samuel Johnson associated with dictionary-making. The combing of printed matter for new words or old words with new meanings, the tracing of etymologies, the writing of definitions—these chores are ever reserved for mortals. (Dr. Johnson, in his *Dictionary of the English Language,* defined the word *dull* thus: "Not exhilarating; not delightful; as, *to make dictionaries is* dull *work.*") Computers will also never make the intellectual decisions about purpose and function that underlie every dictionary. But computerizing the text of dictionaries—creating an electronic version that can be amended at will and set in type at any time—will make them easier to revise and produce. More important, a computerized dictionary is no longer just a dictionary. It becomes a data base; a source of new kinds of knowledge not only for those interested in language but for specialists of all kinds.

Questions for Class Discussion

1. What questions would you like to ask the computer?
2. With computerized dictionaries, possibilities for additions are practically endless. Are there types of words that should not be there? How many people need to use a word before it goes into the dictionary?
3. Cullen Murphy writes that this dictionary can be useful "for specialists of all kinds." How could people in business, law, or science take advantage of this computerized dictionary?

Making a New World

For Class Discussion

1. Some people use dictionaries too much; some people never use one. If you are reading and you run across a new word, how do you decide whether to look it up?
2. What is the value, if any, of providing etymologies and citations?
3. Some people want dictionaries to "purify" the language by saying how words should be used. Others say that dictionaries should reflect real speech even if most people violate the rules, because rules will change as habits allow. Which side are you on? What are the gains and losses in each system?

Collaborative Learning

1. Usage
   Purpose: To test the proposition "All of us deserve the chance to make decisions about usage."

    A. Your group has been hired as a usage panel for a new dictionary. You will choose from these labels to describe words (you do not need to use all the labels): standard, colloquial, slang, nonstandard, derogatory.

    B. Now, label these words and phrases: howdy, ain't, lousy (meaning "bad"), sales rep, idiotic, and cool guy. Do not consult a dictionary; you are the usage panel.

    C. Give your reasons for assigning each label.

    D. Report to the class and see if you agree. Optional: check dictionaries now to see if you are more strict or more liberal than they are.

2. Flattering or Derogatory Language
   Purpose: To develop sensitivity to connotations.

    A. Make sure each group has a dictionary and a thesaurus.

    B. Look up these words: womanly, manly, rich, poor. Keep using cross-references until you find a flattering synonym (or definition) and a derogatory synonym (or definition) for each word. (Use your judgment: the synonyms need not have labels.)

    C. Write down why these words seem flattering or derogatory.

    D. Report your findings to the class. See if you and the class believe these synonyms and definitions to be true and fair. Why or why not?

Ideas for Writing

1. In a paragraph, advise a friend about when to use a dictionary and when not to use one when reading.

2. In a page, write a letter to Joe. Joe knows how to use the pronunciation guide in his dictionary, but he is worried that his strong Brooklyn accent might make him mispronounce words anyway. Encourage Joe to try using new words in spite of his accent.

3. The eighteenth-century writer Daniel Defoe hoped that in the future it would "be as criminal to coin new words as money." Yet dictionaries are continually adding new words from other languages, from science, and from slang. At home, write an essay on why the English language needs to grow or does not need to grow. Discuss what you think a person should do to foster either change or stability.

More Words for Chapter 3

amend: to correct an error, mend

attribution: indicates who wrote or first coined a word

cognate: having the same source or origin, sharing etymology

declension: variation of the form of a noun

derivation: place from which something derives, comes from; origin

diacritical mark: a sign used in pronunciation keys to indicate that a letter has a particular sound

Germanic: having German origins; typically short words from Anglo-Saxon

homonym: word with the same spelling or sound as another but a different meaning (e.g., sale and sail)

Indo-European: of the family of languages spoken in most of Europe and parts of Asia

idiolect: the unique pronunciation or use of words by one person

idiom: the language as used by most people

inflection: change of a word to show a grammatical relationship; ''bring'' inflects to ''brought''

Latinate: having Latin origins; Spanish, French, and Italian are Latinate languages; longer words in English

linguistics: the scientific study of language structure and use

lexicography: the practice or art of writing dictionaries

locution: a word or phrase

neologism: a freshly coined or created word or phrase

orthography: correct or standard spelling

palindrome: a word or phrase that reads the same backwards or forwards: ''Madam I'm Adam''

prefix: a word or syllable (pre-, un-) placed before a word to change meaning

root: the source or base syllable or syllables of a word

semantics: the branch of linguistics dealing with meaning

suffix: a word or syllable (-tion, -able) placed after a word to change meaning

variant: differing from standard, a variant form or spelling

Answer Key to Chapter 3

I. THE BOOK ITSELF

Yes-No Questions

1. No; they do not help with usage.

2. Yes; descriptive dictionaries describe usage.

3. Yes; back matters sometimes include names from mythology.

4. No; each field has specialized dictionaries.

Matching

A. (h) B. (i) C. (c) D. (g) E. (b)
F. (a) G. (a) H. (d) I. (d) J. (f)

Using Context: Stranded

unabridged,   general,   prescriptive,
front matter, back matter

II. THE PAGE

Yes-No Questions

5. Yes; *b* comes before *l* in the
   alphabet.
6. No; *aircraftsman* has its own
   entry.
7. Yes; it has two.
8. Yes; see the punctuation key.

True-False

K. F L. F M. F N. T O. T

III. THE ENTRY

Yes-No Questions

9. Yes; air-con-di-tion.
10. No; "ai" is pronounced "eye" as
    in Taiwan.
11. No; it's an adjective: "My ailing
    friend."
12. Yes; see 13: "aestimare (see
    ESTIMATE)."
13. Yes; it has 26 altogether.
14. Yes, though you might admire
    the picture.
15. Yes; synonyms appear at the end
    of the entry.

Matching

P. (g) Q. (f) R. (c) S. (a) T. (b)
U. (d) V. (e)

Using Context: Aiming Higher

definitions, pronunciation (or syllabification), syllabification (or pronunciation), parts of speech, etymology

IV. LABELS AND USAGE NOTES

Yes-No Questions

16. No; it ain't true. See the sample
    dictionary page.
17. Yes; derogatory means insulting.
18. Yes; *ain't* is informal in Britain,
    that is, acceptable in conversa-
    tion, but nonstandard (incorrect)
    in the U.S.
19. Yes; "*Obs.* before."
20. Yes; in formal usage *nauseous*
    means "causing to make nau-
    seated."

True-False

W. T X. T Y. T Z. T a. F b. T
c. F d. T e. F f. T g. F

V. THE THESAURUS

Yes-No Question

21. Yes; the entry says "see **unusual
    2.**"

True-False

h. T i. F j. F k. F l. F

CHAPTER REVIEW

I. Multiple Choice

1. (c) 2. (b) 3. (b) 4. (a) 5. (b)

II. True-False

6. T 7. F 8. T 9. F 10. F 11. T

12. T 13. T 14. F 15. T 16. F
17. F 18. T 19. T 20. F

III. Using Context: Power
and Change

definitions, prescriptive, usage notes, descriptive, abridged, pronunciation, citations, obsolete or rare, slang, derogatory, entry, thesaurus

WORD PARTS: LIFE AND PEOPLE

Quick Reference Word List

amor, eros, philos	cide	mal	ped, pus	son, phon
andr	crat, -cracy	man	phobia	soph, -sophy
anim	cred	mania	poli, polis, civi, civic	soror
anthrop	ego, auto	matri, mater	prud	spirat
audi	fid	mort	pseudo	theo
bene, eu	frater	necro	psycho, psyche	ver
bio	gen	neur	reg	vid, vis
capit	gyn	ocul	scop, spec	viv
cardio	log, logo, -logy	patri, pater		voc, vocal
		ped		

Introduction: English, an International Language

English has been an international language almost from its beginnings. Migrations, conquests, and trade have brought waves of new words into the vocabulary, and trade in products and ideas continues to enrich the English language. The language generally changes slowly, but sometimes it has changed drastically.

Latin and Greek are two important languages for English. Greek was the language of European learning for many centuries. Latin was the language of the Roman Empire and also the parent of such Latinate modern languages as Spanish, Italian, and French. Greek and Latin have contributed both complete words and parts of words to the English language: these word parts form the building blocks of many words. By learning a few parts, you can increase your vocabulary by hundreds or even thousands of words. Also, you can learn to pick apart an unfamiliar word to guess at its meaning. If you are a native speaker of a Latinate language, or if you are studying a Latinate language, many of these buildings blocks may be familiar.

There are three types of word parts: prefixes, suffixes, and roots. A prefix is added in front of a word to change its meaning. *Pre-*, for example, is a prefix meaning "before," so a *pre*fix is fixed *before* the word. A suffix is added to the end of the word. The *-ed* in *added* is a suffix used to indicate the past tense. Prefixes change the meaning of a word more than suffixes. Suffixes make it possible for a word to be used in several parts of speech—as a noun, an adjective, or an adverb. Many prefixes and suffixes can be picked up after a few years of working with English. In most dictionaries, a word part printed with a hyphen after it (*hyper-*) is a prefix. A word part with a hyphen before it (*-sophy*) is a suffix. Roots may appear anywhere. A root is the basic word or word part from which other words are formed. This chapter and the next one emphasize roots.

. . . .

Have You Heard?
Who Is Psyche?

Our word *psychology* comes from the fable of Psyche. As a young woman, Psyche was so beautiful that the goddess of love was jealous and sent her son Cupid to fall in love with the mortal. Cupid visited Psyche only in the dark, forbidding her to look at him. One night she peeked. Struck by the sight of his godly beauty, Psyche let a drop of oil fall from the lamp, which woke him up. The god left her in anger. To win him back, Psyche performed a variety of superhuman tasks. Near the end of the last task, her curiosity prompted her to open a box that turned out to contain a deadly sleeping potion. Still in love, Cupid convinced the gods and goddesses to make Psyche immortal, so the two were married. Psyche's blend of love, curiosity, heroism, and movement from human to immortal make her the perfect symbol of the human soul, mind, or spirit.

I. Body Parts and the Human Sensory System

1. *son* and *phon:* sound.

sonorous: having or producing an impressive sound.

sonic: of or relating to sound.

phonograph: a machine that reproduces sound from a disk.

phonetics: the study of the sounds of speech.

If you know that *tele* means "far" and *phon* means "sound," might you think a telephone conveys sounds over distances?

Yes   No   because _____

2. *audi:* hearing.

audible: capable of being heard.

audience: a gathering of listeners.

auditory: pertaining to hearing.

If you decided to call an auditor, would you be looking for someone to do the talking?

Yes   No   because _____

3. *scop, spec, vid, vis:* see.

microscope: an instrument for observing tiny objects.
spectacles: eyeglasses.
video: pertaining to televised images.
television: device for receiving visual images over a distance.
visual: involving the sense of sight.

If you visualize something, do you form a mental picture of it?

Yes   No   because _____

4. *ocul:* eye.

binoculars: two lenses for seeing at a distance.
oculist: a physician who treats the eyes.

If a speaker provides an ocular demonstration, is that person using a visual aid?

Yes   No   because _____

5. *voc, vocal:* voice, call.

vocal: pertaining to the voice.
vociferate: to cry out loudly.
vocation: a profession for which one feels a calling.
vocalist: singer.

If someone says you are vociferous, are you silent and withdrawn?

Yes   No   because _____

6. *ped* and *pus*: foot.

octopus: eight-footed creature.
biped: creature with two feet.

. . . .

Guess What!
You Can Learn History from Word Parts

Professors sometimes are known as *pedagogues*. The word comes from *ped* (child) and *agog* (leader). The original pedagogues were slaves who led Greek children to school.

Before people knew the disease *malaria* was transmitted by insects, it was thought that breathing swamp air caused the infection. Hence the name *malaria*, from *mal* (bad) and *aer* (air).

pedestrian: one who travels on foot.

pedal: lever operated with one's foot.

If you know that a manicure is cosmetic care for the hands and fingernails, might you guess that a pedicure is that same care for feet?

Yes   No   because _____

7. man: hand.

manicure: cosmetic care for hands.

manual: operated by hand.

manacles: handcuffs or other restraining device.

manifest: clearly apparent (from "grasped by the hand").

Is a fully automated machine doing its work manually?

Yes   No   because _____

8. cardio: heart.

cardiology: the study of heart disease.

cardiovascular: involving the heart and blood vessels.

cardiologist: a doctor specializing in treatment of the heart.

If someone has suffered cardiac arrest, has that person's heart stopped?

Yes   No   because _____

9. *capit:* head.

    capitol: building where heads of state assemble.

    capital city: the official place of government.

    capitulate: to surrender under certain conditions (listed under headings).

If you were studying architecture, would you expect to find the capital of a column at the bottom?

Yes   No   because _____

10. *neur:* nerves.

    neuron: nerve cell.

    neurosis: disorder of the mind or emotions with no clear cause (formerly thought to be caused by nerves).

    neuralgia: pain along the nerves.

    neuritis: inflammation of a nerve.

Would you consult a neurologist for a manicure?

Yes   No   because _____

Matching: Use your knowledge of word forms to match the definitions with the words.

A. ____ A dramatic event that everyone *sees*.	(a) cardiology
B. ____ A profession for which you feel a *calling*.	(b) phonetics
C. ____ An instrument for *seeing tiny* objects.	(c) microscope
D. ____ The study of *heart* disease.	(d) vocation
E. ____ Pain along the *nerves*.	(e) triped
F. ____ A physician who treats the *eye*.	(f) spectacle
G. ____ The study of the *sounds* of speech.	(g) oculist
H. ____ A creature with three *feet*.	(h) audible
I. ____ Capable of being *heard*.	(i) manifest
J. ____ Clearly known, grasped by the *hand*.	(j) neuralgia
	(k) pediatrician

Using Context: Fill in each blank with the word part that completes the word.

Crowds

Last week I went to Washington, D.C., the nation's _____al. I tried to

drive a car, but at every corner I almost hit a _____estrian. These close

calls almost caused me a _____ac arrest, so I quickly parked. You

might think that my nervousness about driving is a sign of

_____osis, but I wanted to see the monuments and museums, not the

inside of a hospital. Hoping to capture some of the scenes, I took my

_____eo camera and bin_____ulars from the car and headed to-

ward the Washington Monument, standing like a needle into the sky.

There I saw _____iferous protesters, who shouted at the tops of their

lungs. Soon they roused the air with a _____orous chanting that must

have been _____ble for two miles. It was _____ifest to me that

our democracy is as vital as ever.

For Your Critical Reflection: How much of a "calling" is required for a job to become a vocation?

_____

_____

II. The Family, Self, and Others

11. *matri* and *mater:* mother.

> *matriarchy:* rule by women or mothers.
> *maternal:* motherly.
> *maternity:* motherhood.
> *matron:* married woman.
> *matrimony:* marriage.

Would you expect a matriarchal society to have men in most positions of social power?

Yes   No   because _____

12. *patri* **and** *pater:* father.

> *patriarchy:* rule by men or fathers.
> *paternal:* fatherly.
> *paternity:* fatherhood.
> *patrimony:* inherited wealth, especially from one's father.

Would a new father be able to request maternity leave from work?

Yes   No   because _____

13. *soror:* sister.

> *sorority:* social club for female students; sisterhood.
> *sororicide:* the killing of one's sister.
> *sororate:* marriage with the sister of a former wife.
> *sorosis:* a society of women.

If your daughter wanted to get to know other female students, might she join a sorority?

Yes   No   because _____

14. *frater:* brother.

> *fraternity:* social club for male students; brotherhood.
> *fratricide:* the killing of one's brother.
> *fraternal:* brotherly.
> *fraternize:* to associate with others in a friendly way.

If you were accused of patricide and fratricide, could you still have a sister?

Yes   No   because _____

15. *ped:* child.

> *pediatrics:* medical care of children.
> *pederasty:* the prohibited practice of sexual relations between an adult and
>   a child.
> *pedagogue:* teacher of the young.

Would a pediatrician be likely to recognize chicken pox?

Yes   No   because _____

16. *anthrop:* people, humanity.

anthropology: the study of the origin and cultural development of humanity.
misanthrope: someone who dislikes people in general.
anthropocentric: seeing all reality in terms of human values and experience.
anthropomorphize: treating nonhuman objects and animals as if they were
   human.

Is a misanthrope likely to enjoy working as an anthropologist?

Yes   No   because _____

17. *gyn:* female.

gynecology: medical study of female physiology.
misogynist: someone who dislikes women.
gynocentrism: seeing female experience as the norm.
gynephobia: fear of women.

If a policy discriminates against women, could the policy be misogynistic?

Yes   No   because _____

18. *andr:* male.

androgen: male hormone.
androgynous: pertaining to male offspring.
misandry: dislike of men.
polyandry: marriage to more than one husband.

Noticing that androgynous contains the roots *gyn* for female and *andr* for male,
would you conclude that the word refers to "both male and female"?

Yes   No   because _____

19. *ego* and *auto:* self.

Ego is used only for people; *auto* may be used for people or things.

    egocentric: self-centered.
    egoistic: promoting one's own interest above the concern for others.
    egotistic: talking and writing about oneself too much; conceited.
    autocracy: government by one person who has total power.
    autobiography: a written account of one's own life.
    automatic: moving by oneself, not susceptible to outside influence.

If your children want more autonomy, are they seeking more guidance from you?

Yes   No   because _____

Matching: Use your knowledge of word forms to match the definitions with the words.

K. ____ Someone who dislikes all *humans*.   (a) sororicide

L. ____ Rule by women or *mothers*.   (b) gynephobe

M. ____ A written account of one's own *life*.   (c) patrimony

N. ____ To associate in a *brotherly* way.   (d) fraternize

O. ____ Inherited wealth from one's *father*.   (e) matriarchy

P. ____ Someone who is *self*-centered.   (f) misanthrope

Q. ____ Someone who fears *women*.   (g) autobiography

R. ____ The medical care of *children*.   (h) egotist

S. ____ The killing of one's own *sister*.   (i) pediatrics

T. ____ Someone who dislikes only *men*.   (j) misandrist

    (k) misogynist

True-False: Write "T" for true and "F" for false. Provide the word part clue.

U. ____ An egotistical person would probably enjoy ruling an autocracy.

    Clue: _____

V. ＿＿ A misandrist would probably not be a polyandrist.

Clue: ＿＿＿＿＿＿＿＿＿＿＿

W. ＿＿ A misogynist would make a good gynecologist.

Clue: ＿＿＿＿＿＿＿＿＿＿＿

X. ＿＿ Someone who liked to anthropomorphize might nickname her car.

Clue: ＿＿＿＿＿＿＿＿＿＿＿

Y. ＿＿ A pedophile would warn you to use the clutch sparingly.

Clue: ＿＿＿＿＿＿＿＿＿＿＿

Z. ＿＿ A matriarch would probably enjoy sorosis.

Clue: ＿＿＿＿＿＿＿＿＿＿＿

For Your Critical Reflection. The words *misanthropy* and *misogyny* are heard much more frequently than the almost unknown *misandry*. What is it about American society that would make the first two words so much more common than the last?

＿＿＿＿＿＿＿＿＿＿＿＿＿＿＿＿＿＿＿＿＿＿＿＿＿＿＿＿＿

＿＿＿＿＿＿＿＿＿＿＿＿＿＿＿＿＿＿＿＿＿＿＿＿＿＿＿＿＿

III. Life and Death

20. *bio:* life.

biology: the study of life and living things.

biochemistry: the chemistry of biological substances.

biography: a written account of someone's life.

microbiology: study of minute forms of life.

symbiosis: the living together of different plants or animals for mutual benefit.

Are biodegradable substances capable of being absorbed through the life processes in nature?

Yes   No   because ＿＿＿＿＿＿＿＿＿＿＿＿＿＿＿＿＿＿＿

"Out! Everyone out! ... I've had it
with this 'symbiosis' baloney!"

The Far Side © 1986 Universal Press Syndicate.
Reprinted with permission.

21. *viv:* living, alive.

vivid: strikingly bright or intense.

vivacious: lively or animated.

vivify: to give life or to make brighter.

vivarium: a place where plants and animals are kept under conditions similar to those in nature.

vivisection: the action of cutting up a live body.

Do animal-rights groups support vivisection?

Yes   No   because _____

22. *anim:* living, breathing.

animal: a living creature that is not a plant or microbe.

animation: liveliness.

animism: the belief that natural objects, actions, and the universe itself have life.

animalize: to turn into an animal.

anima: spirit or soul.

If your drawing class has a unit on animation, can you expect to try to make pictures look alive?

Yes   No   because _____

23. *spirat:* breath, essence of life.

respiration: breathing in and out.

aspiration: strong desire (from panting for something).

inspiration: breathing in; being filled with exalted desire.

If you are inspired to fulfill your aspiration, are you bored and confused?

Yes   No   because _____

24. *gen:* creation or production.

engender: to procreate or produce.

genetics: the study of biological heredity.

geneology: the study of a person's ancestry.

generate: to create or bring into existence.

If you could only trace your geneological tree back one generation, would you know your great grandparents?

Yes   No   because _____

25. *mort:* death.

mortal: subject to death.

mortgage: pledge of property against payment of a debt (from "dead pledge").

mortify: to humiliate or subjugate, dealing a blow to the pride.

mortician: one who prepares the dead for burial.

If you mortify someone in conversation, have you actually killed that person?

Yes   No   because _____

26. *necro:* dead, corpse, death.

> *necrolatry:* worship of the dead.
> *necrophilia:* sexual attraction to corpses.
> *necrophobia:* fear of death.
> *necromancy:* magic, especially witchcraft or communication with the dead.

Do some people employ necromancers to help them speak to dead relatives?

Yes   No   because _____

27. *cide:* murder.

> *matricide:* murder or murderer of the mother.
> *patricide:* murder or murderer of the father.
> *regicide:* murder or murderer of a king or queen.
> *genocide:* murder of a race or people.
> *infanticide:* murder of an infant.
> *suicide:* murder of oneself.

Could someone hire an assassin to commit regicide?

Yes   No   because _____

Matching: Use your knowledge of word forms to match the definitions with the words.

a. ____ The belief that natural objects are *living*.   (a) necrophobia

b. ____ *Murder* of a race or people.   (b) symbiosis

c. ____ Being filled with exalted desire and *breath*.   (c) genocide

d. ____ *Fear* of *death*.   (d) mortal

e. ____ To produce or *procreate*.   (e) animism

f. ____ Subject to *death*.   (f) engender

g. ____ *Lively* or animated.   (g) vivacious

h. ____ The *living together* of different plants or animals   (h) inspired
        for mutual benefit.
                                                                 (i) necrophilia

Using Context: Fill in each blank with the word part that completes the word.

Death and Breath

Mortimer I. Shin was not afraid of the dead. As a student of

_____logy, he knew that death was one part of the cycle of life. In his

_____arium, he kept numerous species alive and well for study. And

when birds or cats were near death, he would try to _____mate them.

His long-term interest was to study _____etics—the sci-

ence of heredity, even though he also found the science of undertaking fas-

cinating. Although he was no _____lator, he found the

process of death as fascinating as that of birth. How are we made? What

makes us die? Answering these questions was his vocation. In the mean-

time, he worked on a strategy to cut air pollution. "The key to life is

healthy re_____ation," he said. "If we don't keep our air clean, we

are commiting sui_____ on a global scale."

For Your Critical Reflection: How far back can you trace your geneology? Can you go back as far on your mother's side as on your father's side?

_____ _____

_____ _____

IV. Feelings, Beliefs, Judgments

28. *amor, eros,* and *philos:* love.

> *amorous:* inclined to love, especially sexual love.
>
> *erotic:* pertaining to sexual love or desire.
>
> *philosophy:* love of wisdom.
>
> *homoeroticism:* the tendency to be sexually aroused by members of the same sex.
>
> *philogyny:* love of or liking for women.

Might you send a Valentine's Day card to someone who makes you feel amorous?

Yes   No   because _____

29. *phobia:* fear.

arachnophobia: fear of spiders.

agoraphobia: fear of open spaces.

claustrophobia: fear of closed spaces.

hydrophobia: fear of water.

If your friend has a phobia about cats, would you give him a kitten for his birthday?

Yes   No   because _____

30. *mania:* exaggerated love or desire.

megalomania: obsession with doing great or extravagant things.

egomania: excessive devotion to oneself.

monomania: exaggerated devotion to a single thing or idea.

pyromania: a compulsion to set fire to things.

If your dinner companion considers you an egomaniac, do you need to talk more about yourself?

Yes   No   because _____

31. *bene, eu:* good or well.

benevolence: desire to do good to others.

benediction: spoken blessing or wish for good.

eudemonia: the state of being happy.

eulogy: high praise.

euphemism: a "nice" or "good" word used in place of a blunt word, such as "pass away" for "die."

Would a minister who ended a speech praising one who had "passed on" with a blessing for all have included a euphemism in the eulogy which he ended with a benediction?

Yes   No   because _____

32. *mal:* bad or unwell.

malediction: curse or slander.
malefaction: bad deed or crime.
malevolence: ill will or hatred.
malady: sickness.

If someone shouted a malediction at you, should you thank that person for benevolence?

Yes   No   because _____

33. *pseudo:* false or sham.

pseudonym: false name used to conceal identity.
pseudointellectual: someone who pretends to be scholarly but is not.
pseudomorph: a mineral with a deceptive appearance of another mineral.

Is your chemistry professor giving a compliment if she calls your report pseudoscientific?

Yes   No   because _____

34. *psycho, psyche:* relating to the mind, spirit, or soul.

psychiatry: the science of treating mental disorders.
psychology: the science of the mind and its processes.
psychedelic: relating to a mental state characterized by intense perceptions.
psychobiology: the study of relations between mind and body.

Would a student of psychobiology need to know about the nervous system?

Yes   No   because _____

35. *cred:* belief.

credit: trustworthiness.
credible: capable of being believed.
incredible: not capable of being believed, astonishing.
credulous: too willing to believe, gullible.

Might a credulous person give credit to an incredible tale?

Yes   No   because _____

36. *fid:* faith.

   fidelity: faithfulness.
   infidel: unbeliever.
   infidelity: unfaithfulness.

Would you want to marry a person who promised regular infidelities?

Yes   No   because _____

37. *ver:* truth.

   veracious: truthful, habitually telling the truth.
   veracity: personal truthfulness.
   verify: to test the truth of something.
   veritable: truly or very much so.

Is someone known for veracity likely to be credible?

Yes   No   because _____

38. *theo:* God.

   theology: the study of religion.
   theocentric: having God as the focus or interest.
   theocrat: a person who rules or governs as a representative of God.
   theologian: a person who is versed in theology and studies it.
   atheist: one who does not believe in a supreme being.

Can a nation that separates church and state be described as theocentric?

Yes   No   because _____

Matching: Use your knowledge of word forms to match the definitions with the words.

i. —— *Good words* about someone.

j. —— The study of the relation between *mind* and *body.*

k. —— To test the *truth* of something.

l. —— Exaggerated devotion to *one* thing or idea.

m. —— *Ill* will or hatred.

n. —— The study of religion or *God.*

o. —— Capable of being *believed.*

p. —— Unbeliever.

q. —— Desire to do *good* to others.

r. —— *False name* used to conceal identity.

s. —— Fear of *water.*

t. —— Pertaining to sexual *love* or desire.

(a) erotic

(b) pseudonym

(c) infidel

(d) credible

(e) malevolence

(f) monomania

(g) psychobiology

(h) eulogy

(i) verify

(j) theology

(k) benevolence

(l) hydrophobia

(m) infidelity

True-False: Write "T" for true and "F" for false. Provide the word part clue.

u. —— A theologist would probably not be an infidel.

   Clue: _____

v. —— An incredulous person would probably verify things before believing.

   Clue: _____

w. —— A psychiatrist would be disturbed to be called pseudo-intellectual.

   Clue: _____

x. —— A malediction would please you as much as a benediction.

   Clue: _____

y. —— An egomaniac would enjoy hearing many eulogies on herself.

   Clue: _____

z. ___ An arachnophobic would probably not feel amorous toward spiders.

Clue: _____

For Your Critical Reflection: What are your chief phobias or manias?

_____

_____

V. Civics, Knowledge, Study

39. *poli, polis, civi, civic:* city.

metropolis: city.
politics: the science or art of government.
civic: pertaining to a city or citizenship.
civilization: an advanced state of human society.
civil: pertaining to citizens or citizenship.

Do civil rights have to do with people's rights as citizens?

Yes No because _____

40. *reg:* rule, ruler (king, queen).

regicide: murder of a queen or king.
regent: someone who rules while a monarch is absent or underage.
regime: a mode or system of government.
regina: queen.

If a dieter goes on a strict regimen, is he strictly ruling over his desires for food?

Yes No because _____

41. *crat, -cracy:* ruler, rule, governing body.

democracy: rule by the people.
autocrat: one person who rules with absolute authority.
aristocracy: the elite members of a society.

bureaucracy: government characterized by many rigid hierarchies of officials.

If your college administration seems highly bureaucratic, are there many people who seem to be in charge of many different things?

Yes   No   because _____

42. *soph, -sophy:* wisdom, skill, or the science of something.

philosophy: the love (and study) of wisdom.

sophism: an argument that appears to be wise but is deceptive.

sophomore: a student in the second year of high school or college (combining roots for "wisdom" and "foolishness").

sophistication: worldly wisdom.

Would a sophomore sometimes appear to practice sophism in a philosophy class?

Yes   No   because _____

43. *-logy:* body of knowledge or study of something.

theology: the study of religion.

biology: the science of life processes and forms.

paleontology: the science of life forms existing in earlier eras.

psychology: the study of the mind.

Would you expect a cardiologist to study the heart?

Yes   No   because _____

44. *prud:* practical wisdom.

prudence: cautious wisdom in practical deeds.

prudery: excessive modesty or restraint in conduct.

jurisprudence: the science of law and legal matters.

imprudence: rashness, lack of discretion.

Would you like to make an imprudent investment of your money?

Yes   No   because _____

45. *log, logo:* word, language, reason.

logic: the science of correct reasoning.

logocentric: making language and reason the center of attention.

logorrhea: pathologically incoherent, repetitive speech.

logotherapy: psychological treatment emphasizing nonmedical language, such as looking for the meaning of life.

Is someone likely to accuse a philosophy teacher of being logocentric?

Yes   No   because _____

Matching: Use your knowledge of word forms to match the definitions with the words.

A. ___ A person with worldly *wisdom* has this.

B ___ A person who keeps all power to him or her*self.*

C. ___ Knowledge of the *psyche* or mind.

D. ___ A group that rules like a *king.*

E. ___ The practical wisdom of judges and *juries.*

F. ___ Holding *logic* and rationality as central.

G. ___ Having to do with *cities* and *citizens.*

(a) civil

(b) regime

(c) autocrat

(d) sophistication

(e) psychology

(f) jurisprudence

(g) logocentric

(h) sophomoric

Using Context: Fill in each blank with the word part that completes the word.

Asking the Big Questions

Asking hard questions is simple, but it is what college students do best. Here are some of the classic questions that students have asked since the first _____sopher in ancient Athens put on his toga. What is a just so-ciety? How do we solve _____itical conflicts? Is it proper to kill a king, or is _____cide condemned by the gods? Should all people be equal in a society, or can _____cracy lead to mob rule and chaos? Should a country be run by the values of priests and ministers, or should _____ology be kept separate from government decisions? The general pattern of history tells us that people must use _____ence and common sense when answering these questions. Otherwise we lose our ability to reason and our _____ic goes out the window with a storm of emotions.

For Your Critical Reflection: Why might the words *civilization* and *politics* trace their origins to words meaning "city"?

_____

_____

Chapter Review

I. Yes-No Questions

1. Might an oculist write a prescription for spectacles?

   Yes   No   because _____

2. Might a cardiologist and a pediatrician use microscopes in their training?

   Yes   No   because _____

3. Would an expert in phonetics be interested in things audible?

   Yes   No   because _____

4. Might neurosis be manifest in a person who was too nervous to put up a tripod?

   Yes   No   because _____

5. Would a patriarchal college run by gynephobes like sororities on campus?

   Yes   No   because _____

6. Would genocide be fascinating to a necrophiliac?

   Yes   No   because _____

7. Can you have symbiosis between a mortal being and a vivacious animal?

   Yes   No   because _____

8. Would an infidel find theology credible?

   Yes   No   because _____

9. If your best friend was a monomaniac, would you wish him benevolent?

   Yes   No   because _____

10. Would a proper eulogy express malevolence toward the deceased?

    Yes   No   because _____

11. Can hydrophobia be verified?

    Yes   No   because _____

12. Would a civilized regime be democratic?

    Yes   No   because _____

13. Can a logical psychologist be sophisticated?

    Yes   No   because _____

14. Would pediatricians fraternize with pedophiles?

    Yes   No   because _____

15. Would misanthropes join a fraternity?

    Yes   No   because _____

16. Would an autobiography be the kind of thing an egocentric person might write?

    Yes   No   because _____

17. Would a misandrist and misogynist agree?

    Yes   No   because _____

18. Does jurisprudence require logic?

    Yes   No   because _____

19. Might a psychotherapist use logotherapy?

    Yes   No   because _____

20. Would sorosis be feared by a gynephobe?

   Yes   No   because _____

II. Using Context: Use the word part list at the beginning of the chapter to fill in the blanks. You might not use all the word parts, or you might use a word part more than once.

Fiends, Lovers, and Frightened Folks

The annual meeting of the greatest fiends, lovers, and phobics had begun. The fiends spoke first. One fiend advocated _____cide—especially for brothers who eat the last of the ice cream. Another advocated

_____cide for sisters who brush their hair at the breakfast table. One recommended _____cide for mothers who never make chocolate chip cookies and _____cide for fathers who hog the television set. A radical democrat argued for _____cide across the globe, even if the kings or queens were _____volent, or good willed. Finally, a fiend who hated everyone suggested that mis_____ unify to create _____cide on the planet. She preferred insects to humans. The fiends mumbled among themselves, but the lovers buzzed with anticipation. The first lover praised God, logic, and mothers, inspiring all _____philes, _____philes, and _____philes to applaud. A new father and mother were some- what _____tistical; they wanted _____philia and _____philia to become heroic ideals. The lovers of all humanity, the _____philes, smiled, cheered, and spoke politely. The phobics suffered stage fright, of course. The _____phobes stayed away from the women, and the _____phobes stayed away from the men. The _____ophobes feared their hands, and the _____ophobes were scared by their feet. The _____phobes feared death, and the _____phobes feared life. The _____phobes plugged their ears: they did not want to hear any- thing. And the _____phobes, who feared crowds, of course never showed up.

Reading for Chapter 4

RICHARD SENNETT

The Evolution of Paternalism

In his book Authority, *sociologist Richard Sennett tells us how authority shapes societies and individuals. This passage illustrates how one root,* patri *or* pater, *for* father, *spawns several related words.* Patri *plus* archy *(rule) creates* patriarchy, *or "rule by the fathers."* Patri *plus* mony *(wealth) creates* patrimony, *the wealth of the father, and* patrimonialism, *a system of authority based on inherited wealth.* Pater *plus suffixes meaning "of or pertaining to" creates* paternalism, *or a system of authority based on dominance and support by fathers.*

Words to Notice

Optional Exercise: Use your knowledge of root words to help you answer *Yes* or *No* the following questions about words from the reading.

A. **Discrimin** is the Latin root meaning distinguish. Is using a word **indiscriminately** being precise?

B. Coming from a long **line** of MacDougals, she described herself by **lineage**. Did she mention family?

C. A mental **conception** yields a **concept**. Is something **conceived** thought up?

D. The **prime** is the first. **Primogeniture** means inheritance by the

_____ son.

E. **Senior** means eldest in rank. If you belonged to a **seignor**, would you follow a young man?

F. To **defer** is to yield to out of respect. Is showing **deference** a way of honoring?

G. **Archy** means rule or governor. Do some people rule others in a **hierarchy**?

H. A **diffuser** is a frosted screen that softens a light. Does a **diffuse** pattern get clearer?

I. **Flux** comes from a Latin word *flow*. Do things **in flux** stay exactly the same?[1]

[1]*Answers:* A. No B. Yes C. Yes D. eldest, first E. No F. Yes G. Yes H. No I. No

1   Paternalism is often used indiscriminately as a synonym for patriarchy or patrimonialism, an error which comes from assuming that all forms of male domination are basically the same. There are in fact important structural and historical differences in the meaning of these words.

2   A patriarchy is a society in which all people are *consciously* related by blood ties. Each person defines his or her relationship to anyone else in the society in terms of lineage: "He is the uncle of my second cousin's brother" or "He belongs to the family made by the daughter of my niece's third cousin by her marriage to my father's uncle twice-removed." In a patriarchy, males are the linchpins of these family relationships. They decide who marries whom, property passes through male lines, and so on. In a matriarchy, females are the linchpins. In a polyarchy, neither sex is dominant, but all social relations are still conceived in terms of family ties. The most familiar examples of patriarchy are Old Testament families; the most celebrated, if largely mythical, example of matriarchy are the Brazilian Amazons; and the striking examples of polyarchy are the actual tribes of the Brazilian Amazon described by Claude Lévi-Strauss.

3   A patrimonial society is like the patriarchal in one way, unlike it in another. Property passes from generation to generation through male relatives; for instance, primogeniture in England and France passed property from eldest male in one generation to eldest male in the next. It is considered legitimate for the male heads of household to determine the marriages of the people in that household. Patrimonialism is different from patriarchy in that people do not conceive of their social relationships exclusively in terms of family. They may think of themselves as "belonging" to a medieval seigneur even though they are not related to him. The male bloodline has become a model for the inheritance of property and position in a society which consciously recognizes there to be ties beside family which knit people together.

4   A medieval manor is the most obvious example of a patrimonial society, but not the most interesting one. Modern Japan is. Until a few years ago, the patterns of deference and age-grading which ruled the Japanese family were expected to rule in industry as well. Often the younger generation inherited the position of its elders in shops, factories, and corporations, at all levels of the hierarchy. Although these patterns are now beginning to become diffuse, the male bloodline was indeed the principle for the inheritance both of property and position; even when males of different generations were in fact not related by blood, they acted as though they were. As Ronald Dore has pointed out in a comparative study of industrial life in Japan and Britain, the patrimonial model was in no way a brake on Japanese industrial growth. In fact, patrimonialism gave the society a coherence and discipline which may be one of the principal causes Japanese industry grew fast and efficiently.

5   Paternalism differs from patrimonialism in the most basic way: the patrimony itself does not exist. Property no longer passes legally from father to eldest son according to the principle of primogeniture. Nor does society legally guarantee that the position held by a person in one generation will be held by a relative in the next.

. . .

6   In a paternalistic society, males continue to dominate. The domination is based on their roles as fathers: protectors, stern judges, the strong. But this basis is symbolic rather than material as in a patrimonial order. In a paternalistic society no father can guarantee to his children a known place in the world; he can only act protectively.

7   In one way, paternalism may seem the only form of male dominance possible in a society of great change like that of the 19th Century. The material organization of life was in so much flux that a man was in danger who based his claims to power on his ability to pass on a fixed amount of property to someone else in thirty or forty years. If a male were to legitimate his power, he would have to do so in terms of symbols and beliefs cut loose from such material tests. The Japanese example is a warning against thinking paternalism the only form of male dominance suited to the rapid development of capitalism. And it is also true that in modern capitalism families of the rich and poor tend in general to reproduce their social conditions; the son of a corporation president has a much better chance of going to Eton, joining the right clubs, and becoming a corporate president himself than does the son of a plumber. But this is only in general; no particular father can employ the law to give a guarantee. Paternalism is male domination without a contract.

Questions for Class Discussion

1. Do you see evidence of paternalism in society today? How about patrimonialism and patriarchy?
2. How can fathers help their children succeed? What about mothers? Should women and men help their children the same ways or different ways?
3. Most social scientists agree that males continue to dominate society. Why do you think men still have more power than women?

Making a New World

For Class Discussion

1. Do you see any patriarchal elements in today's society? How about matriarchal elements? What is the place of fraternity? Sisterhood? What about your own family?
2. Describe the actions or behavior of the following: A misanthrope. A misogynist. A misandrist. Do you know any people like those?
3. What should a person do who wants to attain eudemonia?

Collaborative Learning

1. The Self
   Purpose: To use word parts in context.

    A. Describe the characteristics of an egocentric person, an egoistical person, and an egotistical person. For each description, use at least one word part from the chapter.

    B. Report your results to the class.

2. Neologisms

Purpose: To develop flexibility in using and understanding word parts.

    A. Check the list of word parts. Then combine roots to invent at least four new words. Write appropriate definitions.

    B. Optional: Check your dictionary to see if any of your neologisms actually exist.

    C. Pick two neologisms you like best and have the class guess their meanings.

Ideas for Writing

1. In a paragraph, write a brief autobiography, using at least three word parts from the chapter.
2. In a page, describe your chief phobias, philias, and manias.
3. At home, explore the relationship between philosophy and theology. How have you used or not used each in your own life?

More Word Parts for Chapter 4

aer: air (aerobic, aerosal, aerospace)

agr: field (agriculture, agribusiness)

alter: other (alternate, altercation, alterity, alterego)

aqu, hydr: water (aquatic, hydraulic)

arm: weapon (armistice, armament)

art: craft (artistic, artful)

astr: star (asteroid, asterisk, disaster)

avi: bird (aviary, aviation)

bel, bell: war (belligerent, bellicose, antebellum)

biblio: book (bible, bibliography, bibliophile)

carn: flesh (carnal, carnivore)

cogn: know (cognitive, cognition, incognito)

crypt: secret (cryptic)

dent: tooth (dental, dentist)

derm: skin (epidermis, dermatology)

doc, doct: teach, prove (docile, doctor, indoctrinate)

geo: earth (geothermal, geology, geocentric)
graph, graphy, scrib, scrip: write (monograph, photograph, scribe, scriptures)
grat: please, favor (gratuity, gracious)

litera: letter (literal, literature)
loq, loc: talk (loquacious, eloquent)

mut: change (mutation, mutable, immutable)

nom: name (nominate, nominal)

onym: name (patronym, eponym)
orth: right, straight, true (orthopedic, orthodontia)

paleo: ancient (paleography, paleontology)
path, pathy: feeling, disease (pathetic, homeopath)
phos, phot: light (photo, photocopy)
physi: nature (physiology, physics)
pyr: fire (pyromania)

rat, ration: reason (ratio, rational, ratiocination)

sanct: holy (sanctify, sanctimonious)
scop: see, watch (microscope)
sign: sign (signature, signify)

techn: skill (technical, technician)
terra: earth (terrestrial, extraterrestrial)

vinc, vic: conquer (invincible, victory)

zo: animal (zoology, zoo)

Answer Key to Chapter 4

I. BODY PARTS

Yes-No Questions

1. Yes; a telephone conveys sounds.
2. No; auditors listen.
3. Yes; visualize means to imagine.
4. Yes; it appeals to the eye.
5. No; you are using your voice.
6. Yes; a pedicure takes care of feet.
7. No; it is not doing it by hand.
8. Yes; to arrest is to stop.
9. No; capital means the head, top.
10. No; unless you were nervous about it.

Matching

A. (f) B. (d) C. (c) D. (a) E. (j)
F. (g) G. (b) H. (e) I. (h) J. (i)

Using Context: Crowds

capital, pedestrian, cardiac, neurosis, video, binoculars, vociferous, sonorous, audible, manifest

II. THE FAMILY, SELF, AND OTHERS

Yes-No Questions

11. No; matriarchies are run by women.
12. No; but he might request parental leave.
13. Yes; sororities are female social clubs.
14. Yes; only your father and brother died.
15. Yes; chicken pox is a children's disease.
16. No; a hater of humanity would not study it.
17. Yes; it could be a sign of anti-women bias.
18. Yes; androgynous means having both features.
19. No; they want to be more independent.

Matching

K. (f) L. (e) M. (g) N. (d)
O. (c) P. (h) Q. (b) R. (i) S. (a)
T. (j)

True-False

U. T (ego + auto)
V. T (mis + poly)
W. F (mis + gyn)
X. T (anthro)
Y. F (ped)
Z. T (mat + sor)

III. LIFE AND DEATH

Yes-No Questions

20. Yes; degrade in bio (nature).
21. No; they oppose cutting living beings.
22. Yes; animate means bring to life.
23. No; *spir* is breath, essence of life.
24. No; one generation is your parents.
25. No; you've "killed" the pride only.
26. Yes; necromancers practice magic.
27. Yes; kings and queens can be killed.

Matching

a. (e) b. (c) c. (h) d. (a) e. (f)
f. (d) g. (g) h. (b)

Using Context: Death and Breath

biology, vivarium, animate, genetics, necrolater, respiration, suicide

IV. FEELINGS, BELIEFS, JUDGMENTS

Yes-No Questions

28. Yes; *amor* means love.

29. No; your friend is afraid of cats.
30. No; you are in love with yourself anyway.
31. Yes; *eu* and *bene* mean good.
32. No; malediction suggests malevolence.
33. No; your report is falsely scientific.
34. Yes; nerves link mind and body.
35. Yes; a credulous person believes easily.
36. No; the person is not faithful.
37. Yes; this person tells the truth.
38. No; the church is not the center.

Matching

i. (h) j. (g) k. (i) l. (f) m. (e)
n. (j) o. (d) p. (c) q. (k) r. (b)
s. (l) t. (a)

True-False

u. T (a theologian is probably not a doubter)
v. T (incredulous persons do not believe)
w. T (psychiatrists should be intellectual)
x. F (*mal* is the opposite of *bene*)
y. T (*ego* = self; *eu* = good)
z. T (*phobic* = fear; amorous = love)

V. CIVICS, KNOWLEDGE, STUDY

Yes-No Questions

39. Yes; civil rights are citizen's rights.
40. Yes; regimen is a strict government.

41. Yes; bureaus are in charge.
42. Yes; foolishness equals false wisdom.
43. Yes; cardiology equals the study of the heart.
44. No; imprudent means unwise.
45. Yes; philosophy makes reason central.

Matching

A. (d) B. (c) C. (e) D. (b) E. (f)
F. (g) G. (a)

Using Context: Asking the Big Questions

philosopher, political, regicide, democracy, theology, prudence, logic

CHAPTER REVIEW

I. Yes-No Questions

1. Yes; ocu/spect = eye. 2. Yes; both are doctors. 3. Yes; phon/aud = sound. 4. Yes; neur = nerves. 5. No; it dislikes women. 6. Yes; lots of death. 7. Yes; they share life. 8. No; infidels don't believe. 9. Yes; a good interest. 10. No; needs good words. 11. Yes; people do fear. 12. Yes; one hopes. 13. Yes; wordly wise. 14. No; pedophilia is illegal. 15. No; they hate people. 16. Yes; written by self. 17. No; one hates men. 18. Yes; it requires reason. 19. Yes; talking cures. 20. Yes; afraid of women.

II. Using Context: Fiends, Lovers, and Frightened Folks

fratricide, sororicide, matricide, patricide, regicide, benevolent, misanthropes, genocide, theophiles, logophiles, matriphiles, egotistical, patriphilia, matriphilia, anthrophiles, gynephobes, androphobes, manophobes, pedophobes, necrophobes, biophobes, audiophobes, agoraphobes

WORD PARTS: SPECIFICATIONS AND MOVEMENTS

Quick Reference Word List

ambi	equi-	meter	proxi-
an-, a-	greg	micro	retro
ante-, pre-	hetero	morph	rupt
anti-, con, contra	homo	mov, mot, mob	semi
bi, di, du	hyper-	multi, poly	stat, stas
cent	hypo-	nov, neo	sub, infer
chron, temper	-ic, -al, -ous	omni, pan	super, sur, meta
circum	inter	plastic, plasty,	ten, tain
con, com, co	intra, intro	plast, plasto	trans
deca, deci	kilo, mille	post-	tri
dist, tele	macro	prim	turb
duct, duc	medi-	pro-	uni, mono

Introduction: More Word Parts

This chapter continues your study of word parts. The word parts contained here emphasize specifications, such as number, form, placement, and measure, as well as movements, such as direction and speed. Again, learning the building blocks of words can help you to figure out and remember the meanings of many new words you encounter.

I. Numbers

1. *uni, mono:* one.

unify: to form into a single whole.

unilateral: occurring on one side only.

universe: the whole totality of known and unknown things and actions throughout space.

monolingual: able to speak only one language.

monogamy: marriage with only one person at a time.

If you were interested in unilateral disarmament, would you wait for the other side to disarm?

Yes   No   because _____

. . . .

Have You Heard?
About Panic

The root *pan*, meaning ''all,'' comes from the Greek god named Pan. He had the body of a goat and the head, chest, and arms of a man. He loved to play tunes on a pipe made of seven reeds. He also fell in love with woodland nymphs, who, instead of loving him back, fled from him in fright. From their scattering, we get the word *panic*.

2. *bi, di, du:* two.

> *bisect:* to cut in two.
>
> *bilateral:* occurring on both sides.
>
> *diphthong:* a single vowel that causes you to pronounce two sounds (eye = ah + ee).
>
> *dichromatic:* having two colors.
>
> *dual:* of or pertaining to two.
>
> *dualism:* division into two, as in mind and body.
>
> *bilingual:* able to speak two languages.

In bilateral disarmament, does one side wait until the other also is ready to disarm?

Yes   No   because _____

3. *tri:* three.

> *triad:* a group of three.
>
> *triangle:* a three-angled plane in geometry.
>
> *triathlon:* athletic contest of three events, such as swimming, bicycling, and running.
>
> *triarchy:* government by three persons or sets of persons.
>
> *trinity:* the state or condition of being three.

Would you have to be a good all-around athlete to win a triathlon?

Yes   No   because _____

4. *deca, deci: (deca* for multiples, *deci* for divisions): ten.

decade: ten years.
decameter: ten meters.
decimeter: one-tenth of a meter.
decimal: pertaining to tenths.

Is a decagram more than a decigram?

Yes   No   because _____

5. *cent:* one hundred.

century: one hundred years.
cent: in the United States, one-hundredth of a dollar.
centurion: in Roman times, the commander of one hundred soldiers.
centennial: a one-hundredth anniversary.

If a nation celebrates its bicentennial, is it three hundred years old?

Yes   No   because _____

6. *kilo, mille:* one thousand.

millennium: one thousand years.
millimeter: one-thousandth of a meter.
kilometer: one thousand meters.
kilobyte (K): 1,024 bytes of memory in a computer; loosely, one thousand bytes.

Would a lazy person rather walk a kilometer than walk a millimeter?

Yes   No   because _____

7. *prim:* first.

primordial: existing at or near the beginning.
primitive: being the first or earliest of its kind in existence.
primeval: pertaining to the first ages, particularly of the world.
primary: first.

"Unicycle . . . Impossicycle" copyright 1978 by Roz Chast. Reproduced by permission of Roz Chast.

Was the earth's primeval era the time when people were wicked?

Yes   No   because _____

8. *ambi:* both.

> ***ambivalent:*** in two directions at once, such as feeling love and hate for the same person.
> ***ambiguous:*** having two or more possible meanings, obscure, unclear.
> ***ambidextrous:*** equally skilled in using the right and left hands.

Can ambiguous and ambivalent have the same meaning?

Yes   No   because _____

9. *multi, poly:* many.

> ***polyphonic:*** consisting of many voices or sounds.
> ***polyglot:*** knowing many languages.

multilingual: knowing many languages.

polytheism: belief in more than one or many gods.

multicultural: of many cultures.

multitude: a great number of persons or things.

Can multilingual and polyglot have the same meaning?

Yes   No   because _____

10. *semi:* half.

semiannual: half yearly.

semiliterate: barely able to read and write.

semiformal: partly formal.

semicircle: half circle.

Does land that is semiarid get any water at all?

Yes   No   because _____

11. *omni, pan:* all.

omnipotent: all-powerful.

omniscient: all-knowing.

omnivorous: eating all kinds of food.

panacea: cure-all.

pandemonium: chaos, uproar.

panorama: wide or comprehensive picture or view.

Could an omnipotent doctor create a panacea?

Yes   No   because _____

Fill in the Blank: Use the proper number or amount.

A. A unilateral decision occurs on only _____ side.

B. A monogamous person is a partner with only _____ person at a time.

C. If you bisect an orange it falls into _____ pieces.

D. Dualistic philosophers like to break the world into _____ things.

E. A triarchy is a government of _____ persons.

F. A decimeter is _____ of a meter.

G. A decameter is _____ meters.

H. A centurion is in charge of _____ soldiers.

I. A millenium is a period of _____ years.

J. A three kilometer race is a race of _____ meters.

K. A primeval forest is one from the _____ age of the world.

L. A ambidextrous person can use _____ hands.

M. A multilingual person can speak _____ languages.

N. A polyphonic sound contains _____ voices.

O. A semicircle is only a _____ of a circle.

P. An omnivore eats _____ foods.

Q. A panacea cures not just a few things but _____ of them.

Using Context: Fill in each blank with the word part that completes the word.

Language and Schools

Because English is not our family's native language, my wife and I enrolled our young children in the _____lingual education program (in which they learn two languages) at the local _____mary school. We had mixed feelings, so we decided to discuss our _____valence with the school principal. Mr. Carlos said we did not have to worry about our children's literacy. They would be fully literate in both languages instead of only _____literate, as we had feared. He said that nowadays many children study in two languages, because parents and educators agree that in today's _____cultural world no one wants to be _____lingual. Even native speakers of English are learning one or two more languages, hoping to become bilingual or even _____lingual. At first I argued that the mixing of all these languages could result in _____demonium at school, in the community, and in the country. But my wife disagreed. She said that if our son or daughter could be a _____glot, that kid would be practically _____potent in the future. I don't know about that, but if I had a penny, I'd bet that _____ on the good talkers.

For Your Critical Reflection: What are some things you feel ambivalent about?

_____

_____

II. Forms and Measures

12. *morph:* form.

morphology: the branch of biology dealing with forms and structures of life.
metamorphosis: a total change in form.
polymorphous: having many shapes or forms.
morphogenesis: the evolution of forms of life or organs.

Gregor Samsa awoke to find himself turned into a giant insect. Had he undergone a metamorphosis?

Yes   No   because _____

13. *plastic, plasty, plast, plasto:* formed or molded.

plastic: capable of being molded or formed.
dermatoplasty: skin grafting.
cytoplasty: in biology, the forming of cell material outside the nucleus.

Does a plastic surgeon re-form body parts?

Yes   No   because _____

14. *-ic, -al, -ous:* made of or characterized by (used to turn some words into adjectives).

poetic: in the form or spirit of a poem.
porous: having pores.

aquatic: of the water.

regal: like a queen or king.

metric: measured by meters.

If your bearing is regal, are you one of the normal people?

Yes   No   because _____

15. *meter:* measure.

thermometer: an instrument that measures heat.

meter: a measurement of length equal to 39.37 U.S. inches.

altimeter: an instrument that measures height above sea level.

kilometer: a thousand meters.

If you know that *chron* means "time," do you know that a clock is a chrono-meter?

Yes   No   because _____

16. *macro:* large.

macroeconomics: the branch of economics that deals with broad and general issues.

macroscopic: large enough to be seen by the naked eye.

macrocosm: the great world or universe.

macrobiotics: the art of lengthening a life, often used to refer to a vegetarian diet.

Is your face macroscopic?

Yes   No   because _____

17. *micro:* small.

microeconomics: the branch of economics that deals with the economic behavior of individuals.

microscopic: too small to be seen by the naked eye.

microcosm: a little world or universe in miniature.

microphone: an instrument for enlarging "small" sounds.

If your family is a microcosm of society, are you unlike all others?

Yes   No   because _____

18. *chron, temper:* time.

temporary: for a limited time.
contemporaneous: living or occurring at the same time.
temporal: pertaining to time.
chronological: in the order of time.
anachronistic: chronologically out of place, such as having George Washington use a computer.
chronic: occurring continually over time.

If your uncle has a chronic disease, will he get well soon?

Yes   No   because _____

19. *nov, neo:* new.

novel: new (the storybook form of the novel got its name when it was new).
novice: someone who is new to something.
neophyte: someone newly converted to a belief or religion.
neologism: a new word.

Can a neophyte also be a novice?

Yes   No   because _____

20. *homo:* same.

homogenous: essentially alike.
homonyms: words that sound or are spelled alike but differ in meaning.
homosexuality: sexual desire for those of one's own sex.
homophone: a word pronounced the same as another but differing in meaning.

Are *heir* and *air* homonyms?

Yes   No   because _____

21. *hetero:* different or other.

> *heterogeneous:* essentially different or of various types.
>
> *heterodox:* not in accordance with established doctrines, especially in theology.
>
> *heterosexuality:* sexual desire for those of the opposite sex.
>
> *heteroplasty:* surgical repair that uses tissues from another individual or species.

If your classroom has many types of students, is it heterogeneous?

Yes   No   because _____

Matching: Use your knowledge of word forms to match the definitions with the words.

R. ___ A group of people who are all the *same*.

S. ___ A person *new* to a crowd or profession.

T. ___ A device that tells *time*.

U. ___ The study of the economic system as a *whole*.

V. ___ Sounds like *poetry*.

W. ___ Use this to *mold* or *shape* a statue.

X. ___ Changing *form* into a butterfly.

Y. ___ Something that *measures altitude*.

Z. ___ The study of economic behavior of *individuals*.

a. ___ Something that lasts only a short *time*.

b. ___ Someone who holds a *different* belief.

(a) metamorphosis

(b) plaster

(c) poetical

(d) altimeter

(e) macroeconomics

(f) microeconomics

(g) chronograph

(h) temporal

(i) neophyte

(j) homogenous

(k) temperature

(l) heterodox

True-False: Write "T" for true and "F" for false. Provide the word part clue.

c. ___ A heterodox person would hold a different belief.

     Clue: _____

d. ___ A polymorphous pleasure would have many forms.

     Clue: _____

e. ___ A material with high plasticity would be hard to mold.

Clue: _____

f. ___ An aquatic animal would enjoy the water.

Clue: _____

g. ___ A micrometer would measure large quantities.

Clue: _____

h. ___ Two contemporaneous events would occur at the same time.

Clue: _____

i. ___ A novel idea would be one that everyone knew.

Clue: _____

j. ___ A homosexual person would probably marry a heterosexual person.

Clue: _____

For Your Critical Reflection: Many thinkers believe that the family is a microcosm of the whole society. In what ways is this idea true or not true for your family?

_____

_____

III. Movement

22. *mov, mot, mob:* movement.

mobile: moving.
movement: the passing from one place to another.
motion: the process of moving.
motivity: the power of producing or starting motion.

If someone is upwardly socially mobile, is that person moving up in the world?

Yes   No   because _____

23. *stat, stas:* standing, motionless.

thermostat: instrument for keeping heat constant.

static: pertaining to a fixed condition.

stasis: state of inactivity caused by equal forces.

stationary: standing still.

Is writing paper called (and spelled) stationary?

Yes   No   because _____

24. *retro:* backward.

retroact: to act in opposition or to react.

retrofit: to modify older equipment.

retrogression: backward movement.

retrospection: contemplation of the past.

Does an automobile retrospective feature older models of cars?

Yes   No   because _____

25. *circum:* around.

circumscribe: draw a line around, restrict.

circumlocution: to talk around a subject.

circumspect: discreet, not crossing social boundaries (particularly by saying too much).

circumvent: to go around, bypass, either with motion or (figuratively) by cleverness.

If you consider yourself circumspect, would you also consider yourself a gossip?

Yes   No   because _____

26. *rupt:* break.

disrupt: to interfere with normal activities or cause disorder.

rupture: a break in friendly relations or physical wholeness.

interrupt: to break into a process, such as a conversation, by intruding.

If your phone line was ruptured, would anyone be able to interrupt your conversation?

Yes   No   because _____

27. *turb:* spinning, rapidly moving.

> *turbine:* a type of machine with a rotor driven by the pressure of moving liquid or gas.
>
> *turbulence:* disorder, commotion, or irregular movement.
>
> *disturb:* to interrupt, agitate, or unsettle.
>
> *turbid:* murky because of stirred up sediment (water) or muddled because of stirred up ideas or emotions (thought or feeling).

If a book you have just read seems turbid, are you likely to praise its clearness?

Yes   No   because _____

28. *ten, tain:* hold.

> *abstinence:* self-restraint, especially from bad habits.
>
> *tenable:* capable of being held, maintained, or defended.
>
> *tenacious:* holding fast, stubborn.
>
> *container:* something that holds objects inside of it.

If someone says your views are untenable, does that person hold your ideas as true?

Yes   No   because _____

29. *trans:* across.

> *translate:* to render something in another language.
>
> *transgress:* to break a moral code or violate a law.
>
> *transitory:* not lasting or permanent.
>
> *transform:* to change in form.
>
> *translucent:* permitting light to pass through but diffusing it.

Is someone who seeks transitory pleasures interested in taking each moment as it comes?

Yes   No   because _____

30. *duct, duc:* lead.

> *deduction:* subtraction or a process of reasoning from known premises.
>
> *induction:* a process of reasoning by which one has to interpret evidence.

abduction: kidnapping.

conductor: one who leads or assists.

educate: to lead to learning.

If you are conducting a scientific experiment, are you practicing induction?

Yes   No   because _____

Matching: Use your knowledge of word forms to match the definitions with the words.

k. ____ The *leading* of reasoning from known premises.

l. ____ Tending to *hold* tightly to a goal.

m. ____ A machine that *spins* very fast.

n. ____ To travel *around* the globe.

o. ____ Remaining *motionless.*

p. ____ Something that *moves.*

q. ____ To oppose progress by looking *backward.*

r. ____ To *break* the skin.

s. ____ To write *over* a letter from notes.

(a) mobile

(b) static

(c) retrograde

(d) circumnavigate

(e) rupture

(f) retain

(g) tenacious

(h) transcribe

(i) deduction

(j) turbine

True-False: Write "T" for true and "F" for false. Provide the word part clue.

t. ____ A mobile home remains static.

Clue: _____

u. ____ A thermostat keeps the temperature moving.

Clue: _____

v. ____ A retrogression is not static.

Clue: _____

w. ____ Circumlocution can help prevent ruptures among friends.

Clue: _____

x. ____ To disrupt a funeral is to be circumspect.

Clue: _____

• • • • • • • •

Guess What!
Roman Roots

Decimation now refers to widespread destruction, but it used to have a more limited meaning. When an officer in the Roman army did not know which of his soldiers had committed a crime, he randomly selected one out of ten (deci) for punishment.

We all know the meaning of *trivia*. But did you know that its roots (*tri* three, and *via* way) link it to Roman crossroads? At the places where three roads met, women often stopped to chat and to discuss politics on their way to market.

y. ___ A tenacious person would be unperturbable.

Clue: _____

z. ___ A transitory container would be ideal for toxic waste.

Clue: _____

A. ___ An abductor of children might take transcontinental trips.

Clue: _____

For Your Critical Reflection: *Educate* has its roots in "to lead to learning." Does that mean that others can educate you, or must you educate yourself?

_____

_____

IV. Location in Place, Time, or Value

31. *super, sur, meta*: beyond or above.

metaphysical: above or beyond the physical level, spiritual.
supernumerary: extra, beyond the usual or proper.
surname: last name or family name.

metaethics: the branch of philosophy that looks beyond specific cases of right and wrong to look for the nature of ethics and morality themselves.

superlative: of the highest or best kind.

Would you like to have dinner at the home of a superlative cook?

Yes   No   because _____

32. *sub, infer:* below

subcontractor: a person who contracts (agrees) to perform the task of another contract or job.

subatomic: pertaining to a process that occurs below the atomic level, usually within the atom itself.

subordinate: someone who is below another in authority.

inferior: someone or something that is not as good as another.

infernal: pertaining to the underworld.

Is it likely that a subcontractor is subordinate to the contractor?

Yes   No   because _____

33. *ante-, pre-:* in front of, before.

antechamber: a small room one enters before going into a main room.

antecedent: someone or something that has gone before another (in time or order).

anterior: situated toward the front.

precede: go before.

prenuptial: before the wedding.

preamble: an introductory statement.

If someone has precedence over you, might that person have priority in rank or importance?

Yes   No   because _____

34. *post-:* behind, after.

posterior: situated toward the rear.

postscript (P.S.): a section added to a letter that already has been finished and signed.

postgraduate: pertaining to scholarly work done after graduation.

postmortem: pertaining to the time following death.

If you skied down a hill on your posterior, would you be proud of yourself?

Yes   No   because _____

35. *medi-:* in the middle.

intermediary: a go-between.

medieval: the time between the ancient world and the modern era, the Middle Ages.

media: the means of communication that reach large numbers of people.

mediate: to settle a dispute by acting as an intermediary.

If you mediate in a dispute, must you side with one party or another?

Yes   No   because _____

36. *proxi:* near or next.

approximate: being nearly as specified, or being similar.

proximity: nearness.

proxy: a person or agency authorized to act as a substitute.

proximal: situated toward the point of origin or attachment (as in a bone).

To reduce commuting time, does one want to live in close proximity to work?

Yes   No   because _____

37. *dist, tele:* apart or far.

distinguish: to mark off one as different from another.

distal: located away from the point of origin or attachment (as in a bone).

distance: the amount of space between two things.

telescope: instrument for seeing things that are far away.

telecommunications: the transmission of information over great distances, as by telegraph.

Does a telegraph convey information over long distances?

Yes   No   because _____ _____

Matching: Use your knowledge of word forms to match the definitions with the words.

B. ____ An electronic meeting with people *far* away.	(a) superhuman
C. ____ An ice cream whose taste is *below* average.	(b) submarine
D. ____ A study of the world *above* the physical world.	(c) inferior
E. ____ Someone who steps in *between* two fighting companies.	(d) antebellum
F. ____ A discussion *after* the final game of the season.	(e) postmortem
	(f) distant
G. ____ A person who is clearly *above* normal humanity.	(g) approximate
H. ____ A ship that goes *under* the water	(h) teleconference
I. ____ Life *before* the war.	(i) metaphysics
J. ____ Something *close* but not exactly the same.	(j) mediator

Using Context: Fill in each blank with the word part that completes the word.

Remodeling

My brother Kenny is thinking about remodeling his condo. As an expert in

_____communications, he has _____lative judgment about

_____physical matters, but his judgment about daily life sometimes is

_____ior to that of his cat. Anyway, he got into an argument with

the _____contractor, who could not believe Kenny wanted to turn his

_____chamber into a second bathroom. When Kenny finally

realized that his guests would walk through the front door right into the

toilet, he asked the subcontractor to _____ate between him and the

main contractor so he could get his money back. The subcontractor

laughed and said, "When you have that discussion, I don't want to be in

close _____mity. Just call me for the _____mortem."

For Your Critical Reflection: Are telecommunications making you a more educated person? How?

_____

_____

_____

V. Relationships

38. *equi-:* equal.

> *equidistant:* of equal distances.
>
> *equitable:* fair and just.
>
> *equilibrium:* at rest or balance due to the equal action of opposing forces.
>
> *equipotent:* equal in power, ability, or effect.
>
> *equivocate:* to use unclear expressions in order to mislead or dodge a question.
>
> *equity:* fairness, impartiality.

Should judges make decisions that are equitable?

Yes   No   because _____

39. *an-, a-:* without.

> *asymmetrical:* not symmetrical.
>
> *amoral:* lacking in both morality and immorality.
>
> *apathetic:* uncaring.
>
> *anarchy:* without rule or law.

Is anarchy always the same as chaos?

Yes   No   because _____

40. *con, com, co:* with, together.

> *convivial:* fond of companionship, feasting, and good living.
>
> *concur:* to agree.
>
> *compass:* an instrument for telling direction by means of a needle that is drawn to the magnetic north.
>
> *collaborate:* to work together.

community: a social group whose members reside in one location or share a common heritage.

If you are accused of collaborating with the enemy, does someone think you have been a traitor?

Yes   No   because _____

41. *greg:* flock.

congregate: to come together, to assemble.

segregate: to separate, often on the basis of race or sex.

gregarious: friendly.

aggregate: the combined total.

egregious: severe, against the group (flock).

Is the congregation of a church composed of the members of the church?

Yes   No   because _____

42. *anti-, con, contra:* against.

contrary: opposite or opposed.

controversy: disputes, debates, or strife.

antisocial: against society or socializing.

antonym: words with opposite or nearly opposite meanings.

antibiotic: a drug that attacks bacteria in the body.

Does everyone agree about controversial issues?

Yes   No   because _____

43. *pro-:* for, in favor of, forward.

proslavery: in favor of slavery.

prognosis: forecast of the probable cause of disease or recovery.

prologue: preface or introductory part of a poem, play, novel, speech, etc.

progeny: children.

protuberant: swollen.

If your doctor wishes to discuss the prognosis of your heart condition, should you remind him that this has nothing to do with your nose?

Yes   No   because _____

44. *intra, intro:* within.

   intravenous: within the vein.
   intrastate: within one state.
   intramural: involving members of a single school, as in sports.
   intracultural: involving members of one cultural group.
   introverted: shy, quiet, or withdrawn.

Do intracellular reactions take place between two different cells?

Yes   No   because _____

45. *inter:* between.

   intervene: to come between people or events.
   intercultural: between or among cultures.
   interfere: to come into opposition, especially to hamper an action.
   interpolate: to alter (a writing) by inserting new matter, especially without permission.

If you were asked to intervene in a dispute, would you be expected to mediate?

Yes   No   because _____

46. *hyper-:* excessive.

   hyperventilate: to breathe too rapidly and deeply.
   hypercritical: overly critical.
   hyperactive: excessively active.
   hyperbole: obvious exaggeration.

If you say, "I waited forever for that lunch today," are you using hyperbole?

Yes   No   because _____

47. *hypo-:* insufficient, under.

> *hypoglycemia:* abnormally low level of blood sugar.
>
> *hypothesis:* a provisional explanation that needs testing.
>
> *hypocrite:* a person who pretends to have the approved morality but does not practice it.
>
> *hypothermia:* abnormally low body temperature.

Are *hypoglycemia* and *hyperglycemia* likely to be opposites?

Yes   No   because _____

Matching: Use your knowledge of word forms to match the definitions with the words.

K. ____ *Excessive*ly high rise in prices.　　　　(a) equivocate

L. ____ Activities *within* Colorado.　　　　(b) atheist

M. ____ A statement that is *against* another statement.　　　　(c) commingling

N. ____ To act against the group or *flock*.　　　　(d) egregious

O. ____ A person *without* a god or theology.　　　　(e) antibiotic

P. ____ To speak two *equally* true statements.　　　　(f) contradiction

Q. ____ Going to a party to *come together* with others.　　　　(g) contravene

R. ____ A medicine that works *against* disease.　　　　(h) intrastate

S. ____ An introduction or a *foreword*.　　　　(i) interlinear

T. ____ Writing *between* the lines.　　　　(j) hyperinflation

U. ____ An *insufficient* thesis that must be proved.　　　　(k) hypothesis

　　　　(l) prologue

True-False: Write "T" for true and "F" for false. Provide the word part clue.

V. ____ Two equipotent leaders would share the same amount of power.

Clue: _____

W. ____ An amoral person would be highly interested in social equity.

Clue: _____

X. ___ People in a community would probably collaborate together.

   Clue: _____

Y. ___ A gregarious person would probably not like being segregated.

   Clue: _____

Z. ___ An antisocial person would probably be gregarious.

   Clue: _____

a. ___ The antonym of prologue is epilogue.

   Clue: _____

b. ___ An intercultural movement might interfere with intracultural communities.

   Clue: _____

c. ___ A hyperactive child might speak in hyperbole.

   Clue: _____

For Your Critical Reflection: What is more important in your community—intercultural activities or intracultural activities? Why?

_____

_____

Chapter Review

I. Yes-No Questions

1. Would a socially mobile person enjoy a static social structure?

   Yes   No   because _____

2. Would a retrograde person be interested in progress?

   Yes   No   because _____

3. Would a circumspect person often interrupt?

   Yes   No   because _____

4. Would things be smooth during turbulence?

   Yes   No   because _____

5. Would a turbid idea be tenable?

   Yes   No   because _____

6. Would a translation of Chinese poetry into English help most American readers?

   Yes   No   because _____

7. Would a conductor be handy on a transcontinental train trip?

   Yes   No   because _____

8. Would the best metaphysics be superlative?

   Yes   No   because _____

9. Would a subterranean world be infernal?

   Yes   No   because _____

10. Could you make a prenuptial agreement part of the postscript of a proposal?

    Yes   No   because _____

11. Would a good mediator have to be in close proximity to the quarreling groups?

    Yes   No   because _____

12. Can a telescope allow you to distinguish between planets far away?

    Yes   No   because _____

13. Would an anarchy have a governor helping to ensure equity among citizens?

    Yes   No   because _____

14. Would people who like to congregate be likely to enjoy convivial conversation?

    Yes   No   because _____

15. Would a proslavery view be controversial?

    Yes   No   because _____

16. Should you interfere with intravenous feeding?

    Yes   No   because _____

17. Could a hypocrite be hypercritical of others but not himself?

    Yes   No   because _____

18. Would an introverted person be likely to enjoy intramural activities?

    Yes   No   because _____

19. Would an amoral and atheistic person be apathetic about morals and theology?

    Yes   No   because _____

20. Would an antebellum period occur after the war?

    Yes   No   because _____

II. Using Context: Use the word part list at the beginning of the chapter to fill in the blanks. You might not use all the word parts, or you might use a word part more than once.

Plastic Surgery

Before my new job, I thought that a drastic change was needed and that _____ic surgery would be the answer. It would so _____form me that no one would recognize me after my _____osis. I believed that my new beauty would make me _____potent, able to turn the short-term, _____ary admiration of others into adoration. I wanted to be upwardly and socially _____ile, and I hoped that my new looks would make me less shy and _____verted. My family had seemed too narrowly limited, too _____scribed by a small, unchanging circle of friends. I was eager to become more _____arious. I wanted action, even if it was _____archy. I wanted the sun, moon, and stars to be mine: I was ready to take on the whole _____verse. Most members of my family were supportive. They always have been a _____vivial bunch. Only my brother was _____ary. He made a gloomy _____gnosis of debt and disappointments. But his criticisms seemed so outlandish that they sounded like _____bole. I just laughed off his exaggerated claims because I know he never would seriously _____fere with anything I really wanted to do.

Well, it has been years now, a whole _____ade since my huge nose turned into a cute little _____angle in the middle of my face. The surgeon may have trimmed only a few _____meters, but it felt like a lot to me. And I think I'll be paying the bill well into the next _____ury. You may wonder whether I have become a social success, someone who can charm even the most _____geneous group with my splendid face. The strongest reaction has been from that same brother. "What happened to you?" said that _____nal little devil the next time he saw me, "Did you get a haircut?"

Reading for Chapter 5

JOHN BOYLE

Anatomical Terminology

Scientists often use Greek and Latin roots to create new vocabulary and to communicate with professionals around the world. Here is a portion of a real college lecture in anatomy from Professor John Boyle of Cerritos College. The topic is "anatomical terminology." Notice how the professor uses Latin roots to explain new terms.

Words to Notice

Optional Exercise: Use your knowledge of root words to help you answer the following questions about words from the reading:

A. **Ana** is up; **temnein** is to cut. Does **anatomy** come from the roots to cut or dissect?

B. **Terminus** is expression; **logy** is study. Is the **terminology** of a science how people talk about it?

C. **Con** is together; **spirare** is to breathe. Is a **conspiracy** a breathing together to form a plot?

D. **Con** is together; **duct** is to lead. Can we **conduct** a discussion if we are alone?

E. **Concisus** means to cut up. Is being **concise** a way of cutting out extra words?

F. **Nov** is new. Would you want a **novice** in anatomy to operate on you?

G. The **denotation** is the dictionary meaning. If you **denote** something, do you explain or reveal it?[1]

1   Why do we learn anatomical terminology? Is it a conspiracy by anatomists to write a secret code of long, unfamiliar words? No, on the contrary. Scientific terminology is a precise tool. It allows people of different times and languages to conduct complex discussions in a small number of words. Conciseness is necessary in scientific discussion, for it actually saves time and ensures clarity of understanding. Anatomical terminology is the map that helps us move around the territory of the human body.

2   As a novice student in world geography, you must first learn the rudiments of global terminology: *longitude* and *latitude,* the locations of north and south pole, the terms *equator* and *continent,* as well as the directions north, south, east and west. In the same way, beginning anatomy students must learn the principal directional landmarks of the body and the proper directional terms.

ANATOMICAL POSITION

3   When you study geography, the locations of the continents and poles do not move but remain stable in relation to one another. The north and south poles, for instance, are always at opposite ends, and the north pole is always on top. That is not the case, however, with the human body. We can fold our arms, cross our legs, even stand on our heads—putting our south poles on top of our north poles. So to effectively study our anatomy, we need to have one constant body position to which we always refer. That position is called the "anatomical position." (*Position* derives from the Latin word meaning "place.") You are in the anatomical position when you stand erect, with your arms at your sides and *your palms pointing forward.* Whenever anatomists refer to the positions and directions of the body, they presume this position.

Anterior/Ventral and Posterior/Dorsel

4   The anatomical terms for the human body are derived from zoological terms for animals. All vertebrate animals (those with spinal columns) are related. And they are all bilaterally symmetrical (*bi* is Latin for "two" and *latus* is Latin for "side"). That is, the form of vertebrate bodies can be divided into roughly equal right and left sides. This body form also implies a "front" end, with which the organism meets its environment when moving, and a "rear" end. Consider a dog. We say that its head is at the "anterior" end (*ante* is Latin for "before") and its tail is at the "posterior" end (*posterus* is Latin for "come after"). The underside of the dog is referred to as "ventral" (*venter* is Latin for "belly") and its top or back side is referred to as "dorsal" (*dorsum* is Latin for "back").

[1] *Answers:* A. Yes. B. Yes. C. Yes. D. No. E. Yes. F. No. G. Yes.

5   All human anatomical terms, however, are based upon the anatomical position—that is a person standing erect. In this position, the *ventral* ("belly") surface meets the environment and is, therefore, also *anterior*. Likewise, the *dorsal*, or back surface, and the *posterior* surface are the same (they both "come behind"). Now, how shall we denote the "top" or "head" of a human body and its opposite? For the direction toward the head we use "superior" because the Latin word *super* means "above." And for its opposite we use "inferior" (*inferus* is Latin for below). Thus, we can say that our chin is *superior* to our navel and our nose is *inferior* to our forehead. Our sternum (or "breastbone," *sternon* being New Latin for "breast") is, therefore, *anterior*, or *ventral*, to our heart, and our vertebral column is *posterior*, or *dorsal*, to our stomach.

Medial and Lateral

6   Consider again the bilateral symmetry of the human body. Imagine a plane (a square flat surface) running from the anterior surface of the body to the posterior that bisects the body into virtually equal right and left halves. Using this plane as your reference, you describe any direction that moves away from the plane as *lateral* (*latus* is Latin for "side"). Thus, the ears are lateral to the nose. The opposite direction, moving toward the midline, is called *medial* (*medius* is Latin for "middle"). Thus, the little finger is medial to the thumb. (Remember, all terms refer to the anatomical position and thus the palms are forward.)

Proximal and Distal

7   Certain limbs, organs, and processes of the body have a defined point of attachment to another part. The arm, for example, is attached to the shoulder. When we want to describe a position or movement moving away from the point of attachment, we use the term *distal* (*distare* is Latin for "standing apart" and forms the words *distant* and *distance*). The opposite position or movement towards the point of attachment is referred to as *proximal* (*proximus* is Latin for "nearest to"). For the arm and forearm, the point of attachment is the shoulder. So the wrist is distal to the elbow, but the elbow is proximal to the wrist. In the lower extremity, the knee is proximal to the ankle, but the ankle is distal to the knee.

Questions for Class Discussion

1. Why don't scientists simply say "top" and "bottom"? When should they keep the complex language, and when should they use simpler words?
2. Which of the root words here are also used in common speech? In what ways are the meanings slightly different?

3. Ordinary words often shift in meaning through the generations. Scientists, however, want precise and unchanging meanings for their terms. Do you think that using Latin roots will help keep scientific language stable? Why or why not?

Making a New World

For Class Discussion

1. What do you feel ambivalent about when it comes to learning and using new words?
2. In what ways is your college or university a microcosm of the whole society? In what ways is it not?
3. Sometimes it seems as if every advertiser and politician is offering a panacea. Can you think of some panaceas that have been offered lately?

Collaborative Learning

1. Neologisms
   Purpose: To develop flexibility in using and understanding word parts.
   A. Check the list of word parts. Then combine roots to invent at least four new words. Write appropriate definitions.
   B. Optional: Check your dictionary to see if any of your neologisms actually exist.
   C. Pick the two neologisms you like best and have the class guess their meanings.
2. More Words
   Purpose: To see word parts in multiple contexts.
   A. Using your dictionary, find words that *do* contain word parts listed in this chapter but do not appear in the chapter. For example, *multiplicity* means "a great number."
   B. Write down at least five words and definitions.
   C. Hand in your list or report to the class.

Ideas for Writing

1. In a paragraph, describe some things you expect to see in the next decade. Try to use at least two word parts from this chapter.
2. In a page, describe some things you expect to see in the next century. Try to use at least five word parts from this chapter.
3. At home, write an essay discussing three ways in which our society should try to be *homogeneous* and three ways in which our society should try to be *heterogeneous*. Use at least five word parts from this chapter.

More Word Parts for Chapter 5

aun, enn: yearly (annual, bicentennial)
amphi, peri: around (amphitheater, periscope)
arch: chief (archrival, monarch, archaic)

cyc: wheel (cycle, cyclical)

epi: beside, on (epidermis, epicenter, epitaph, epiphenomenon)
ex-: out of, former (extract, exit)

hex: six (hexagram, hexagonal)

ject: throw (eject, reject, trajectory)

loc: place (locate, locus)

magn-, mega-: large (megalomaniac, magnate)
mit, miss: send (missive, mission, missionary)

nin: nine (ninety, ninefold)

oct: eight (octave, octopus, octopod)

pent: five (pentagon, pentagram)
per: through, by (percent, per capita, perchance)
pon, posit: place (position, positive)
port: carry (portable, portage)

quasi: to some degree but not truly (quasi-victory, quasi-scientific)
quatr, quad: four (quadrangle)

re-: again (reentry, repeat, redundant)

sept: seven (septuagenarian, septet)
sect, seg: cut (section, segment)
sol: alone, single (solitary, solitude, solitudinous)
-sperse: scatter (disperse, dispersion)

tort: twist (torque, tort, distort)
-tion, -scion, -ion: one who, something that (action, traction, condescension)
tract: pull (extract, traction)

ultra: beyond, very (ultraconservative, ultrahigh frequency, ultramodern)

un-, in-: not (uninterested, uninformed)

vert, vers: turn (divert, versify)

vac: empty (vacuum, vacuous, vacate)

Answer Key to Chapter 5

I. NUMBERS

Yes-No Questions

1. No; you act on your own.
2. Yes; both sides must agree.
3. Yes; it has three events.
4. Yes; *deca* = ten times; *deci* = one-tenth.
5. No; it is two hundred years old.
6. No; a kilometer is one million millimeters.
7. No; it is the time when people were ancient.
8. Yes; you can be confused about two things.
9. Yes; they both mean many tongued.
10. Yes; it gets water half the year.
11. Yes; a know-it-all might be able to cure all.

Fill in the Blank

A. one B. one C. two D. two
E. three F. one-hundredth G. one hundred H. one hundred I. one thousand J. three thousand
K. first L. both M. many
N. many O. half P. all Q. all

Using Context: Language and Schools

bilingual, primary, ambivalent, monoliterate, multicultural, monolingual, multi or polylingual, pandemonium, polyglot, omnipotent, cent.

II. FORMS AND MEASURES

Yes-No Questions

12. Yes; his form was changed.
13. Yes; plastic means form.
14. No; you are royalty.
15. Yes; it measures time.
16. Yes; you can see it without a microscope.
17. No; you are a miniature society.
18. No; it will last a long time.
19. Yes; both are beginners.
20. Yes; they sound alike.
21. Yes; *hetero* means many.

Matching

R. (j) S. (i) T. (g) U. (e) V. (c)
W. (b) X. (a) Y. (d) Z. (f) a. (h)
b. (l)

True-False

c. T (hetero = many)
d. T (poly = many)
e. F (plast = moldable)
f. T (aqua = water)
g. F (micro = small)
h. T (contemp = same time)
i. F (novel = new)
j. F (homo = same)

III. MOVEMENT

Yes-No Questions

22. Yes; mobile means moving.
23. No; stationary means static.
24. Yes; it looks back on old cars.
25. No; you would be discrete, careful.
26. No; the line would be broken.
27. No; it is murky and hard to read.
28. No; they cannot be held by another.
29. Yes; transitory means not permanent.
30. Yes; you are looking for evidence.

Matching

k. (i) l. (g) m. (j) n. (d) o. (b)
p. (a) q. (c) r. (e) s. (h)

True-False

t. F (mobile = move)   u. F (stat = same)
v. T (gress = move)   w. T (circum = around)
x. F (rupt = break)   y. T (ten = holds tight)
z. F (trans = impermanent)   A. T (trans = across)

IV. LOCATION IN PLACE, TIME, OR VALUE

Yes-No Questions

31. Yes; it would be above average.
32. Yes; *sub* means below.
33. Yes; precede means go before.
34. No; you would be embarrassed.
35. No; mediators come between.
36. Yes; proximity means near.
37. Yes; *tele* means far.

Matching

B. (h) C. (c) D. (i) E. (j) F. (e)
G. (a) H. (b) I. (d) J. (g)

Using Context: Remodeling

telecommunications, superlative, metaphysical, inferior, subcontractor, antechamber, mediate, proximity, postmortem

V. RELATIONSHIPS

Yes-No Questions

38. Yes; they should be fair and just.
39. No; without law does not mean without order.
40. Yes; you have worked with the enemy.
41. Yes; they are people who flock together.
42. No; controversies spark debate.
43. No; prognosis is not probiscus.
44. No; *intra* means within
45. Yes; *inter* and *medi* both mean between.
46. Yes; you are exaggerating.
47. Yes; *hyper* is above; *hypo* is below.

Matching

K. (j) L. (h) M. (f) N. (g)
O. (b) P. (a) Q. (c) R. (e) S. (l)
T. (i) U. (k)

True-False

V. T (equi = equal)

W. F (amoral = no morals)

X. T (comm/coll = common)

Y. T (greg = group)

Z. F (greg = crowd)

a. T (pro = before; epi = on top, after)

b. T (inter is not intra)

c. T (hyper = excess)

CHAPTER REVIEW

I. Yes-No Questions

1. No; it allows no movement.
2. No; she looks backwards.
3. No; he speaks around topics.
4. No; they would be shaken.
5. No; it would be hard to hold.
6. Yes; most Americans do not read Chinese.
7. Yes; she leads you across.
8. Yes; above and beyond.
9. Yes; it is below earth.
10. Yes; last point on note.
11. Yes; she needs to be near.
12. Yes; it makes them clear.
13. No; no ruler exists.
14. Yes; *con* means together.
15. Yes; it creates a fight.
16. No; it could mean a life.
17. Yes; strict on others only.
18. No; he would hate groups.
19. Yes; he would have no feelings.
20. No; *ante* means before.

II. Using Context: Plastic Surgery

plastic, transform, metamorphosis, omnipotent, temporary, mobile, introverted, circumscribed, gregarious, anarchy, universe, convivial, contrary, prognosis, hyperbole, interfere, decade, triangle, millimeters, century, heterogeneous, infernal

WORDS OF EMOTION AND POWER

Quick Reference List

adroit	credulous	ephemeral	ostentatious	succumb
affable	cryptic	immutable	ostracize	transcend
altruistic	dissemble	lurid	rapacious	vehement
ambivalent	dogmatic	meticulous	rectify	vicarious
apathy	enigmatic	mollify	skeptical	vindictive
assimilate				

Introduction: The Power of Describing

The Russian poet Anna Akhmatova [ock-MAH-teh-vah] knew the importance of powerful description. During the worst years of Stalinist oppression, Akhmatova was waiting outside a prison to visit her son, who was imprisoned for political reasons. One day, while waiting outside the gates in the cold, another woman in line recognized her as the famous poet. She asked the poet, "Can you describe this?" When Anna replied, "I can," the woman was pleased, and, the poet writes, "a smile crossed what used to be a human face." Describing well is important not only to poets of witness, but to the ordinary person as well. You gain more social prestige and power if you can accurately describe people, events, or phenomena in nature or society. Describing your own feelings well helps people understand you. In this chapter you will learn a few of the most important words to describe feelings, people, or actions that give you social power and some key words for understanding deceptive uses of language.

I. Words to Describe How You Feel

1. vehement [VEE uh mint]: passionate, powerful, fervent feelings.

Have you ever been told "Don't get carried away"? If so, you know your feelings were vehement. Vehement combines the roots *vehere*, which means "to carry," with *mens*, which means "mind" (as in "vehicle" and "mental"). To be vehement, then, is to be "carried out of one's mind."

Would you likely have vehement feelings if you leaped up at a town meeting and shouted, "I protest!"?

Yes   No   because _____

· · · · · · · · · ·

**Have You Heard?
Are You an Altruist?**

The word *altruistic* comes from philosophy. The French philosopher Auguste Comte (1798–1857) wanted a philosophy to oppose the selfish "egoism" he saw all around him. He coined the word *altruism* to describe his belief that people should be devoted to the interests of others, even at personal sacrifice. He got the idea because the Greek word *alter* means "other," whereas the Greek *ego* means "I." The modern writers Max Stirner and Ayn Rand believe that altruism is unnatural to humans. What do you think?

2. ambivalent [am BIV uh lint]: feeling two strong—but opposite—emotions at once.

Have you ever strongly regretted the end of summer but also been excited about the start of school? That's ambivalence. Ambivalent emotions, such as love/hate, are favorite topics for poets and psychologists. Ambivalence combines the Latin prefix *ambo*, meaning "both" (as in ambidextrous) with the root *valens*, meaning "to be strong" (as in valiant).

If you were ambivalent about a Memorial Day parade, would you vehemently want to march in it?

Yes   No   because _____

3. apathy [AP uh thee]: empty of feelings, indifferent, uncaring.

Apathy is a lack of care or feeling. Some people complain vehemently about the excessive apathy in society. Other people are apathetic about other people's vehemence. Can you "feel apathy"? Not really. Apathy combines the Greek word for suffering or feeling (*pathos*) with the prefix *a*, which means "without."

If your valentine were apathetic toward you, would that person be a good romancer?

Yes   No   because _____

4. vicarious [vie CARE ee us]: to enjoy through imagination or sympathy instead of direct action.

Vicarious experiences let us enjoy (or suffer) without danger. People read literature, watch movies, and attend sports events for vicarious pleasure, thrills, and suffering. If you cover your eyes during the frightening parts in movies or leave the room when a television character is about to be embarrassed, you are sensitive to vicarious experience.

If you cried when Little Nell died in Dickens's *Old Curiosity Shop*, would you have vicarious grief?

Yes   No   because _____

Practice with Word Forms: Fill in each blank with the proper form of the word.

A. **vehemence, vehement, vehemently:** The defendant

_____ proclaimed her innocence in the courtroom.

But her _____ did not inspire confidence in the

members of the jury. They reasoned that an innocent person should be

as calm as a slug, and so anyone so _____ must be

guilty.

B. **ambivalence, ambivalent:** Should I marry, or not? My

_____ causes me to toss and turn at night. I am both

excited and filled with dread. I suppose _____ feel-

ings are natural the night before the wedding.

C. **vicarious, vicariously:** There is no substitute for life, but sometimes a

_____ experience can be safer and more instructive

than the real thing. Who wouldn't rather experience imprisonment, the

death of a close friend, or starvation _____ than

directly?

D. **apathy, apathetic, apathetically:** When I asked about the election,

he _____ replied that he was not voting. "Not voting!" I exclaimed. "Do you know how hard people struggled to pass the Twenty-third Amendment? If eighteen-year-olds in the past were as _____ as you are, where would we be?" He said, "I care even less about the previous generation's _____ than I do about my own."

Using Context: Fill in each blank with the vocabulary word that best suits the context.

Returning to College as an Adult

That first cool morning in the middle of August reminded me of my decision to return to college in the fall. I was enthusiastic about getting my degree but also insecure about my talents. This _____ kept me from immediately going to register. I got little encouragement from my children, because they were _____ about my college career; they did not care either way. My spouse, on the other hand, was _____ about the value of a college degree. He said: "Education is the only thing no one can take from you." My younger sister prefers the active life. When she asked, "So what do you get from books, anyway?" I explained that while studying I could be the Queen of Egypt like Cleopatra, win the Nobel Prize in physics with Marie Curie, tour Asia with Marco Polo, or suffer ignominious, that is, shameful, defeat at Gettysburg. "Yes," she answered, "but these are all _____ experiences, not real ones." "Better than nothing," I replied, "Call me next time *you* ride down the Nile with Mark Antony."

For Your Critical Reflection: Ambivalence describes two competing emotions. Have you ever had two emotions competing with one another? When? Can you describe it?

_____

_____

II. Words to Compliment People You Admire

5. altruistic [al TROO is tick]: devoted to the interest of other people.

Altruism is the belief that one should be concerned first for the welfare of others. An altruist is a person fully dedicated to the ideal of altruism. Altruistic behavior is often praised, so a humorist might say, "I am altruistic; my friend is unselfish, but you, sir, are a pushover." Altruism comes from the Latin *alter* for "other."

Would an altruist say, "I refuse to give money to beggars; these people care too little for themselves"?

Yes   No   because _____

6. skeptical [SKEP tih kul]: inquiring, thoughtful, disbelieving.

Skeptikos was an ancient Greek word meaning "thoughtful." The skeptics were Greek philosophers who questioned what they were told and believed that human knowledge could advance only by doubting. Being skeptical today means that you are not easily fooled. You tend to check things out for yourself, withhold judgment. "She was skeptical of the report that said married women live longer."

If you were skeptical of the occult, would you change your plane tickets after reading your horoscope?

Yes   No   because _____

7. affable [AFF uh bul]: easy to talk to, pleasant, civil, courteous.

An affable person is easy to approach. Sometimes high officials, famous people, and professors are surprisingly affable—even when we expect them to be unfriendly. Affable, then, is a more precise word for being "nice."

Would an affable person be likely to tap a pencil to show impatience with you?

Yes   No   because _____

8. adroit [uh DROIT]: skillful in the use of hands, nimble, mentally quick, resourceful.

Adroit people are handy, deft, or quick on their feet. The agile tightrope walker must be adroit. People who stumble, drop things, or bungle jobs are *maladroit*.

Adroit also describes people who can use words or arguments cleverly—especially in difficult situations. Adroit comes from the Latin *directus*, meaning "to set in a straight line."

Would an adroit dancer necessarily be adroit at talking a police officer out of a speeding ticket?

Yes   No   because _____

9. meticulous [meh TIK yoo lus]: careful over details, particular.

From the Latin *metus*, meaning "fear," meticulous used to describe someone terrified of mistakes—too careful, picky, or finicky. Today, meticulous is a complimentary term for someone who works painstakingly to make sure every detail is exact.

If you meticulously studied your road map, would you be likely to get lost?

Yes   No   because _____

Practice with Word Forms: Fill in each blank with the proper form of the word.

E. **altruistic, altruism, altruist, altruistically:** Lee is a firm believer in

_____ and once argued that only a genuine

_____ can unselfishly promote the welfare of others.

Open palm extended, Lee asked me to show how _____

I was by handing over a thousand dollars. But I refused, adding,

"_____, I prefer to give it to people less fortunate

than myself."

F. **skepticism, skeptic, skeptical, skeptically:** Most scientists are

_____ about diet fads. They listen

_____ to the promises of the advertisers to help people to lose a hundred pounds in a hundred days. Scientific

_____ derives from the findings of scientific researchers. Sometimes only the _____ can ask the tough

questions society needs.

Using Context: Fill in each blank with the vocabulary word (or form) that best suits the context.

Working at Slim Wood's

Working at Slim Wood's Health Food Store was the best job I ever had. At first I was _____ about interviewing for the job; I had my doubts about how any food could be "healthier" than another. But my fears were calmed during my first interview with the relaxed and _____ Slim. Slim answered all my questions and explained that the reasons for opening the store were as _____ as they were businesslike. "Everyone deserves good food," he added. Each morning Slim _____ studied the catalogs and ordered only organically grown food that contained no pesticide residue, no preservatives, no artificial flavors, no red dye, no agar, and no cholesterol. "Miraculously, these semisweet chocolate chips meet my rigid scrutiny," he said, and _____ flipped one into his mouth.

For Your Critical Reflection: A skeptic might agree with the famous saying, "Who never doubted, never half believed." Is this true? Do you need to doubt to affirm your faith in something? How can doubt help you to believe better?

_____

_____

_____

III. Words to Describe People You Do Not Like

10. rapacious [rih PAYSH us]: devouring, grasping, greedy.

Rapacious and rape share the same Latin root, *rapere*, meaning "to seize." Rapacious people seize what they want, even by force or treachery. Grasping and greedy, the Snidely Whiplash shows his rapacity by foreclosing mortgages. Because *rapacious* has a negative tone, you might say, "You are rapacious, madam; my friend is ambitious; and I, myself, am a go-getter."

If you scared a widow from her home so that you could buy it at a cheap price, would you be rapacious?

Yes   No   because _____ _____

11. **credulous** [KRED yoo lus]: lacking doubt or skepticism, ready to believe.

A credulous person is easily convinced. Credulous comes from the Latin root *credere*, meaning "to trust" (as in *cred*it, *creed*, incre*d*ible). Credulous has a slightly negative tone, so you might say, "I am trusting; my friend is credulous; but you, my dear, are gullible."

If you were a credulous person, would you be likely to get the best deals at a yard sale?

Yes   No   because _____

12. **vindictive** [vin DIK tuv]: revenging, unforgiving, resentful.

Vindictive people hold grudges. An entire society can turn vindictive, which means that people become more interested in punishing criminals than preventing or avoiding crime. Vindictive comes from the Latin *vindicta*, meaning "revenge."

Would vindictive people be likely to forgive you for accidentally running over their dog?

Yes   No   because _____

13. **dogmatic** [dog MAT ik]: arrogant, dictatorial; always right.

Although we all have dogmas, we probably do not insist dogmatically on their absolute truth. Dogmatic has a negative connotation; so people will say, "I am steadfast; my friend is firm; but you, madam, are dogmatic." From the Greek *dogma*, meaning "what one believes."

Would you be a dogmatist if you insisted dogmatically that all dogmas are always wrong?

Yes   No   because _____

14. **ostentatious** [ah sten TAY shus]: showy, boastful, attracting notice, pretentious.

Do you know a person who buys a new ring and stretches it before your face until you blurt, "Oh, a new ring?" That person is ostentatious. From Latin *ob*, "before" and *tendere*, "to stretch" (as in tender, tendon), ostentatious means to "stretch before" others.

"Would you say you're 'dogmatic'?"

Herman © 1989 Jim Unger. Reprinted with permission of
Universal Press Syndicate.

Would you be ostentatious if you wore a mink coat to a baseball game on the
Fourth of July?

Yes   No   because _____

Practice with Word Forms: Fill in each blank with the proper form of the
word.

G. **credulous, credulously, credulity:** Simple Simon believed what you

told him. His sweet _____ endeared him to many

kind people, but it also got him in trouble. Among his fellow

_____ friends, Simon was safe and happy. But one

time he listened _____ to a sales pitch about develop-

ment in Florida, and now he is working on an alligator farm.

H. **rapacious, rapacity, rapaciousness:** The extreme _____

of the rulers and warlords of the Middle Ages is well documented.
Some warlords were so _____ that they would keep
looting, pillaging, and raping even when war ended. The Vikings, once
infamous for their _____, eventually became traders
who helped develop the economy of medieval Europe.

Using Context: Fill in each blank with the vocabulary word (or form) that
best suits the context.

A Party at the Smythereens'

I never should have gone. My ex-neighbors, the Smythereens, were celebrating the completion of their custom-built house in the mountains. Syl-
via Smythereen told me to dress casually, because my quiet style would
be perfectly welcome. That was a lie! How could I have been so
_____ as to believe a woman who wears
_____ feathered boas and gold rings to plant zucchini?
Samuel Smythereen is a _____ real estate agent who
scares senior citizens about crime in their neighborhood until they sell their
homes to him at a bargain price. Even though his sales are only average,
he still _____ insists that everyone should adopt his
magic method. The party was a disaster. Besides being bored to tears, I accidentally sat on the Smythereens' toy poodle, which they bought to match
their mohair couch. It squealed and limped away. I barely endured the
_____ remarks of the unforgiving Ms. Smythereen for
the rest of the evening.

For Your Critical Reflection: The French philosopher Jean-Paul Sartre says
that people confuse ''Being'' with ''Having.'' Ostentatious people certainly
seem to do that, thinking that they are only as good as their possessions.
What advice would you give these people?

_____

_____

IV. Action Words for Power

15. transcend [tran SEND]: to go beyond, to rise above, to surpass.

You might transcend your performance in golf and thereby reach a new level of excellence. But you can also transcend, or "rise above," daily circumstances through philosophy. Transcendence is sometimes a form of mental escape; it comes from Latin *trancendere*, meaning "to climb over."

If you ignore the petty criticisms of your classmates to become a great poet, are you transcending your circumstances?

Yes   No   because _____

16. rectify [RECK tuh fie]: to make right, correct when wrong, to remedy.

To rectify is to "make right." Rectify comes from Latin *rectus*, meaning "right," and *facere*, meaning "to make" (as in factory). Sometimes misunderstanding between friends needs to be rectified.

If you crash a neighbor's car, could paying for repairs rectify the damage?

Yes   No   because _____

17. mollify [MOLL uh fie]: to soften a person's temper; pacify, appease, mitigate.

To mollify is to soften temper, diminish pain, appease demands, calm fears, and so on. A child sometimes can be easily mollified. Unpopular political leaders can mollify their citizens with talk of happy days to come. Mollify is formed from the Latin roots *mollis* (soft) and *facere* (to make).

If you placed a pacifier in a crying baby's mouth, would you be trying to mollify her?

Yes   No   because _____

18. succumb [suh KUMM]: to yield to a superior force, submit.

Succumb is a popular word in romantic fiction, where it has sexual overtones: "She succumbed to his overwhelming desires." But succumb has a general meaning of submitting to any unrelenting pressure or plea. In polite discourse,

. . . .

Guess What!
If You Can't Beat 'em, Transcend 'em!

The word *transcend* is from the Latin *transcendere*, meaning "to cross a boundary" or "rise above." A person famous for transcending circumstances was the medieval statesman Boethius (480–524). Unjustly jailed and eventually executed, Boethius wrote a book in prison about how Lady Philosophy comforted him in his cell by directing his thoughts to universal ideas instead of the petty and worldly squabbles of the court: "While they fight over things of no value, we laugh at them from above, safe from their fury and defended by a strength against which their aggressive folly cannot prevail."

American transcendentalism was founded in 1836, when the Transcendental Club of Boston met to discuss the ideas of Ralph Waldo Emerson (1803–1882). Disappointed with the growing commercialism and materialism of American society, Emerson lectured and preached to inspire people to think about great ideas and noble philosophers. The key to the knowledge of the universe, he said, was in the human intuition, not science. His friend, Henry David Thoreau, chose to transcend the busy city by deliberately moving to Walden Pond, where he could live a simple life and quietly consider his thoughts. What do you do if you need to transcend the world around you?

succumb can refer to dying: "He struggled till the end, but at eight this morning, he succumbed."

If you succumbed after hearing the sales pitch of a street vendor, have you bought something?

Yes   No   because _____

19. ostracize [OST ruh size]: reject, eject, cast out, exile, banish from favor.

To ostracize means to exclude a person from a social sphere or group. You can feel ostracized, even if you are not, when a member of your group snubs or rejects you, but a full-scale ostracism takes place only when everyone knows it is happening. Sometimes ostracized people form their own groups and ostracize others. The word *ostracize* goes back to an ancient Greek custom of temporarily banishing one person from the city. The votes were cast on shells or chips of clay pots, called *ostrakon*.

If three of your friends refused to answer your phone calls, might you feel ostracized?

Yes   No   because _____

20. assimilate [uh SIM ih late]: take in, absorb, adjust, fit in.

To assimilate is to "make similar." The body assimilates food by transforming it into digestible material. People assimilate into a group by becoming like the members of that group. Assimilate is an important word in the history of immigration.

Would you be trying to assimilate if you moved to France but never learned to speak French?

Yes   No   because _____

Matching: Match the definition with the vocabulary word.

I.   ___ Make yourself similar to others in your new club.   (a) transcend

J.   ___ Think of eternal truths instead of daily tasks.   (b) rectify

K.   ___ Eject someone from your church group.   (c) mollify

L.   ___ Calm the child's frantic emotions.   (d) succumb

M. ___ Yield to the beggar's relentless appeals.   (e) ostracize

(f) assimilate

Using Context: Fill in each blank with the vocabulary word (or form) that best suits the context.

All in the Family

When my grandparents emigrated from Poland, they faced many conflicts.

The immigration troubles at Ellis Island were easily _____,

but trying to _____ into American culture required pati-

ence. My grandparents settled in a large and friendly Polish community in

South Chicago. When my father, who learned both Polish and English, de-

cided to move away from the neighborhood to open a restaurant in the

countryside, his family complained bitterly. And he could not easily

_____ their worries and fears. In fact, it might have been

easier if he were rejected or _____ from the community, because then he could have moved away with a clear conscience. Nevertheless, he never _____ to the repeated demands of the family to move back to the city. And he was always proud that he _____ his limited situaton to imagine and create a new life for his wife and children in a lake village of Wisconsin.

For Your Critical Reflection: The assimilation ideal holds that the United States is a "melting pot" in which all new immigrants are assimilated into the common culture. But some people choose not to assimilate; they choose instead to maintain the unique identity of their own culture. How important or unimportant do you believe assimilation to be?

_____

_____

V. Words to Describe Confusion and Deception

21. ephemeral [eh FEM ir uhl]: existing or important only for the day; transitory.

Ephemeral things are short-lived. Many daily news events can be called "mere *ephemera*," which means that they are insignificant in the long run. Ephemeral comes from the Greek words *epi*, meaning "on," and *hēmera*, meaning "day."

If you were accused of spending your money on ephemera, would you love to buy cars, houses, and land?

Yes   No   because _____

22. immutable [ih MYOOT uh bul]: not changing, invariable, unalterable, constant.

Immutable things are unchanging and everlasting—the opposite of ephemeral. We refer to "immutable facts," "immutable problems," "immutable joys," or "immutable values." "We must acknowledge the immutable desire for justice." "Mutability is the only immutability" is another way to say "The only constant is change."

If you wanted to study the immutable themes of human civilization, would you be concerned mostly with the ephemeral events of the day?

Yes   No   because _____

23. enigmatic [en ig MAT ik]: riddling, puzzling, mysterious, hard to know.

We can be intrigued by enigmatic people, messages, or art. Enigmatic people keep to themselves or speak in secret and cryptic messages. People who solve enigmas (such as detectives or scientists) are highly praised, even heroic: Oedipus solved the enigma of the Sphynx; Daniel interpreted the enigmatic dreams of King Nebuchadnezzar. Enigmatic comes from the Latin *ænigma*, meaning "riddle" or "dark saying."

Would enigmatic people be likely to reveal their life stories on the bus?

Yes   No   because _____

24. dissemble [dih SEM bul]: to hide, conceal, disguise, veil.

When you tell the truth, your words "resemble" reality. If you try to lie, your words "dissemble" reality. To dissemble is to hide truth. Dissembling is a polite word for lying in public. Dissemblers include famous people who dissemble their lives in "tell-all" biographies, revealing only respectable parts. Public relations experts may dissemble about the danger of a toxic spill to avoid public alarm.

Would you dissemble if, when accused of cheating, you said, "Cheating is a word I don't understand."

Yes   No   because _____

25. cryptic [KRIPT ik]: hidden, secret, involving secret codes or ciphers.

A cryptic message requires decoding. A cryptic reply raises more questions than it answers. A cryptic correspondence demands another letter. Professors sometimes mark "cryptic" on a student paper, meaning "Please stop writing in an abbreviated secret code. Explain your ideas for people who do not know as much as you; be explicit; that is, *write more.*" Cryptic comes from the Latin *kryptein*, meaning "to hide."

If you wrote your term paper on a note card, might your professor view this as a cryptic correspondence?

Yes   No   because _____

26. lurid [LIR id]: vivid in a harsh, ghastly, or sensational way.

Lurid things are characterized by violent passion or crime, such as in a lurid detective story. Lurid camera shots cast a lurid light on lurid details to excite viewers. The Latin word *luridus* means "pale-yellow, ghastly."

If you liked a quiet life, would you want the lurid details of your past discussed on a talk show?

Yes   No   because _____

Matching: Match the message with the word that best describes it.

N. ____ A message in a bottle: "Herodotus rules; avoid Xenophon."

O. ____ A message on television: "See the gritty details of Elvis's death."

P. ____ A message on radio: "Now, for the daily traffic report."

Q. ____ A message from the boss: "We must slow the growth of raises."

R. ____ A message from the *Koran*: "Is not a pure worship due to God?"

(a) ephemeral

(b) immutable

(c) enigmatic

(d) cryptic

(e) dissembling

(f) lurid

True-False: Write "T" for true and "F" for false.

S. ____ The statement "All things are ephemeral" is an immutable truth.

T. ____ An enigmatic message would create more curiosity and less frustration than a cryptic one.

U. ____ A dissembling news reporter might cover the falsehoods with lurid details.

V. ____ An immutable truth, such as "To be is to be perceived," can also be cryptic.

W. ____ An enigmatic philosopher might actually turn out to be a dissembler.

For Your Critical Reflection: Ephemeral news is unimportant. On the other hand, ephemeral pleasures (a sunrise or first spring robin) are highly valued *because* they are fleeting. Poets celebrate them: "O where are the snows of yesteryear?" How are ephemeral joys both important and unimportant?

_____

_____

Chapter Review

I. **True-False:** Mark "T" for true and "F" for false.

1. ____ A vehement person is likely to marry someone who is apathetic.

2. ____ Vicarious experiences do not cause physical reactions.

3. ____ An altruistic person is likely to invest in child care to make a profit.

4. ____ An ambivalent decision gives you a clear sense of security.

5. ____ Rapacious people are perfectly content with their fate.

6. ____ An ostentatious student might say "ostentatious" instead of "show off."

7. ____ To succumb is to yield to an overwhelming force, such as love or death.

8. ____ A rectifiable problem is one that can be made right.

9. ____ An unmollified baby will continue to cry.

10. ____ One way to transcend your circumstances is to think of immutable ideas.

11. ____ An enigmatic smile from an attractive person is a clear message.

12. ____ Being a parent can be called one of the ephemeral joys of life.

13. ____ Dissemblers love to show one face but hide another behind their words.

14. ____ An ephemeral desire passes quickly.

15. ____ A cryptic message makes us want to know more.

16. ____ A lurid story is likely to avoid cryptic descriptions.

II. Matching: Match the action with the word that describes it.

17.____ Leaps over the fence and plucks the baseball from the rose patch.

(a) altruistic

18.____ Studies all religions before believing any one of them.

(b) skeptical

(c) affable

19.____ Triple checks all arithmetic before submitting a tax return.

(d) adroit

(e) meticulous

20.____ Establishes a free counseling center for runaway teenagers.

III. Using Context: Use the word list at the beginning of the chapter to fill in the blanks. You might not use all the words, or you might use one word more than once.

The Scandal

Representative Haipher was infuriated. Although she knew reporters considered her hard to understand, an _____ official if there ever was one, she did not realize they would sink to _____ her life to grab a juicy headline. Haipher welcomed press scrutiny as one of the _____ facts of public service. Yet the press was frustrated with her, because instead of providing "sound bites" about the petty and _____ battles on Capitol Hill, she _____ bickering. She either shared the statistics from her _____ reports or talked philosophically about the _____ American values—initiative, industry, and _____ concern for other people, especially those who seek freedom. After one inspirational speech, some reporters showed their deep and _____ disappointment by booing. Another one sent only a _____ message to his editor: "Haipher the Knifer plays the philaisopher." Finding nothing sensational in her broad-minded ideas, and hungry for a shocking story, two local reporters _____ seized on a story about Haipher's brother, a friendly and _____ chap, who was, unfortunately, a professional gambler. _____ to believe that the reporters had his sister's best interest at heart, he allowed the reporters to follow him through every casino in Las Vegas; they recorded his _____ opinions about foreign policy and focused their camera on his gaudy and _____ jewelry, vulgar quips to the bartender, and other sordid and _____ details. He even _____ to their requests to attack the opposite party. The reporters closed the story with this quote: "When asked why he gambles so much, Haipher's brother replied, 'How else will my sister get the money to run for the White House?'" But Representative Haipher did not seek revenge; she was not _____ at heart. She knew a better way to _____ her angry constituents and dodge the attacks like an _____ boxer. Her campaign slogan for reelection was the simple and _____ "Bet on Haipher. Her brother does."

Reading for Chapter 6

DAISETZ T. SUZUKI

Aspects of Japanese Culture—*Wabi*

This reading describes the Japanese traditional value of wabi, *a "presence of something of the highest value in the simplest and most austere circumstance." Suzuki finds connections between* wabi *and the American tradition of transcendentalism, represented by David Henry Thoreau. Suzuki provides an excellent example of the difficulty we all have when we lack the words to describe feelings or states of mind.*

Words to Notice

Prepare for the reading by reviewing the following key words:

characterize: describe
retaining: holding or keeping
vastness: a wide expanse
primitive: simple, crude
audacious: bold, daring
turbulent: tossed, violent
braving: facing courageously
incomprehensibility of the
  Absolute: the quality of God
  that cannot be understood

encompassing: encircling
luxurious: rich, plentiful
pensive: thoughtful
ungrudgingly: generously
aloofness: the quality of being
  cool, remote
ineradicable longing: a deep
  desire
marshaling thoughts: organizing
  ideas

1   Among things which strongly characterize Japanese artistic talents we may mention the so-called "one-corner" style, which originated with Bayen (Ma Yüan, *fl.* 1175–1225), one of the greatest Southern Sung artists. The "one-corner" style is psychologically associated with the Japanese painters' "thrifty brush" tradition of retaining the least possible number of lines or strokes which go to represent forms on silk or paper. Both are very much in accord with the spirit of Zen. A simple fishing boat in the midst of the rippling waters is enough to awaken in the mind of the beholder a sense of the vastness of the sea and at the same time of peace and contentment—the Zen sense of the Alone. Apparently the boat floats helplessly. It is a primitive structure with no mechanical device for stability and for audacious steering over the turbulent waves, with no scientific apparatus for braving all kinds of weather—quite a contrast to the modern ocean liner. But this very helplessness is the virtue of the fishing canoe, in contrast with which we feel the incomprehensibility of the Absolute encompassing the boat and all the world. Again, a solitary bird on a dead branch, in which not a line, not a shade, is wasted, is enough to show us the loneliness of autumn, when days become shorter and nature begins to roll up once more its gorgeous display of luxurious summer vegetation. It makes one feel somewhat pensive, but it gives one opportunity to withdraw the attention toward the inner life, which, given attention enough, spreads out its rich treasures ungrudgingly before the eyes.

2   Here we have an appreciation of transcendental aloofness in the midst of multiplicities—which is known as *wabi* in the dictionary of Japanese cultural terms. *Wabi* really means "poverty," or, negatively, "not to be in the fashionable society of the time." To be poor, that is, not to be dependent on things worldly—wealth, power, and reputation—and yet to feel inwardly the presence of something of the highest value, above time and social position: this is what essentially constitutes *wabi*. Stated in terms of practical everyday life, *wabi* is to be satisfied with a little hut, a room of two or three *tatami* (mats), like the log cabin of Thoreau, and with a dish of vegetables picked in the neighboring fields, and perhaps to be listening to the pattering of a gentle spring rainfall. The cult of *wabi* has entered deeply into the cultural life of the Japanese people. It is in truth the worshiping of poverty. . . . Despite the modern Western luxuries of comforts of life which have invaded us, there is still an ineradicable longing in us for the cult of *wabi*. Even in the intellectual life, not richness of ideas, not

brilliancy or solemnity in marshaling thoughts and building up a philosophical system, is sought; but just to stay quietly content with the mystical contemplation of Nature and to feel at home with the world is more inspiring to us, at least to some of us.

Questions for Class Discussion

1. Is there a place for *wabi* in your life? Why or why not?
2. How could *wabi* make people more altruistic? Less altruistic?
3. Suzuki ends the passage by implying that not all Japanese people long for *wabi* equally. What kinds of things would keep people from appreciating *wabi*, even if they once did?

Making a New World

For Class Discussion

1. Some people say that society benefits from the faults of its members. Describe the benefits to society of the following kinds of people: dogmatic, credulous, ostentatious, rapacious.
2. People in public authority have the opportunity to mollify and to dissemble. Do you know any examples of mollification or dissembling?
3. The ideal of America is one in which all new immigrants assimilate into the culture. The American culture is supposed to be welcoming to those who assimilate, and new immigrants are supposed to be eager to assimilate. Is this ideal being realized today? What is lost and what is gained by assimilating?

Collaborative Learning

1. Describing People
   Purpose: To use emotions and brainstorming to add to descriptive ability.
   A. Appoint a scribe. List the words you use to describe (1) people you admire, (2) people you despise, or (3) people you think enjoy deceiving others. (Your instructor may assign one group or all three.)
   B. Use a thesaurus or dictionary to add more words or make the existing words more precise.
   C. Select the "Top or Bottom Ten."
   D. Share your conclusions with the class.
2. People and Philosophy

Purpose: To assign different people to a dominant philosophy of life. Note: "Have You Heard" in the beginning of the chapter supplies some background.

A. Appoint a scribe. List the kinds of people (individual persons or types) who you think can be called altruists, that is, people who follow the altruistic ideal that one should be devoted to the interests and welfare of others, even at personal sacrifice. Include reasons for your selections. Select the best three.

B. (Optional) List the kinds of people (individual persons or types) who you think can be called skeptics, that is, people who doubt the truth of leading ideas, philosophies, governments, or religions. Include reasons for your selections. Select the best three.

C. (Optional) List the kinds of people (individual persons or types) who you think can be called transcendentalists, that is, people who seek to transcend their existing world by concentrating on high ideals or who seek to pursue knowledge of reality by using mystic intuition. Include reasons for your selections. Select the best three.

D. Share your conclusions with the class.

Ideas for Writing

1. In a paragraph, explain why someone you know is a good example of one of the descriptive words in this chapter.
2. In one page, write a letter of praise to a coworker, fellow student, or employee. Use at least four words from the chapter.
3. At home, write a letter of blame to a person, business, or institution, using at least two words from the chapter.

More Words for Chapter 6

allege: declare without being able to prove; "alleged culprit"

dubious: doubtful; "dubious reasoning"

evolving: changing, growing, developing; "evolving concern"

frenetic: frantic, frenzied; "frenetic activity"

harbinger: person, event, thing announcing the approach of another; "harbinger of doom"

indigenous: native to an area or region; "indigenous custom"

ineffable: too great to be destroyed; "ineffable joy"

inexplicable: not easy to explain; "inexplicable behavior"

inherent: existing in something as a natural or permanent character or quality; "inherent flaw"

inscrutable: impossible to understand or interpret; "inscrutable decision"

insidious: developing or acting in a subtle but harmful or evil way; "insidious rumor"

insular: island-like, isolated, narrow-minded; "insular prejudices"

invidious: likely to cause resentment because of a real or imagined unfairness; "invidious comparison"

magnanimous: noble and forgiving, not petty; "magnanimous nature"

marginal: unimportant, placed to the outside, very slight; "marginal activities"

notable: worthy of notice or attention; "notable idea"

obligatory: required, necessary; "obligatory handshake"

odious: hateful, detestable; "odious tasks"

paradoxical: contradicts normal expectations; "paradoxical conclusion"

plausible: probable or believable but not proven; "plausible explanation"

precocious: having developed certain abilities or knowledge earlier than is usual; "precocious vocabulary"

propensity: tendency, inclination, habit; "propensity to interrupt"

salient: projecting, prominent, most notable; "salient features"

unwieldy: awkward to move or handle because of size or shape; "unwieldy load"

volatile: quickly changing in nature, likely to change in mood; "volatile behavior"

Answer Key to Chapter 6

I. WORDS TO DESCRIBE HOW YOU FEEL

Yes-No Questions

1. Yes; you show strong feelings.
2. No; ambivalence is a mixed feeling.
3. No; valentines should care.
4. Yes; the death did not happen to you.

Practice with Word Forms

A. vehemently, vehemence, vehement

B. ambivalence, ambivalent
C. vicarious, vicariously
D. apathetically, apathetic, apathy

Using Context: Returning to College as an Adult

ambivalence, apathetic, vehement, vicarious

II. WORDS TO COMPLIMENT PEOPLE

Yes-No Questions

5. No; altruists believe people should be selfless.
6. No; skeptics would not believe in astrology.
7. No; affable people are civil and courteous.
8. No; physical adroitness is not mental adroitness.
9. No; meticulous means paying attention.

Practice with Word Forms

E. altruism, altruist, altruistic, altruistically
F. skeptical, skeptically, skepticism, skeptic

Using Context: Working at Slim Wood's

skeptical, affable, altruistic, meticulously, adroitly

III. DESCRIBING PEOPLE YOU DO NOT LIKE

Yes-No Questions

10. Yes; rapacious means greedily seizing.

11. No; credulous people are easily deceived.
12. No; vindictive people get mad, then even.
13. Yes; dogmatic people insist they are right.
14. Yes; the coat is for showing off, not warmth.

Practice with Word Forms

G. credulity, credulous, credulously
H. rapacity/rapaciousness, rapacious, rapacity/rapaciousness

Using Context: A Party at the Smythereens'

credulous, ostentatious, rapacious, dogmatically, vindictive

IV. ACTION WORDS FOR POWER

Yes-No Questions

15. Yes; you are rising above the criticisms.
16. Yes; to rectify means to make right.
17. Yes; mollify means to pacify or calm.
18. Yes; succumb means to give in or submit.
19. Yes; ostracized means being excluded, snubbed.
20. No; you should assimilate into French culture.

Matching

I. (f) J. (a) K. (e) L. (c) M. (d)

Using Context: All in the Family

rectified (rectifiable), assimilate, mollify, ostracized, succumbed, transcended

V. WORDS TO DESCRIBE CONFUSION AND DECEPTION

Yes-No Questions

21. No; ephemeral purchases are consumed in a day.
22. No; immutable themes transcend the daily news.
23. No; enigmatic people keep to themselves.
24. Yes; you would be trying to use words to hide.
25. Yes; too much would be unexplained, hidden.
26. No; lurid means passionate, criminal, crude.

Matching

N. (c) or (d)   O. (f)   P. (a)   Q. (e)
R. (b)

True-False

S. T   T. T   U. T   V. T   W. T

CHAPTER REVIEW

I. True-False

1. F 2. F 3. F 4. F 5. F 6. T
7. T 8. T 9. T 10. T 11. F
12. F 13. T 14. T 15. T 16. T

II. Matching

17. (d) 18. (b) 19. (e) 20. (a)

III. Using Context: The Scandal

enigmatic, dissembling, immutable, ephemeral, transcended, meticulous, immutable, altruistic, vehement, cryptic, rapaciously, affable, credulous, dogmatic, ostentatious, lurid, succumbed, vindictive, mollify, adroit, cryptic

YES, IT IS YOUR BUSINESS

Quick Reference Word List

assets	downturn	indictment	nominal/real
bonds	exchange rates	inflation	precedent
bull market/bear	fiscal policy	injunction	prosperity
market	global market	investment	recession
collective	goods and services	laissez-faire	recovery
bargaining	gross national	litigation	regulation
corporation	product (GNP)	management/labor	stocks
de jure/de facto			

Introduction: The Key to Business Success

> If ignorance paid dividends, most Americans could make a fortune out of what they don't know about economics.
>
> [Luther Hodges]

Many students enter college planning to major in business. Business news rings from newspapers, magazines, and air waves. Bookstores are filled with how-to books offering schemes to make money in business. People approach economic issues urgently, but they are often frustrated by the new vocabulary—long lists of specialized words, which seem to require background to understand and which seem to change weekly. Where are the leveraged buyouts of yesteryear? This chapter starts your fortune in vocabulary from business, economics, and law.

I. The Business Cycle

Did you know that economists consider recessions a normal part of the business cycle? Each stage in this four- to five-year cycle helps produce the next stage. To soften the pain of the downturn, both governments and individuals often draw on their savings and borrow money. Although many experts say that today's business cycle is hard to predict, they still use the following words to describe it.

1. prosperity [pros PAIR ih tee]: increased wealth.

We are in prosperity when the real value of goods and services goes up, unemployment is low, and people feel better off. Consumers spend money, so business activity steps up and profits increase. More people invest in business because it is doing so well.

. . . .

Have You Heard?
Capitalism, Communism, Socialism

There are three major economic systems in the world today. That is, there are three different approaches to the production, development, and management of wealth. None of these systems operates in a "pure" state, partly because they have to deal with each other, and partly because citizens apply pressure for compromise.

Communism is based on the theory of ownership by all people. In pure communism, there are no classes of rich and poor, because people own the means of production (the factories, farms, and so on), and they make economic decisions together for the benefit of all. In all but the most radical communes, individuals do own their furniture, clothing, and other personal property.

Socialism is a middle ground between communism and capitalism. Business is administered by the state, which should represent the people. Sometimes market forces, such as competition, play a limited role. Again, private ownership is limited to personal property.

Capitalism, the free-enterprise system, allows for private ownership of the means of production. Individuals compete with each other to accumulate wealth, when possible, or to work for wages. Businesses take risks for profit, losing or gaining accordingly. In pure capitalism, there is no regulation of economic activity, such as a minimum wage, because individuals and firms decide what to do with their own wealth. The United States is a capitalist country, so this chapter focuses mostly on words relevant to this system.

If food costs more each week but your pay is not going up, are you participating in prosperity?

Yes   No   because _____

2. downturn [DOWN turn]: movement toward recession.

When economic activity is high, businesses want to borrow money to expand. The demand for credit then pushes interest rates up, which raises the cost of starting a business. If competition is still holding down prices, profits are lower. As profits decline, some workers are laid off. People cannot afford to buy as much, so businesses slow down.

If unemployment starts to rise, could we be entering a downturn?

Yes   No   because _____

3. recession [ree SESH un]: temporary decline in prosperity.

Because some businesses have slowed down, they do not buy goods or use services of other businesses. So all businesses slow down and more people are unemployed. Less investment causes layoffs among financial workers as well. Wages decline because more people are looking for work. Prices start to fall in hopes that people will be able to afford some things. A depression is a severe and sustained recession. One joke has it that "When your neighbor is out of work, it's a recession. When you are out of work, it's a depression."

If business is booming, are we likely to be in a recession?

Yes   No   because _____

4. recovery [ree CUV ir ee]: movement toward prosperity.

Traditionally, the stage is set for recovery when enough spending can be encouraged to get businesses back on their feet. The cost of doing business is low now, so businesses can make better profits. Interest rates are low because investment has fallen off, so people who *can* borrow money for investment can get low interest rates. Business is stimulated, leading toward prosperity.

If people have enough money to spend on some things, is recovery easier?

Yes   No   because _____

5. inflation [in FLAY shun]: widespread increase in prices.

Inflation happens when your money cannot buy as much as it used to buy. As the economy grows from a recession, businesses raise prices to make more profits and employees ask for increases in wages to keep up with rising prices. In the past, economic downturns were accompanied by deflation (falling prices). In recent decades, prices have continued to creep upward through all phases of the cycle.

If all your expenses go up but your salary remains the same, are you suffering from inflation?

Yes   No   because _____

6. nominal/real [NOM in ul/RE uhl]: two types of changes in costs, prices, or value.

Nominal means "in name only." *Real* means after making allowances for inflation. If your wages increase 5 percent but inflation also increases 5 percent, you have experienced a nominal increase in earnings but no real increase in wealth. Watch out for these terms when they are used to describe freezes and cutbacks, however. If the president freezes education spending in real terms, he allows spending to rise with inflation. If he freezes education spending in nominal terms, the numbers will remain the same no matter what happens to inflation.

If your wages increase 5 percent but inflation is 10 percent, is your prosperity nominal?

Yes   No   because _____

Matching: Match the conditions with the best description.

A. ____ Unemployment is low, consumers spend money, wealth increases.

B. ____ Wages decline because people are looking for work.

C. ____ Everything seems to cost more.

D. ____ After adjusting for inflation, you are still making more money.

E. ____ Your weekly paycheck is higher, but you only keep up with inflation.

F. ____ The demand for credit pushes interest rates up and business slows.

G. ____ People are encouraged to spend money and business gets stimulated.

(a) inflation

(b) nominal raise

(c) real raise

(d) recovery

(e) downturn

(f) recession

(g) prosperity

Using Context: Fill in each blank with the vocabulary word that best suits the context.

Whose Cycle Is It?

Your perspective on the business cycle often depends on where you fit into society. Most owners of large businesses are not too worried about a certain amount of unemployment; joblessness can be useful to keep wages down and therefore to keep prices down, preventing widespread

_____. Owners of small businesses also dislike inflation,

but in a full slowdown, called a _____, it is difficult for

them to survive. Because they often deal directly with the public, they are

hurt if ordinary people face a decline in their standard of living. Owners of

small businesses look forward to the next stage, signs of a _____,

as much as their employees. The good times of _____

make almost everyone happy. As long as wages keep up with inflation,

higher prices for working people are merely _____. For

those on fixed incomes, however, who do not make more money even if

inflation is high, all price increases are _____.

For Your Critical Reflection: What stage in the cycle best seems to fit today's economy?

_____

_____

II. The Markets

Any time people come together to buy and sell, there is a market. People can buy products, land, services, stocks, bonds, even money. In today's world, markets can be run entirely through computers, with no actual market "place" needed.

7. stocks [STOCKS]: portions of a firm entitling holders to earnings and assets.

If you buy shares of stock, you are buying little pieces of the company. If the company makes a profit, you receive your portion in payments called dividends. If a company is doing well, many people want to buy shares of stock; then the value of each share rises. If the company does badly, owners of stock lose some or all of the money they invested. When shares can be bought and sold at a stock market, such as the ones in New York, London, and Tokyo, the company is said to be publicly owned. In the United States, 2 percent of the population owns one-half of all public stock. Nevertheless, people watch the stock market anxiously, because its prosperity is often thought to mirror the economy of the nation.

If everyone wants to buy shares of stock in your company, are your stock prices rising?

Yes   No   because _____

8. bonds [BONDS]: agreements to pay back borrowed money plus interest; bonds are issued by governments or businesses.

If you buy a bond, you have lent money to someone. That someone agrees to pay you back, with interest. In most cases, the interest is paid gradually; the amount borrowed is paid back in a lump sum at a certain date. People buy and sell bonds as well as stocks.

If you have bought bonds, are you trusting someone to pay you back?

Yes   No   because _____

9. bull market/bear market [BOOL/BAIR MAR ket]: ways of describing the activity of the financial market; in a bull market everyone buys, whereas in a bear market everyone sells.

Bulls hope that prices will rise, so they buy stocks, bonds, or whatever else they hope to trade. Enough bulls create a bull market, which sometimes does raise prices simply because of the demand. That kind of market is called an inflated market, because prices are higher than the stocks' real worth. According to Andrew Maurois, "Artificial inflation of stocks must be considered a crime as serious as counterfeiting, which it closely resembles." Bears sell because they believe that prices are going to fall. One slow-moving trader remarked, "I am neither a bull nor a bear—I'm a chicken."

If you decide to sell all the stocks you own, are you feeling bullish?

Yes   No   because _____

10. global market [GLOW bull MAR ket]: worldwide buying and selling by companies whose activity can help or hurt the economies of many nations, not just one.

You might buy a car from Ford, an American company. But that car might contain parts made in many countries. An increase in the sale of automobiles, then, could increase profits in firms from many nations, all of which depend on each other for their prosperity. The global market affects even such products as wheat. Too much wheat in one country could bring prices down all over the world.

If you are selling candies and need to watch the sugar prices in Europe in order to price your own candies, are you participating in the global market?

Yes   No   because _____

11. exchange rates [eks CHAYNJ rayts]: the price at which one country's money can be converted into another's.

The exchange rate between the U.S. dollar and the British pound is different from the rate between the dollar and the German mark. Most exchange rates change slightly each day. The buying and selling of currency to make profits from changes in the exchange rates is common, giving rise to the term *currency market*. A favorable exchange rate means that the dollar buys more marks, pounds, and yen than it did yesterday.

Would it be best to take a trip to Paris when the exchange rate is favorable for the dollar?

Yes   No   because _____

Matching: Match the definition with the vocabulary word. Use one answer twice.

H. ____ Agreement to pay back borrowed money plus interest.

I. ____ Worldwide buying and selling.

J. ____ Price at which you can convert your dollars into yen.

K. ____ Piece of a company allowing you earnings and assets.

L. ____ Everyone is buying stocks, bonds, or whatever.

M. ____ Everyone is selling stocks, bonds, or whatever.

N. ____ A booming company in Germany affects New York real estate.

(a) stock

(b) bond

(c) bull market

(d) bear market

(e) global market

(f) exchange rate

True-False: Write "T" for true and "F" for false.

O. ____ Even though only a handful of Americans own public stock, many people watch the market.

P. ____ If you buy a bond, you are actually lending.

Q. ____ A bull market is also an inflated market because prices are higher than the stock's real worth.

R. ____ A bear market suggests that people think they are losing money by holding stock.

S. ____ A global market means that the prosperity of one country is often tied to that of another.

T. ____ If the dollar is weak against other currency, it means that the exchange rate is not favorable.

For Your Critical Reflection: Centuries ago, Anacharvis said, "A market is a place set apart for men to deceive and get the better of one another." Do you agree?

_____

_____

III. Commercial Life

12. corporation [core puh RAY shun]: a group of people allowed, within limits, to do business as one person.

Ambrose Bierce described a corporation as "an ingenious device for obtaining individual profits without individual responsibility." Corporations register with the state or federal government. They can own property, incur debts, sue, or be sued. The people who invest in corporations can lose only what they invested, even if the corporation goes bankrupt. People like to incorporate (form corporations) so that they can pool their resources and create a bigger business.

If you and three other people wanted to form a business together, would you be likely to form a corporation?

Yes   No   because _____

13. management/labor [MAN ij ment/LAY bir]: people within a business; management sets and administers business policy, whereas labor works under the management to perform particular jobs.

Traditionally, management and labor are the two opposing forces in corporations: management wants labor to do more work for less pay; labor wants more pay, less work, and more participation in decisions. Today, more jobs are being classed as "management" positions even though people work at specific jobs, and labor is more involved in setting policy.

If you work as a clerk-typist for a corporation, are you management?

Yes   No   because _____

14. **collective bargaining** [cuh LEK tiv BAR gehn eeng]: negotiations by an organized group of employees to improve working conditions, pay, and so on.

This term was coined in 1891 by Beatrice Webb, who worked to improve conditions for labor. Collective bargaining allows employees to join together rather than having to ask for raises separately. Unions are collective bargainers.

If you ask your boss for a raise because your nine children need to go to college, are you engaged in collective bargaining?

Yes   No   because _____

15. **goods and services** [GOODS and SER vis es]: products of any economy.

When people say that we have become a service economy, they mean that human tasks, such as cleaning, word processing, or providing medical care, have become a bigger part of our economy than the making of objects, such as shoes and automobiles.

If you are a lawyer giving advice to clients, are you providing a service?

Yes   No   because _____

16. **gross national product (GNP)** [GROHS NASH un uhl PRAH duct]: the total value of the goods and services produced by everyone in a nation in one year.

Economists use the growth of the GNP as the primary indicator of the health of the economy. "The gross national product is our Holy Grail," Stewart Udall once said, meaning that we spend most of our effort chasing after it. Remember, however, that the GNP can look good even if we have polluted our air, destroyed our resources, and otherwise hurt the economy in the long run.

If the GNP increases by 10 percent in one year, is it likely that the nation is prosperous?

Yes   No   because _____

17. assets [ASS ets]: anything owned that has value.

Assets are things you can convert to pay off debts. They include real estate, personal property, savings accounts, and so on. In business, you can list as an asset the money other people owe you. However, if some of those people cannot pay what they owe, your business may not have the assets you think it has. In general usage, assets are values beyond money, as in "Her understanding is her greatest asset as a human being."

If you are filling out a form that requires you to list your assets, should you include your car?

Yes   No   because _____

18. investment [in VEST muhnt]: commitment of money in hopes of profit.

If you purchase stocks, bonds, land, corporations, or old furniture to make money, you have made investments. High-risk investment is called speculation. Your investment flow is the money you have available to invest.

If you collect old china simply because it is beautiful, are you interested in investment?

Yes   No   because _____

Matching: Match the definition with the vocabulary word. Use one word twice.

U. ___ Wealth you can convert to cash to pay debts.

V. ___ The products of any economy.

W. ___ People who work at particular tasks.

X. ___ Negotiations by an organized group of employees.

Y. ___ Commitment of money or time in hopes of profit.

Z. ___ Group of people doing business as one person.

a. ___ People who set and administer policy in business.

b. ___ The total value of all goods and services produced.

c. ___ The primary indicator of the year's economy.

(a) corporation

(b) management

(c) collective bargaining

(d) labor

(e) goods and services

(f) gross national product (GNP)

(g) assets

(h) investment

True-False: Write "T" for true and "F" for false.

d. ____ Traditionally, management and labor are two opposing forces in corporations.

e. ____ Collective bargaining includes negotiations for improved working conditions.

f. ____ A service economy makes more wealth from medical care than from manufacturing cars.

g. ____ The gross national product includes costs of destroyed natural resources.

h. ____ You can list the money someone owes you as an asset.

i. ____ If you purchase a house to live in forever, you have made an investment.

j. ____ Corporations cannot own property, incur debts, sue, or be sued.

For Your Critical Reflection: Do you think collective bargaining is good or bad? Why?

_____

_____

IV. Legal Activities

19. fiscal policy [FIS cul POL ih cee]: using government spending and taxation to influence the economy.

How can the government regulate the economy? The British economist John Maynard Keynes (1883–1946) believed government spending was the key. To avoid depression, he argued that the government increase spending and make money easy to borrow, resulting in more investment, more jobs, and more spending. Monetarists such as Milton Friedman, in contrast, believe that the money supply (how much money is in circulation and in savings) has a greater impact on the economy than government spending. Supply-side economists assert that drastic reductions in tax rates for the wealthy will stimulate investment for the benefit of all.

Was John Maynard Keynes a supply sider when it came to fiscal policy?

Yes   No   because _____

Guess What!
Fiscal Policy

Here are the names and brief descriptions of some federal agencies that help guide the economy.

Securities and Exchange Commission (SEC): This federal agency supervises and regulates the selling of stocks and bonds. The SEC protects investors by preventing unfair trade practices and by maintaining order.

Federal Trade Commission (FTC): The purpose of the FTC is to protect free enterprise by preventing price fixing, boycotts, fraudulent advertising, and other unfair methods of competition. Of its five members, no more than three may be of the same political party.

Office of Management and Budget (OMB): This agency presents the president's recommended budget to Congress, reviews fiscal policies of the government, and advises several other agencies as they develop fiscal programs.

The Federal Reserve Board: Informally known as the Fed, this board establishes bank regulations, such as how much cash on hand (reserves) banks need; sets the interest rates banks must pay for money they borrow (which affects the interest rates of the money banks lend); and helps regulate the availability of credit.

---

20. regulation [reg yoo LAY shun]: a rule designed to govern actions and policies.

Regulations are designed to ensure that businesses serve the interests of the people while making profits. Some industries are highly regulated by law. Utilities, such as gas and electricity, often have their prices and profits regulated.

If a law requires toymakers to use materials that do not catch fire easily, is that law a regulation?

Yes   No   because _____

21. laissez-faire [LAY ZAY FAIR]: belief that economic regulation is bad.

Adam Smith's *The Wealth of Nations* (1776) described laissez-faire economics in terms of an "invisible hand" that would provide for all if investors were free to pursue profits as they wish. The term comes from the French for "let them do it."

Would supporters of laissez-faire believe in a minimum wage?

Yes   No   because _____

22. litigation [lih ti GAY shun]: legal action or process, often used to refer to lawsuits.

Litigation tests legal rights and responsibilities. For example, employees who sue a company that forces them to use dangerous chemicals are testing their right to a safe workplace against their employer's right to get the work done. Parties involved in litigation are called litigants, whether they are plaintiffs (bringing the action) or defendants (defending themselves).

Are all litigants in a case of litigation likely to agree with each other?

Yes   No   because _____

23. precedent [PREH suh dent]: a decision that may be used as a standard for later cases.

In law, judicial decisions are often based on earlier decisions about similar cases, which is why some Supreme Court judgments receive so much attention in the newspapers. Once a precedent is set, it is standard not to overturn it.

If a piece of litigation sets a precedent, do people involved in similar situations need to pay attention?

Yes   No   because _____

24. de jure/de facto [dee ZHIR/dee FACT oh]: according to law/as a matter of practice.

There are two types of truths or rights in law. If you are entitled to something *de jure*, then a rule has been made that covers your situation. If you are entitled to something *de facto*, then custom suggests that you have a right to it. Like many legal terms, these two can be informally used in daily life. Some people continued to experience de facto segregation, even after it was made illegal by the Supreme Court.

Might a clever child say "I have had dessert every day this week, so, *de facto*, I should get it today"?

Yes   No   because _____

Drawing by Koren; © 1970 The New Yorker Magazine, Inc.

25. injunction [in JUNK shun]: a legal order requiring someone to do, or to avoid doing, certain things.

If an individual or corporation is doing something you consider to be wrong, you may be able to get the court to issue an injunction. Injunctions can be issued to stop polluters, noisemakers, wifebeaters, or builders who violate codes. They can be issued to force a person or corporation to clean up their mess, to practice fair trade, and so on.

If citizens in your community wanted to prevent a local business from blasting its advertisements over loudspeakers, might the citizens seek an injunction?

Yes   No   because _____

26. indictment [in DITE ment]: a formal accusation by a grand jury.

An indictment does not mean that the accused person is guilty. It only means that the grand jury has reviewed the case and decided that there is enough evidence to merit a trial.

If your local mayor is indicted for misuse of funds, should you presume that the mayor is guilty?

Yes   No   because _____

Matching: Match the definition with the vocabulary word.

k. ___ Legal action or process, often refers to lawsuits.

l. ___ A rule designed to control business actions and policies.

m. ___ A formal accusation by a grand jury.

n. ___ A decision used as a standard for later cases.

o. ___ Government spending or taxing to influence the economy.

p. ___ Belief that government regulation is bad.

q. ___ Not law but a matter of practice or custom.

r. ___ According to law.

s. ___ Legal order requiring you to do or stop doing something.

(a) fiscal policy

(b) de facto

(c) laissez-faire

(d) litigation

(e) precedent

(f) de jure

(g) regulation

(h) injunction

(i) indictment

Using Context: Fill in each blank with the vocabulary word that best suits the context.

Those Coles

Members of the Cole family are involved in legal difficulties. Steve Cole wants to prevent his neighbor from buying more dogs, which bark all night long, so Steve asked the court for an _____ banning ownership of more than one hundred and one dalmations. Lisa Cole has a more mysterious case. She collected evidence that another neighbor murdered his wife, and she expects the grand jury to issue an

_____ any day. Carole Cole is reviewing prior decisions in racial discrimination cases, hoping there is a _____ that will help her. She will turn to customary behavior to find

_____ evidence for her case if she cannot find anything _____. You might think that the Coles are unpleasant people. But, really, you should not be surprised to learn that a family of lawyers is involved in _____.

For Your Critical Reflection: Are you a supporter of a laissez-faire economy? Why or why not?

_____

_____

Chapter Review

I. Yes-No Questions

1. Would you be wealthier if your assets experienced a nominal increase in value?

   Yes   No   because _____

2. If you bought bonds from someone who made bad investments, should you worry?

   Yes   No   because _____

3. If you just bought stock, would you want a bull market?

   Yes   No   because _____

4. Would supporters of laissez-faire believe collective bargaining should set prices?

   Yes   No   because _____

5. If a corporation is served an injunction, are stockholders personally responsible?

   Yes   No   because _____

6. Can you receive an indictment for breaking de facto practices?

   Yes   No   because _____

7. Could transnational fiscal policy help regulate global markets?

   Yes   No   because _____

8. Before getting involved in costly litigation, is it wise to investigate precedents?

   Yes   No   because _____

9. Can the gross national product help you predict a downturn or recession?

   Yes   No   because _____

10. If the prices for all goods and services increased, is there inflation?

    Yes   No   because _____

11. If de facto rules were changed into de jure ones, would the customary ways change much?

    Yes   No   because _____

12. Could the fear of excess regulation in the stock market inspire a bear market?

    Yes   No   because _____

13. Would management be displeased if a recession lowered wages for labor?

    Yes   No   because _____

14. In a global market, do exchange rates tell you about the prosperity of different nations?

    Yes   No   because _____

15. Does recovery affect the GNP?

    Yes   No   because _____

16. Does a nominal increase in your salary help you keep up with real price increases?

    Yes   No   because _____

17. Is prosperity characterized by inflation and recession?

    Yes   No   because _____

18. Is an indictment a good thing to receive?

    Yes   No   because _____

19. Is downturn a nice way of saying recession?

    Yes   No   because _____

20. Are your bonds considered to be assets?

    Yes   No   because _____

II. Using Context: Use the word list at the beginning of the chapter to fill in the blanks. You might not use all the words, or you might use one word more than once.

Black Thursday

October 24, 1929, helped produce the Great Depression. A depression occurs when the low end of the business cycle, the _____,
hits hard and lasts a long time. The late 1920s had seen economic boom,
but that _____ ended when Black Thursday signaled a
sudden _____ in the economy with a stock market crash
on Wall Street in New York City. At nine that October morning, prices of
_____ were high. By afternoon, everyone was selling.
Right up to the crash, people were buying like crazy, but that
_____ reversed, turning into a _____
that created losses of $26 billion by nightfall. Why the sudden shift?
Prices had risen all over the country, but widespread national
_____ was nothing compared with Wall Street. The
bull market wildly inflated the value of stocks, making their
_____ worth lag way behind the _____
increase in their prices. Even worse, many people had borrowed money
to get into this bull market, leaving them with debts they could not
pay. Owners of companies used borrowed money for high-risk
_____, called speculation, and then had to convert valu-
able _____ into cash to pay their debts. Even large
_____ with many owners and good profits lost money on
Black Thursday: General Motors was cut in half, Montgomery Ward lost almost two-thirds, and U. S. Steel was down over one hundred points.

In those days, there was little government _____ to
protect investors or the public. To the extent that there was an economic
_____ in American business, it was the no-interference
philosophy of _____. Since Black Thursday, the stock
market has had a long history of ups and downs, including a Black

Monday 1987. That crash was smaller than the crash in 1929, but Black
Monday sent shivers to London, Tokyo, and almost the whole
_____. There are no actual written laws about who may
put money into the stock market, but strict _____ restrictions are not needed to keep many people away. As everyone knows who
has tried it, the stock market is, _____ , only for the
tough at heart.

III. Practice with Word Forms: Fill in each blank with the proper word
form.

    A. **litigate, litigation, litigant, litigious:** With all the _____
    in society today, people have come to believe that they must
    _____ to receive justice. Being a member of a
    _____ society can be annoying, but some experts ar-
    gue that suits are actually "little people" trying to defend rights against
    "big people." A person sometimes has to become a _____
    to get justice.

    B. **regulate, regulators, regulations:** According to an old saying, "Citi-
    zens break laws; businesses do not comply with _____."
    The government must _____ business to secure safe
    products, clean and safe working conditions, and just treatment of con-
    sumers. People whose profits suffer from _____ like
    to avoid them.

    C. **inflate, inflation, inflationary:** What is the cause of _____?
    Do increases in wages _____ the costs of items, or do
    the increases in prices require higher wages to maintain people's stan-
    dard of living? Increased costs and higher wages—both of these contrib-
    ute to an _____ cycle.

    D. **indict, indictment, indictable, indictee:** Many people do not know
    that a suspect who receives an _____ may not be
    guilty. It only means that the suspect is an _____ in a

court case. That is, a judge has examined the evidence and found that there is an _____ offense and enough evidence for a trial. Americans are innocent until proven guilty. To _____ someone is only to charge that person.

Reading for Chapter 7

PETER F. DRUCKER

Transnational Economy—Transnational Ecology

Peter Drucker is a widely admired economist with a knack for spotting trends. In this essay he writes from the perspective of management to help readers understand the global market. Drucker calls the global economy "transnational" rather than "international" to emphasize the way countries are joined rather than the way they compete.

Words to Notice

Prepare for the reading by reviewing the following key words:

OPEC: Organization of Petroleum Exporting Countries; countries that periodically join together to set prices instead of competing with one another

floating dollar: currency in which exchange rates vary from day to day

factors of production: all the things that make business possible—Drucker mentions land, labor, money, and management

protectionism: a policy that protects a nation's industry from cheap foreign goods

free trade: laissez-faire

reciprocity: give and take

1   Everybody talks about the "world economy." It is indeed a new reality. But it is quite different from what most people—businessmen, economists, politicians—mean by the term. Here are some of the world economy's main features, its main challenges, its main opportunities:

2   In the early or mid-seventies—with OPEC and with President Nixon's "floating" of the dollar—the world economy changed from being international to transnational. The transnational economy has now become dominant, controlling in large measure the domestic economies of the national states.

3   The transnational economy is shaped mainly by money flows rather than by trade in goods and services. These money flows have their own dynamics. The monetary and fiscal policies of sovereign national governments increasingly react to events in the transnational money and capital markets rather than actively shaping them.

4   In the transnational economy the traditional "factors of production," land and labor, increasingly become secondary. Money, too, having become transnational and universally obtainable, is no longer a factor of production that can give one country a competitive advantage in the world market. Foreign-exchange rates matter only over short periods. Management has emerged as the decisive factor of production. It is management on which competitive position has to be based.

5   In the transnational economy the goal is not "profit maximization." It is "market maximization." And trade increasingly follows investment. Indeed, trade is becoming a function of investment.

6   Economic theory still assumes that the sovereign national state is the sole, or at least the predominant unit, and the only one capable of effective economic policy. But in the transnational economy there are actually *four* such units. They are what the mathematician calls "partially dependent variables," linked and interdependent but not controlled by each other. The national state is one of these units; individual countries—especially the major, developed, non-Communist ones—matter, of course. But increasingly decision-making power is shifting to a second unit, the region—the European Economic Community; North America; tomorrow perhaps a Far Eastern region grouped around Japan. Third, there is a genuine and almost autonomous world economy of money, credit, and investment flows. It is organized by information that no longer knows national boundaries. Finally, there is the transnational enterprise—not necessarily a big business, by the way—which views the entire developed non-Communist world as one market, indeed, as one "location," both to produce and to sell goods and services.

7   Economic policy implies increasingly neither "free trade" nor "protectionism," but "reciprocity" between regions.

8   There is an even newer transnational ecology. The environment no more knows national boundaries than does money or information. The crucial environmental needs—the protection of the atmosphere, for instance, and of the world's forests—cannot be met by national action or national law. They cannot be addressed as adversarial issues. They require common transnational policies, transnationally enforced.

9   Finally: while the transnational world economy is reality, it still lacks the institutions it needs. Above all it needs transnational law.

Questions for Class Discussion

1. Do you think there should be transnational laws to guide a transnational economy? If so, what laws would you like to see?

2. According to Drucker, good management is the key to success. What, in your view, is good management?
3. To "maximize" is to make something as large as possible. Why might "market maximization" be more important than "profit maximization?"

Making a New World

For Class Discussion

1. Based on your experience and observation, where do we seem to be now in the business cycle?
2. What kinds of investments seem to be worthwhile these days? Which ones are more risky? How can you tell?
3. Some people say that there is too much litigation in today's society. Others say that litigation is the only way to protect the "little" person. What do you think and why?

Collaborative Learning

1. Guiding the Economy
   Purpose: To learn how to create fiscal policy.
   A. Your group is dissatisfied with the GNP: the nation is not producing enough goods and services. First, explain why the GNP is not producing what it should be. Then decide which fiscal policy is the best to solve the problem.
   B. Choose among these three: Keynesian, monetarist, or supply-side economics.
   C. Make a list of recommendations to help Congress stimulate the economy.
   D. Present your findings to the class.
   E. Optional: See where you agree and disagree with your classmates.
2. Running a Business
   Purpose: To practice managing a small business.
   A. Select one of the following businesses for your group to run:
       ChipCo, makes computer chips
       ChipCo 2, makes chocolate chips
       CleanCo, recycles waste products
       CleanCo 2, cleans office buildings
   B. Using at least four vocabulary words from this chapter, describe how your firm is unique. Consider management/labor relations, investments, policies, and so on. Consult the list of More Words if needed. Use your imagination.
   C. Present your findings to the class.

Ideas for Writing

1. In a paragraph, argue for strengthening or weakening one regulation placed on business and industry, such as minimum wage, disposal of toxic waste, or job safety.
2. In a page, write one of the following: (a) If you are management, describe how you could involve labor in setting policy for your firm. (b) If you are labor, describe how your firm should involve you in setting policy. (c) If you are a student, describe how you hope management and labor should work together in your future career.
3. At home, write an essay in which you support either a laissez-faire economy or a planned economy, which is a highly regulated economy.

More Words for Chapter 7

ad valorem: tax or duty in proportion to the value of the item

affidavit: sworn written statement that is officially witnessed

amortization: the gradual payment of a debt

beneficiary: person who receives money or assets under terms of a will, trust, or other agreement

broker: someone who buys and sells securities for customers

budget: estimate of money coming in and going out, or "a way to go broke systematically"

capital: money or other property that can be used to do business

caveat emptor: "let the buyer beware"—purchase at your own risk; a philosophy among capitalists

collateral: anything used to guarantee payment of debt if money is not paid on time

commodity: any good that can be bought or sold

common stock: stock that is not preferred stock

debt ratio: percentage of assets and income tied up in debt

deficit, federal: excess of U.S. government spending over revenue

deficit, trade: excess of imports over imports; a country is buying more than selling

dividends: profits of a corporation distributed among stockholders

Dow Jones & Company: issues financial information and publishes *The Wall Street Journal* and *Barron's*

downsize: kind word for reducing the scale of a corporation, often through layoffs or selling assets

dumping: selling goods in another country for less than cost to gain an edge; selling unacceptable goods in another country; offering large amounts of stock for low prices, regardless of market effects

economic indicators: key statistics showing the state of the economy
encumbrance: a claim on property

franchise: the right to vote; a special privilege granted to run a certain business

income distribution: the way that income is spread over the various classes in society
interest rates: rate of return for an investment; percentage of a sum of money charged for its use

jurisprudence: a philosophy or pattern of law

leveraged buyout: a type of merger where one company has borrowed money to purchase another
liability: money owed; obligation to do something; legal responsibility
libel: false or malicious writing about someone with the intention to harm
liquid assets: cash or assets easily convertible to cash
long wave: a fifty- to sixty-year period in which the business cycle is thought to experience an extreme up and down

merger: combination of two companies
money supply: stock of currency in circulation and savings
mortgage: agreement that property will be used to pay off a debt if money cannot be paid

negotiable: something that can be transferred to someone else for payment, such as a check

preferred stock: stock that enjoys priority in distribution, dividends, and, if the company dissolves, assets
private stock: stock controlled by a tight group of investors
protectionism: restricting imported goods or charging high tariffs to protect domestic producers
proviso: special condition attached to an agreement
public stock: stock that can be traded on the stock exchange

securities: stocks, bonds, or other written guarantees that entitle the holder to receive payment of money or to participate in profits
slander: false or malicious talk about someone with the intention to harm
solvent: a person or corporation able to pay all its debts

stock exchange: organized marketplace for buying and selling stocks

subpoena: order to appear before a court

supply and demand: law of economics; when supply is high, prices drop, when demand is high, they rise

tight money: credit is hard to get, usually because the Federal Reserve has set high interest rates

tort: damage over which someone can sue

voucher: receipt showing that payment has been made

Answer Key to Chapter 7

I. THE BUSINESS CYCLE

Yes-No Questions

1. No; in prosperity income does not lag.
2. Yes; it is one of the first signs.
3. No; in a recession business suffers.
4. Yes; some spending signals an upturn.
5. Yes; expenses are beating salaries.
6. Yes; it is in numbers only, not real.

Matching

A. (g) B. (f) C. (a) D. (c) E. (b)
F. (e) G. (d)

Using Context: Whose Cycle Is It?

inflation, recession, recovery, prosperity, nominal, real

II. THE MARKETS

Yes-No Questions

7. Yes; more demand increases price.
8. Yes; to buy bonds means to lend money.
9. No; bulls buy, bears (and chickens) sell.
10. Yes; your candy needs Europe's sugar.
11. Yes; you would get more francs per dollar.

Matching

H. (b) I. (e) J. (f) K. (a) L. (c)
M. (d) N. (e)

True-False

O. T P. T Q. T R. T S. T T. T

III. COMMERCIAL LIFE

Yes-No Questions

12. Yes; you would be acting as one.
13. No; you perform particular jobs.
14. No; you are bargaining alone.
15. Yes; your product is knowledge.
16. Yes; growth this decade is 1.5 percent.
17. Yes; you can convert it to cash.
18. No; only if you want to sell it.

Matching

U. (g) V. (e) W. (d) X. (c)
Y. (h) Z. (a) a. (b) b. (f) c. (f)

True-False

d. T e. T f. T g. F h. T i. F
j. F

IV. LEGAL ACTIVITIES

Yes-No Questions

19. Yes; the Fed sets interest rates.
20. Yes; it regulates safe toys.
21. No; let the market decide, they say.
22. No; their disagreement led to it.
23. Yes; it may explain their case.
24. Yes; custom has it so.
25. Yes; courts can say cease and desist.
26. No; innocent before proven guilty.

Matching

k. (d) l. (g) m. (i) n. (e) o. (a)
p. (c) q. (b) r. (f) s. (h)

Using Context: Those Coles

injunction, indictment, precedent, de facto, de jure, litigation

CHAPTER REVIEW

I. Yes-No Questions

1. No; only a real increase makes a difference.
2. Yes; they might not be able to pay you.
3. Yes; your stock would be worth more.
4. No; they want no interference in market.
5. No; stockholders risk only their investment.
6. No; they are for breaking laws, not customs.
7. Yes; fiscal policy helps guide markets.
8. Yes; precedents help decide the case.
9. Yes; decreases in GNP growth signal bad news.
10. Yes; increases in prices mean inflation.
11. No; the customs were only legalized.
12. Yes; people will sell if profits get scarce.
13. No; some unemployment keeps wages low.
14. Yes; a dramatic fall may signal decline.
15. Yes; more jobs, spending, goods, and services.
16. No; nominal increases ignore inflation.
17. No; it is characterized by the opposite.
18. No; it means there is evidence against you.
19. Yes; it is a form of recession.
20. Yes; bonds are a debt owed to you.

II. Using Context: Black Thursday

downturn/recession, prosperity, downturn/recession, stocks, bull market, bear market, inflation, real, nominal, investment, assets, corporations, regulation, fiscal policy, laissez-faire, global market, de jure, de facto

III. Practice with Word Forms

A. litigation, litigate, litigious, litigant

B. regulations, regulate, regulators

C. inflation, inflate, inflationary

D. indictment, indictee, indictable, indict

INTERNATIONAL WORDS AND PHRASES

Quick Reference Word List

angst	chutzpah	jazz	persona non grata
aria	cognoscenti	juggernaut	sangfroid
avant-garde	con amore	Kabuki	savoir faire/vivre
baksheesh	dilettante	kitsch	surrealism
bête noire	faux pas	lagniappe	taboo
bona fide	fin de siècle	nisei	weltschmerz
bonzai	haut or haute	peccadillo	zeitgeist
chiaroscuro	incommunicado		

Introduction: Multicultural English

In today's United States, no one would be surprised to see a Chinese woman eating pizza in front of a Mexican-American grocery store while watching a parade in honor of Jewish war heroes. Such crossing of cultures eventually influences the way people speak. Indeed, the history of the English language has been marked by changes brought about when other languages expand and shift English vocabulary and usage (see the Introduction to chapter 4 for details). Of the twenty thousand or so common English words, over half were imported. New words and uses often are generated by groups as part of a code: generations, classes, professions, and ethnic groups create a sense of belonging and explain their world by using language. Speakers of English also use non-native words to describe achievements in the arts, discoveries in the physical world, or philosophical thoughts that are brought to their attentions by people from other cultures. Many of these words become quite common. Whether you know it or not, you speak a little French every day. However, some of these words never become common. Linguists suggest that today's English language is being pulled in two directions. Our highly mobile population, our systems of mass communication, and our national identity lead us to centralize our language—to welcome some new words and discard others, everywhere, for everybody. But our diverse and varied society also leads groups to cling to their special words and uses without adopting others—to import words differently for different people. This chapter emphasizes but does not limit itself to words and phrases that have "made it" in English from other languages, mostly European. Words from non-European languages probably will become more and more common.

I. Culture Comforts

Some words that enter English describe happy states of affairs: good wishes, love, daring, and knowledge. Instances where words are not entirely complimentary are noted.

• • • • • • • • • • • •

Have You Heard?
What Are Alien Words?

Words that come into English from other languages are classified according to their degree of foreignness. The authoritative *Oxford English Dictionary (OED)* has four categories: natural, denizen, alien, and casual. Words qualify as "naturals" if they have become fully naturalized in use and pronunciation, such as *rose* and *napkin*. Denizens are used like native words but keep their foreign pronunciation and form, such as *faux pas* and *sangfroid*. Aliens include foreign titles, names of objects, and other words that speakers of English may need to use, such as *baksheesh* and *ayatollah*. Casuals are like aliens except that they are less commonly used, such as *sashimi*, sliced raw fish served in Japanese restaurants. Words in the last two categories often move out quickly, either becoming naturals or denizens or dropping from ordinary use.

1. **bonzai** [BON zie] Japanese: ten thousand years.

This word has been used as a patriotic cheer, greeting, toast, and battle cry. When used as a greeting or toast, its meaning is akin to "May you live ten thousand years," or "ten thousand years of happiness." As a battle cry or cheer, the word suggests ten thousand years of triumph. Be careful not to confuse this word with *bonsai*, the art of growing dwarf trees.

Would you say "bonzai" to express your feelings of sadness?

Yes   No   because _____

2. **savoir faire** or **savoir vivre** [SAHV wah FAIR, VEEVR] French: to know what to do or to know how to live.

Savoir means "to know." Someone with savoir faire always seems to know what to do in social situations. People with savoir faire are not likely to drink from the finger bowls at a formal dinner party. Someone with savoir vivre knows how to enjoy life and live it to the fullest. If such a person decided to drink from the finger bowls, you can bet the liquid would taste delicious.

Would someone with savoir faire frequently offend others?

Yes   No   because _____

3. zeitgeist [ZITE GEYEST] German: the spirit of the age.

The taste and outlook of a generation or period of history is its zeitgeist. When politicians say that "a new wind is blowing," they are responding to a change they feel in the zeitgeist.

If you were to describe the zeitgeist of your grandparents' generation, would you think about their attitudes and what they did for fun?

Yes   No   because _____

4. con amore [con uh MORE ay] Italian: with love.

Anything done with dedication and affection can be done con amore. You can cook a meal, paint a picture, or engage in scientific research, con amore. And, of course, the phrase makes a charming closing for a love letter.

If you arranged flowers only because you could make money doing it, would you be arranging flowers con amore?

Yes   No   because _____

5. haut or **haute** [HOHT] French: high.

People who want to distinguish *high*, in the sense of "first class" or "upper class," from *low*, use this French word. It is usually used in combination with another French word: *haut monde* refers to the "high world" of high society; *haute cuisine* is excellent and elegantly prepared food; *haute couture*, or "high sewing" refers to the fashions worn by the stylishly and expensively dressed. French phrases using haut often are invoked for their snob appeal.

Would you describe most good home cooking as haute cuisine?

Yes   No   because _____

6. chutzpah [KHOOTZ puh] Yiddish: brash courage or gall.

If you have chutzpah, you have so much nerve that you risk offending people. The word used to describe only people whose degree of nerve was wrong or inappropriate. Gradually the word has come to include more positive associations.

If you walk into an important business meeting an hour late and then try to change the agenda, have you shown chutzpah?

Yes   No   because _____

7. baksheesh [back SHEESH] Iranian (Persian): a tip or gratuity.

In Turkey, Egypt, India, and other countries, baksheesh can refer to anything from a gift of alms, its older meaning, to regular tipping, to a more extended sense of money given as a bribe. Words for tipping have come into more limited English use from several languages, including the Spanish *propina* (from a Latin word for "drinking one's health"), the French *pourboire* (meaning "for drinking"), and the German *trinkgelt* ("drink money").

If you are paid a salary, have you been given baksheesh?

Yes   No   because _____

8. lagniappe [LON yop] Quechua: a little something extra.

Lagniappe is similar to baksheesh, because it can refer to an unexpected gift or gratuity. There are no undertones of exploitation in lagniappe, however. The word came into common use referring to a small gift presented by store owners to customers along with their purchases. Lagniappe, by extension, now can refer to anything nice and unexpected that is added to one's already good fortune. The word came to English through the Louisiana French, who borrowed it from the American Spanish, who learned it from the American Indians of the South American Incan Empire. The Spanish, who were plundering these peoples, named one group the *Quechua*, meaning, ironically, "plunderer."

If your beloved gives you a birthday present and then surprises you with a dinner, might you regard the dinner as lagniappe?

Yes   No   because _____

9. sangfroid [SAHNG FWAH] French: perfect calmness.

In French, the word *sangfroid* literally means "cold blood." The person who has sangfroid will not show disturbance no matter how distressing the situation.

If you cry during a sad movie, are you responding with sangfroid?

Yes   No   because _____

10. cognoscenti [cog noh SENT ee] Italian: people of superior knowledge or taste.

The singular is cognoscente. The cognoscenti are people in the know. Their information and taste are better than the average.

Would a restaurant reviewer who belonged to the cognoscenti be able to make good recommendations?

Yes   No   because _____

Matching: Match the definition or description with the vocabulary word. Some words will be used more than once.

A. ____ People in the know.

B. ____ Something extra or unexpected.

C. ____ Great nerve or brash courage.

D. ____ Done with love.

E. ____ Knowing what to do in social settings.

F. ____ Ten thousand years of good fortune!

G. ____ The spirit of the age.

H. ____ "High" or sophisticated as opposed to "low."

I. ____ A tip or gratuity.

J. ____ Perfect calmness.

K. ____ Knowing how to live.

L. ____ Done for pleasure instead of money.

M. ____ A person who lives an enviably good life has this.

N. ____ People who seem to have inside knowledge about the way of the world.

O. ____ Someone who can coolly look you in the eye and say "You're fired" has this.

P. ____ An extra appetizer brought to you "on the house."

Q. ____ A five dollar bill slipped to the hostess to guarantee a good table.

R. ____ Telling your boss that you are ready to leave if things do not go your way.

S. ____ An elegant and expensive French meal served at the top of a skyscraper.

T. ____ Turning in your annual report with a rose attached.

U. ____ Something in the air that tells you recycling is the right thing to do.

(a) bonzai

(b) savoir faire

(c) savoir vivre

(d) zeitgeist

(e) con amore

(f) haut or haute

(g) chutzpah

(h) baksheesh

(i) lagniappe

(j) sangfroid

(k) cognoscenti

V. ____ Person who knows if a wine is good or not by examining the cork.

W. ____ A greeting or toast you might hear at a Japanese wedding.

Using Context: Fill in each blank with the vocabulary word that best suits the context.

Suzanne's Wedding

Weddings seem to be in the air these days. Beautiful blends of tradition and surprises just seem to be part of the _____. But the most lovely wedding we have attended was Suzanne's. She and Bob love each other so much that we knew everything would be done _____, which is the most important aspect of a wedding. Everything else is just _____. The ceremony was inspiring, although those of us who had trouble parking thought the minister was a bit stern to order the doors closed promptly at 11:00, an order he issued with perfect _____. People should know to arrive on time to a wedding, though: one does not have to be a member of the _____ to know that much. To show up late takes a lot of _____. Relatives participated in the ceremony by reading stirring passages with as much smooth _____ as if they were trained orators. If the ceremony showed the wedding party's savoir faire, the reception showed their _____. The food was _____ cuisine, and the musicians were gifted. Although one guest tried to give them a tip to reward their fine playing, they were not looking for _____. The best man and Suzanne's father both made funny and heartwarming speeches, ending with a wish for ten thousand years of happiness, "_____!"

For Your Critical Reflection: Can you describe today's zeitgeist? If so, what is it?

_____

_____

II. Culture Discomforts

Words also have entered the language to describe difficulties: blunders, enemies, complexities, even silence.

11. faux pas [FOH PAH] French: false step, blunder.

Someone with savoir faire would never commit a faux pas, which is a social blunder. The plural form is spelled the same way as the singular.

If you went to a funeral and tried to comfort the widow, but you picked the wrong person, would you have committed a faux pas?

Yes   No   because _____

12. peccadillo [peck uh DILL oh] Spanish: small sin.

In Spanish, *pecado* is a sin; a peccadillo is a small transgression or fault. It is sometimes used to describe flirtations. A related word in English is *impeccable*, which means "flawless."

Would you describe a series of murders as peccadillos?

Yes   No   because _____

13. weltshmerz [VELT SMARTZ] German: sadness over the evils of the world.

Too many peccadillos might lead to weltschmerz, which means "world pain." The word usually refers to a sentimental pain, so it may be felt by people who have little actual experience of evil.

If your best friend burned his hand while ironing, would the blisters be called weltschmerz?

Yes   No   because _____

14. fin de siècle [FAN deh see ECK ul] French: end of the century.

Literature written at the end of the nineteenth century tended to exhibit overwrought escapism, decadence, oversophistication, and weltschmerz. The phrase *fin de siècle* captures that mood of fashionable indulgence and despair and is

sometimes used out of the nineteenth-century context. Do you see these signs of a fin de siècle in our own society?

If you wrapped yourself in elegant silk to sigh wearily in the closing days of the twentieth century, might an observer note the mood of the fin de siècle?

Yes   No   because _____

15. angst [ONGST] German: anxiety.

When used in English, angst refers not to nervousness about a test or a dinner party, but to a general feeling of anxiety. Philosophers such as Kierkegaard link angst to our human condition of uncertainty and our desire to believe in and do the right things.

Have most people experienced some amount of angst?

Yes   No   because _____

16. nisei [NEE SIE] Japanese: a person born in America of Japanese immigrants.

Immigration often causes conflicts between the generations along with the difficulties of adjusting to a new society. The Japanese name for a member of the second generation is nisei. You might compare issei, kibei, and sansei.

Might one who is a member of the nisei trace her American ancestry back to the War of 1812?

Yes   No   because _____

17. juggernaut [JUG ir not] Hindi: anything that inspires blind and destructive devotion.

This word derives from a title given to the Hindu god Krishna. Worshippers were said to have thrown themselves to be crushed under the wheels of a carriage drawn in Krishna's honor in an annual procession.

If someone said, "New political policies have rolled through this country like a juggernaut," would the person favor the policies?

Yes   No   because _____

18. taboo [Ta BOO] Tonga: forbidden.

Something is taboo when religious belief, social custom, or widely held emotional responses keep people from using it, mentioning it, or sometimes even approaching it. In most societies, for example, incest is taboo.

If your religion kept you from eating meat on holy days, would meat be taboo on those days?

Yes   No   because _____

19. incommunicado [IN kuh myoon ih CAH do] Spanish: deprived of contact with the outside world.

People who are held incommunicado do not choose silence; they are forced into it. When a hostage is hidden for months without communicating with family or friends, that person is incommunicado.

Are prisoners in solitary confinement held incommunicado?

Yes   No   because _____

20. bête noire [BETT NWOUR] French: a person or thing that one hates and avoids.

You might wish that your bête noire would be held incommunicado someplace. In French, the phrase means "black beast."

Could your mortal enemy be described as your bête noire?

Yes   No   because _____

21. persona non grata [per SOH nuh non GRAH tah] Latin: unwelcome or unacceptable person.

This term is most often used in international diplomacy when a well-known person is denied entrance to a country (even to visit) because that person represents unacceptable values. The phrase can be used more generally. The plural is personae non gratae.

Would your bête noire be a persona non grata at your house?

Yes   No   because _____

Matching: Match the definition or statement with the vocabulary word. Some words will be used more than once.

X. ____ A person unwelcome or unacceptable.

Y. ____ A person hated and avoided, your "black beast."

Z. ____ Something forbidden to talk about.

a. ____ Second generation Japanese.

b. ____ Little sin or mistake.

c. ____ Social blunder.

d. ____ Sorrow for the world.

e. ____ Anxiety.

f. ____ End of the century.

g. ____ Anything that inspires blind or destructive devotion.

h. ____ Deprived of contact with the outside world.

(a) faux pas

(b) peccadillo

(c) weltschmerz

(d) fin de siècle

(e) angst

(f) nisei

(g) juggernaut

(h) taboo

(i) incommunicado

(j) bête noire

(k) persona non grata

i. ___ "Then I mispronounced her name 'Ringworm' instead of 'Ringwald.' "

j. ___ "Oh me, the world is full of hungry, suffering, oppressed people!"

k. ___ "I was stuck in the forest for three days without mail or phone."

l. ___ "I feel terribly anxious, as if the world is about to collapse."

m. ___ "It was a topic no one ever discussed in my family."

n. ___ "I hate him; he is my least favorite person on the planet!"

Using Context: Fill in each blank with the vocabulary word that best suits the context.

The Personnel Office

Working as a chief personnel officer for my company takes a lot of savoir faire, because we do get some strange people coming in. As a person born in the United States with Japanese parents, a _____, I feel as if I understand American culture rather well. But this job brings plenty of surprises. Last week there was a man who had been fired from his last job for taking hostages and secluding them, holding them _____ for six hours. When I asked this guy to explain himself, he said, "Oh, that? It was no big sin, just a small _____." Apparently he had had a big enemy at that job, and he thought he could scare his _____ by playing the hostage prank. Instead, when he showed up for work the next day, he found the locks changed, a new person at his desk, and other signs that he had become a _____ at that place. I did not offer him a job. Someone who blunders that badly without realizing it even now is sure to commit a _____ at any moment. Then there was the gloomy woman who came in yesterday, sighing about the evils of the world. All that _____ was too much for me to take. I realize that the century is drawing to a close, but even at the _____, I look for a little more sparkle. When she started twisting her handkerchief anxiously, I could tell she felt some

_____ as well. At least she cared about the world,

though. This morning a man came in who wanted to reorganize the whole

company. His plans sounded exciting but dangerous, and I could just see

him moving like a _____ through the firm. No personal

details or private matters were _____ to him; anything

could and would be addressed. Maybe you should apply for a job here—

then we would get some sanity.

For Your Critical Reflection: Do you see signs or moods characteristic of a fin de siècle?

_____

_____

Sampling of International English
Here are just a few common cultural terms
borrowed from other languages.

Africa	American Indian	Arabia	China	Egypt
canary	hickory	alcohol	chop suey	gum
chimpanzee	hurricane	algebra	joss	gypsy
gorilla	pony	cipher	ketchup	paper
jazz	skunk	coffee	mandarin	
oasis	succotash	magazine	sampan	
tangerine	tobacco	nadir	soy	
tote	tomahawk	zenith	tea	

France	Germany	Hebrew	Hungary	India
baroque	blitzkrieg	amen	goulash	dungarees
baton	ersatz	balsam	hussar	khaki
cliché	halt	cherub	Tokay	nirvana
connoisseur	kindergarten	jubilee	vampire	pariah
envoy	poker	Sabbath		shampoo
ingenue	strafe	seraph		
matinee	stroll			
resumé	waltz			
vignette				

Ireland	Italy	Japan	Mexico	Netherlands
bard	balcony	geisha	arroyo	dock
hooligan	ditto	haiku	canyon	drawl
smidgen	gusto	kimono	coyote	hull
slogan	incognito	jinrikisha	lariat	leak
whiskey	sonata	jiujitsu	mesa	sloop
	sonnet		mustang	skipper
	stanza		ranch	snap
	trio		tomato	switch
	virtuoso			yacht

Persia	Russia	Spain	Turkey	Yiddish
arsenic	bolshevik	armada	angora	kibitz
bazaar	czar	corral	horde	kosher
chess	glasnost	flotilla	ottoman	mensch
divan	perestroika	guitar		yenta
jackal	polka	mosquito		
pyjama	robot	patio		
seersucker	sable	renegade		
	steppe	tornado		
	vodka			

III. The Arts

Many words relating to music, painting, sculpture, pottery, fashion, architecture, and literature have come into English from other languages. The chart for this chapter includes some of the words; a few appear below.

22. **avant-garde** [AH vant GARD] French: creative people, ideas, or techniques that are ahead of everyone else.

If you are avant-garde, you are untraditional, perhaps inventing new ways to paint or designing new kinds of buildings. Those who are avant-garde are in the vanguard.

Might a conservative person welcome many avant-garde ideas?

Yes   No   because _____

23. bona fide [BOH nuh FEE day or FIDE] Latin: genuine.

In Latin, *bona fide* means "in good faith." A bona fide offer is a genuine offer, one made in good faith. In the arts, something is bona fide if it is real, not an imitation.

Would a collector of bona fide Ming pottery be happy to find one for sale at a reasonable price?

Yes   No   because _____

24. kitsch [KITCH] German: low-quality art designed for popular appeal.

In artistic and literary circles, this word is used to put down works or movements done with showy or slick bad taste. Kitsch usually pretends to be better than it is, such as the Muzak played in elevators. The word derives from the German verb *kitschen*, meaning to sloppily throw together a work of art.

If a serious movie is a box-office hit, but the cognoscenti hate it, might it be called kitsch?

Yes   No   because _____

25. dilettante [DILL uh TAHNT] Italian: someone who dabbles in the arts.

A dilettante "delights" in art but cultivates it as a pastime, not as a professional endeavor. The word sometimes has negative connotations because it can imply lack of knowledge.

If your friend thinks he is an expert but you call him a dilettante, should he be flattered?

Yes   No   because _____

26. aria [AH ree uh] Italian: a solo sung in an opera.

An aria is a beautiful solo song that creates a mood. It is designed to move the audience's emotions. The word *opera*, and indeed many musical terms, come to English from the Italian.

Could you join your friends in singing an aria?

Yes   No   because _____

27. jazz [JAZZ] African-American: music that has strong but flexible rhythms and improvisation.

When asked to define jazz, Louis B. Armstrong said, "If you have to ask, you'll never know." The origin of the word is obscure, with some linguists tracing its history to the Barbary Coast. The word has many slang uses as well, including "to make more interesting or lively," "enthusiasm."

If you were listening to a jazz band, would you be surprised to hear an improvised solo?

Yes   No   because _____

28. chiaroscuro [SHEE ar uh SCYUR oh] Italian: a play of light and shadow.

Chiar means "clear or light"; *oscuro* means "dark or shadowy." In pictures, a strong mixture of bright and shadowy effects is called *chiaroscuro*. Rembrandt is famous for his chiaroscuro.

Would a painting of sunlight filtered through dark leaves be likely to exhibit chiaroscuro?

Yes   No   because _____

29. surrealism [sir REE uh lizm] French: art that draws on dreamlike images to depict psychological reality.

The French poet André Breton launched the surrealist movement in 1924. Today, paintings, film, or literature is described as surrealistic if exaggerated or dreamlike images are used.

Could you call the average snapshot an example of surrealism?

Yes   No   because _____

30. Kabuki [kuh BOOH kee] Japanese: popular Japanese drama featuring elaborate costumes and stylized movements.

Noh theater was the traditional drama for the aristocracy. Kabuki developed in the seventeenth century in contrast to Noh, using similar forms for a middle-class audience. Its mixture of song, dance, and mime influenced such modern dramatists as W. B. Yeats, Bertolt Brecht, and Thorton Wilder.

Is Kabuki a kind of theater only the Japanese can appreciate?

Yes   No   because _____

Matching: Match the description with the vocabulary word. Some words might be used more than once.

o. ____ Popular Japanese drama featuring elaborate costumes.

p. ____ Use of dreamlike images to depict psychological reality.

q. ____ Music with strong rhythms and improvisation.

r. ____ Someone who dabbles in the arts.

s. ____ Genuine.

t. ____ Creative people or ideas ahead of everyone else.

u. ____ Low-quality art designed for popular appeal.

v. ____ A solo sung in an opera.

w. ____ Painting term for the play of light and shadow.

(a) avant-garde

(b) bona fide

(c) kitsch

(d) dilettante

(e) aria

(f) jazz

(g) chiaroscuro

(h) surrealism

(i) Kabuki

True-False: Write "T" for true and "F" for false.

x. ____ An avant-garde artist would probably dress in a three-piece suit.

y. ____ A bona fide painting would be a beautiful imitation.

z. ____ Cartoon jingles, elevator music, and ceramic dogs might all be called kitsch.

A. ____ A dilettante is someone dedicated to studying the arts in depth.

B. ____ An aria would be sung best by a glee club.

C. ____ A live jazz concert might include improvised solos by every player.

D. ____ Rembrandt's mixture of light and dark in painting is called chiaroscuro.

E. ____ A surrealist horror movie might look like a nightmare.

F. ____ Kabuki theater is produced best with no costumes.

Using Context: Fill in each blank with the vocabulary word that best suits the context.

Leonardo at the Art Festival

On Saturday I went with Leonardo to the big cultural festival downtown.

Leonardo clearly is an artist, but I am just a _____, so I

was glad to have him along. Sometimes I cannot tell an imitation from a

_____ masterpiece, so Leonardo explains the differences.

He also helps me appreciate the latest art movements, no matter how

_____ they are. At the festival we saw some extraordi-

nary paintings that showed dreamlike images floating through space in a

manner that reminded us of _____. The funniest exhibit

was a collection of blue ceramic poodles from around the world. The col-

lector said that the poodles would be worth a lot of money some day, be-

cause they once were popular: "Yes, there is a big market for this

_____," the collector informed us. While listening

to the music we sat under a big tree, and Leonardo, with the eye of an

artist, noticed how the mingling of light and shade produced

_____ effects on the lawn. All the music was thrilling.

An opera student sung a beautiful _____, and a Japanese

theater troupe performed _____. The last band was my

favorite. They looked at each other, smiled, and started to play. After the

first improvised solo, we all jumped to our feet to applaud. Then we settled

down to listen to their lively _____ all evening.

For Your Critical Reflection: Could kitsch ever be a good thing?

_____

_____

Chapter Review

I. Yes-No Questions

1. Might a juggernaut gang lord demand baksheesh from everyone on
   the block?

   Yes   No   because _____

2. Would it take chutzpah to ask for lagniappe?

   Yes   No   because _____

3. Would a dilettante practice art con amore?

   Yes   No   because _____

4. Is it common to feel angst at the fin de siècle?

   Yes   No   because _____

5. Would a man with savoir faire make faux pas?

   Yes   No   because _____

6. Would you like your bête noire to be held incommunicado?

   Yes   No   because _____

7. Would the cognoscenti know what is taboo?

   Yes   No   because _____

8. Would a person with savoir vivre be a persona non grata at most parties?

   Yes   No   because _____

9. Can the nisei always exhibit sangfroid?

   Yes   No   because _____

10. Would you cheer bonzai to your bête noire?

    Yes   No   because _____

11. Would it take chutzpah for an artist of kitsch to claim to be avant-garde?

    Yes   No   because _____

12. Would most people maintain sangfroid while watching a surrealistic movie?

    Yes   No   because _____

13. Is it a peccadillo to serve haute cuisine?

    Yes   No   because _____

14. Might someone with savoir vivre enjoy jazz?

    Yes   No   because _____

15. If a restaurant added a free jazz concert to a dinner, might you consider it a lagniappe?

Yes   No   because _____

II. Multiple Choice: Place your choice in the blank.

16. ____ If your guest made a peccadillo, you should
    (a) be careful not to make him a persona non grata.
    (b) enjoy as you would haute cuisine.
    (c) treat him as a bête noire.

17. ____ If your sister were held incommunicado,
    (a) hire a bona fide private investigator.
    (b) give baksheesh to a train conductor.
    (c) sing her an aria.

18. ____ If a new boss declared herself a juggernaut,
    (a) treat her con amore for the faux pas.
    (b) toast her with bonzai for her chutzpah.
    (c) try to control your angst.

19. ____ An avant-garde artist would probably enjoy
    (a) kitsch and traditional Kabuki.
    (b) jazz played with savoir faire.
    (c) a bona fide dilettante.

20. ____ If a child spoke of taboo subjects,
    (a) do not speak until the fin de siècle.
    (b) sit quietly with perfect sangfroid.
    (c) admire the child for its weltschmerz.

III. Using Context: Use the word list at the beginning of the chapter to fill in the blanks. You might not use all the words, or you might use one word more than once.

The Returning Student

I had been out of school for fifteen years, so I did not feel like one of the

_____ when it came to taking college classes. I thought

all those young kids would be hostile to me, and I expected to be treated

like a _____ in every classroom. My son encouraged me,

saying, "Come on, Mom. You have plenty of nerve—just gather up your

_____ and march in there. You'll move through that
school like a powerful _____, grinding up professors
as you go." I laughed, and said that I would sign up the next day.
First, I put on my most exciting outfit, rejecting the expensive
_____ couture in favor of an offbeat and radical
_____ outfit. I grabbed some genuine college books to
give me the look of a _____ student. But then I left
the books in the car, because once I got to school I saw that there
were all kinds of people on campus. Nothing seemed forbidden, or
_____. Instead of a fear of making blunders, I had the
wonderful feeling that it would be difficult to make any mistakes, not even
a _____. The spirit of the age was diverse, and that was a
_____ I could appreciate. My counselor helped me find
some exciting humanities courses. In Music Appreciation 101, I could learn
about the improvised rhythms of _____, the painted
masks of Japanese _____, and maybe even learn to
sing an _____. In Art History 102, I could admire
the way Rembrandt used light and shadow to paint deeply shaded
_____ portraits, and I could study the striking nightmare
visions of _____. Our art history teacher liked popular
art, the counselor said, and therefore did not shy away from
_____. Philosophy 101 would show me all the famous
thinkers who felt anxiety or sadness about the evils of the world, but
that class would cover more than just _____ and
_____. The counselor said that many philosophers really
knew how to live well, and their _____ gave them great
joy in philosophy. For my last class I decided to take Poetry 101, an
English class. I love poetry so much that I can do all the reading
_____, and any good grades will be extra—just
_____ for me. In fact, that is how I am starting to feel
about my whole college experience.

Reading for Chapter 8

RICHARD RODRIGUEZ

Aria

Richard Rodriguez was born in Sacramento, California. His parents were born in Mexico. In this complex passage from ''Aria,'' Rodriguez muses about public and private language. How can language bring people closer together? How can language give speakers power in the world? He concludes that artistic language, such as song or poetry, captures the mystery of intimacy. A particular language—Spanish or English—cannot by itself bring people closer together. Nor do people depend on a common language for intimacy, as you can see by reading about Rodriguez's grandmother.

Words to Notice

Prepare for the reading by reviewing the following key words:

pocho and **gringo:** derogatory terms in Spanish; the first for a Mexican-American who is losing roots, the second for white Americans

Life en Españole (literally ''Life in Spanish''): a magazine about Mexican culture

lyric: the words of a song or a poem about emotion; from the Greek word for ''lyre,'' a stringed instrument that was played while poets sang

intimate: an English word derived from Latin; intimacy refers to emotional closeness and deep understanding between people

1   My grandmother!

2   She stood among my other relations mocking me when I no longer spoke Spanish. *'Pocho,'* she said. But then it made no difference. (She'd laugh.) Our relationship continued. Language was never its source. She was a woman in her eighties during the first decade of my life. A mysterious woman to me, my only living grandparent. A woman of Mexico. The woman in long black dresses that reached down to her shoes. My one relative who spoke no word of English. She had no interest in *gringo* society. She remained completely aloof from the public. Protected by her daughters. Protected even by me when we went to Safeway together and I acted as her translator. Eccentric woman. Soft. Hard.

3   When my family visited my aunt's house in San Francisco, my grandmother searched for me among my many cousins. She'd chase them away. Pinching

her granddaughters, she'd warn them all away from me. Then she'd take me to her room, where she had prepared for my coming. There would be a chair next to the bed. A dusty jellied candy nearby. And a copy of *Life en Español* for me to examine. 'There,' she'd say. I'd sit there content. A boy of eight. *Pocho.* Her favorite. I'd sift through the pictures of earthquake-destroyed Latin American cities and blond-wigged Mexican movie stars. And all the while I'd listen to the sound of my grandmother's voice. She'd pace round the room, searching through closets and drawers, telling me stories of her life. Her past. They were stories so familiar to me that I couldn't remember the first time I'd heard them. I'd look up sometimes to listen. Other times she'd look over at me. But she never seemed to expect a response. Sometimes I'd smile or nod. (I understood exactly what she was saying.) But it never seemed to matter to her one way or another. It was enough I was there. The words she spoke were almost irrelevant to that fact—the sounds she made. Content.

4   The mystery remained: intimate utterance.

5   I learn little about language and intimacy listening to those social activists who propose using one's family language in public life. Listening to songs on the radio, or hearing a great voice at the opera, or overhearing the woman downstairs singing to herself at an open window, I learn much more. Singers celebrate the human voice. Their lyrics are words. But animated by voice those words are subsumed into sounds. I listen with excitement as the words yield their enormous power to sound—though the words are never totally obliterated. In most songs the drama or tension results from the fact that the singer moves between word (sense) and note (song). At one moment the song simply 'says' something. At another moment the voice stretches out the words—the heart cannot contain!—and the voice moves toward pure sound. Words take flight.

6   Singing out words, the singer suggests an experience of sound most intensely mine at intimate moments. Literally, most songs are about love. (Lost love; celebrations of loving; pleas.) By simply being occasions when sound escapes word, however, songs put me in mind of the most intimate moments of my life.

7   Finally, among all types of song, it is the song created by lyric poets that I find most compelling. There is no other public occasion of sound so important for me. Written poems exist on a page, at first glance, as a mere collection of words. And yet, despite this, without musical accompaniment, the poet leads me to hear the sounds of the words that I read. As song, the poem passes between sound and sense, never belonging for long to one realm or the other. As public artifact, the poem can never duplicate intimate sound. But by imitating such sound, the poem helps me recall the intimate times of my life. I read in my room—alone—and grow conscious of being alone, sounding my voice, in search of another. The poem serves then as a memory device. It forces remembrance. And refreshes. It reminds me of the possibility of escaping public words, the possibility that awaits me in meeting the intimate.

Questions for Class Discussion

1. Do you think young Rodriguez was hurt when his grandmother called him *"Pocho"*? Why or why not? Was the grandmother right or wrong to call him that name? Why do you think he was her favorite?
2. Rodriguez suggests that songs and poetry (such as an aria) can make us feel close to others even when we are alone. Can you think of any songs or poems that make you feel this way?
3. By calling this chapter "Aria," Rodriguez suggests that he is like a solo voice conveying intimate feelings to you. What feelings do you think he wants to share?

Making a New World

For Class Discussion

1. What words from other countries (they need not appear in this chapter) have you heard or used recently?
2. Can you describe today's zeitgeist? Example: what counts as a peccadillo today that used to be a major crime or sin? Do you see signs of the fin de siècle? Is angst prevalent?
3. Linguists argue that the English language is moving in two directions—toward sameness (everyone speaking alike) and toward diversity (community differences). Which do you favor and why?

Collaborative Learning

1. Review of the Arts
   Purpose: To practice using words from the chapter in context.
   A. Find a movie, television show, play, piece of music, or exhibit that you all saw or heard.
   B. Working together, write a short review of the piece. Describe the piece and say what you did and did not like. Use at least four words from the chapter. Example: Bart Simpson has a lot of chutzpah, but he does not always have savoir faire. We like to watch his funny peccadillos, and we especially like the show's avant-garde cartoon techniques.
   C. Report to the class.
2. The Zeitgeist
   Purpose: To build conceptual skills while using vocabulary words.
   A. Describe today's zeitgeist, using at least four words from the chapter.
   B. Report to the class.
   C. Your instructor will lead a discussion in which you compare results.

Ideas for Writing

1. In a paragraph, describe a faux pas you recently made or saw.
2. In a page, discuss whether weltschmerz is an appropriate attitude for to-day's world. Why or why not?
3. At home, discuss the signs of fin de siècle in the world around you. If necessary, consult other books for longer discussions of the term. Use as many words and phrases from this chapter as you can.

More Words for Chapter 8

a cappella (Italian): without instrumental accompaniment

ad nauseum (Latin): to a disgusting degree

aficionado (Spanish): devoted followers of some activity, especially art or leisure activities

au contraire (French): on the contrary

azimuth (Arabic): an arc of the heavens; or the angle at which a bomb falls

Bushido (Japanese): a code of loyalty and courage for samurai warriors

cause célèbre (French): a highly publicized lawsuit or other issue

caveat emptor (Latin): a business principle meaning "let the buyer beware"

cloisonné (French): enamelwork with colors separated by wires

de facto (Latin): by custom, not by law (see de jure)

de jure (Latin): according to law

duende (Spanish): the emotion of the bullfighter, combining fiery passion and icelike patience

e.g. (Latin): from exempli gratia, which means "for example"

ersatz (German): an inferior substitute

ex post facto (Latin): having a retroactive impact, as in "The new dean passed ex post facto regulations"

fait accompli (French): an accomplished fact, something finished

fakir (Arabic): a holy man who begs for bread (not a faker)

fortissimo (Italian): musical term for "strongly"

fresco (Italian): a picture painted on a wall before the plaster is dry

glasnost (Russian): "openness," implying increasing freedom of speech, religion, and assembly

Götterdämmerung (German): the twilight of gods, or death of a society

gringo (Spanish): a derogatory term for a white American

haiku (Japanese): a poem of seventeen syllables, suggesting the essence of a season

inamorato, inamorata (Italian): male lover, female lover

injih (Athabaskan): a taboo against predicting or celebrating good luck for oneself

intaglio (Italian): a kind of carving in which the design is below the surface

laissez-faire (French): an economic policy of free enterprise

leitmotif (German): a reappearing theme or element in a piece of music or literature

magnum opus (Latin): a great work

mon frère (French): literally "my brother," used in cases of close comradeship regardless of relationship

naptha (Iranian): a flammable oil obtained from petroleum and used in making plastic

nirvana (Indian): a spiritual state of perfect bliss

noblesse oblige (French): the belief that privilege entails responsibility

nom de plume (French): a pen name, pseudonym

nouveau riche (French): a derogatory term for the newly (vulgarly) rich

palaver (Portugese): long, aimless talk or chatter

perestroika (Russian): "restructuring," implying a shift from socialism to free-market economy

pocho (Spanish): a derogatory term for an assimilated Mexican-American

pro bono publico (Latin): for the public good; lawyers and doctors sometimes do work "pro bono"

quid pro quo (Latin): a deal in which one thing is exchanged for another

raison d'être (French): reason for being

rococo (French): an ornate style of decoration common in the eighteenth century

samurai (Japanese): a warrior from Japan's feudal era

sotto voce (Italian): in a soft voice

status quo (Latin): the existing state of things

sub rosa (Latin): secretly; literally "under the rose"

tour de force (French): a remarkable achievement or work of genius

vox populi (Latin): public opinion; literally "the people's voices"

wunderkind (German): a young person who achieves great things; literally "wonder child"

Answer Key to Chapter 8

I. CULTURE COMFORTS

Yes-No Questions

1. No; bonzai is a cheer, toast, battle cry.
2. No; he would "know what to do."
3. Yes; it would be the spirit of their age.
4. No; you are doing it for money, not love.
5. No; but you might do so to flatter the cook.
6. Yes; you are not afraid to offend people.
7. No; baksheesh is usually "under the table."
8. Yes; it is an extra gift, unexpected.
9. No; you are maudlin, not cool and calm.
10. Yes; she would be "in the know."

Matching

A. (k) B. (i) C. (g) D. (e) E. (b)
F. (a) G. (d) H. (f) I. (h) J. (j)
K. (c) L. (e) M. (c) N. (k)
O. (j) P. (i) Q. (h) R. (g) S. (f)
T. (e) U. (d) V. (k) W. (a)

Using Context: Suzanne's Wedding

zeitgeist, con amore, lagniappe, sangfroid, cognoscenti, chutzpah, savoir faire, savoir vivre, haute, baksheesh, bonzai

II. CULTURE DISCOMFORTS

Yes-No Questions

11. Yes; forgivable perhaps.
12. No; they are hardly small sins.
13. No, though he might say "That hurts!"
14. Yes; fashionable indulgence and despair.
15. Yes, even if they are not philosophical.
16. No; nisei are second generation.
17. No; they must be destructive.
18. Yes; not to be touched.
19. Yes; no one can communicate with them.
20. Yes; your despised and hated "black beast."
21. Yes; hated enemies are usually unwelcome.

Matching

X. (k) Y. (j) Z. (h) a. (f) b. (b)
c. (a) d. (c) e. (e) f. (d) g. (g)
h. (i) i. (a) j. (c) k. (i) l. (e)
m. (h) n. (j)

Using Context: The Personnel Office

nisei, incommunicado, peccadillo, bête noire, personna non grata, faux pas, weltschmerz, fin de siècle, angst, juggernaut, taboo

III. THE ARTS

Yes-No Questions

22. No; avant-garde ideas are ahead of the rest.
23. Yes; it would be quite a find.
24. Yes; popular but badly done art.
25. No; dilettantes merely dabble.
26. No; arias are sung solo.
27. No; improvisation is a mainstay of jazz.
28. Yes; a mixture of light and dark.
29. No; it captures reality, not sur-reality or dream.
30. No; it has influenced many Western writers.

Matching

o. (i) p. (h) q. (f) r. (d) s. (b)
t. (a) u. (c) v. (e) w. (g)

True-False

x. F y. F z. T A. F B. F C. T
D. T E. T F. F

Using Context: Leonardo at the Art Festival

dilettante, bona fide, avant-garde, sur-realism, kitsch, chiaroscuro, aria, Ka-buki, jazz

CHAPTER REVIEW

I. Yes-No Questions

1. Yes; honor and bribes appease the lethal force.
2. Yes; it takes nerve to ask for a gift or surprise.
3. Yes; someone who dabbles in art does it for love.
4. Yes; the end of the century brings anxiety.
5. No; people like this avoid social blunders.
6. Yes; keep your enemy far away and silenced.
7. Yes; they would know what is not to be known.
8. No; people who enjoy life are al-ways welcome.
9. No; sometimes generational con-flicts arise.
10. No; not as a cheer; as a battle cry perhaps.
11. Yes; it takes nerve to assume junk is advanced.
12. No; dreamlike images touch deep emotions.
13. No; it is no sin to serve elegant food, is it?
14. Yes; improvisation requires en-ergy and life.
15. Yes; it would be a pleasant sur-prise.

II. Multiple Choice

16. (a); do not exclude someone for a little sin.
17. (a); he or she might find her.
18. (c); a promise of destruction in-spires anxiety.
19. (b); jazz is often experimental, ahead of its time.

20. (b); you might inspire anxiety if you overreact.

III. Using Context: The Returning Student

cognoscenti, persona non grata, chutzpah, juggernaut, haut(e), avant-garde, bona fide, taboo, faux pas, zeitgeist, jazz, Kabuki, aria, chiaroscuro, surrealism, kitsch, angst, weltschmerz, savoir vivre, con amore, lagniappe

Chapter

9

RELIGION, PHILOSOPHY, AND POLITICS

Quick Reference Word List

anarchy	ecumenical	hegemony	mecca	reactionary
Aristotelian	egalitarian	holocaust	orthodox	right wing
blasphemy	enfranchise	iconoclast	pariah	secular
conservative	epistemology	karma	Pascal's wager	status quo
coup d'état	existentialism	left wing	Platonic	stoic
cynic	hedonist	liberal	radical	

Introduction: How to Start an Argument

Religion, philosophy, and politics—do not talk about these unless you want an argument. Or so we have been told. Fortunately, these topics are studied by college students for discussion and understanding, as well as a rousing argument now and again. Perhaps you do not like to talk about these topics. Then you will be surprised to see how religion, philosophy, and politics have inspired some of the most significant words in the language. Most of the words in this chapter were coined in countries all over the globe; they are some of the oldest words in human history. Yet ancient history mingles with current events. The same words that have shaped people and institutions for thousands of years appear in your newspaper every day.

I. Words from the World Religions

1. orthodox [ORTH uh dox]: holding correct or conventional beliefs.

Orthodox people strictly follow tradition. An orthodox position is uncontroversial. To be unorthodox, then, is to act or think against convention.

Would an orthodox person celebrate Christmas in the middle of summer?

Yes   No   because _____

2. mecca [MEK uh]: a place that enthusiasts are eager to visit.

Eugene, Oregon, is known as a runner's mecca, a great center of activity. When capitalized, Mecca refers to a city in Saudi Arabia which is the birthplace of Muhammad and the holy city of Islam.

• • • • • • • • •

Have You Heard?
The Holocaust

The word *holocaust* came from religion. From the Greek *hol* + *kaustos*, meaning "to burn whole," holocaust originally referred to a sacrifice consumed by fire. It now refers to any large-scale destruction, particularly by fire, as in "nuclear holocaust." When capitalized, Holocaust refers to a historical fact: the genocidal slaughter of European Jews by the Nazis during World War II. The word reminds one of the sacrifice of over six million Jewish people, as well as the gruesome reality that many concentration camps disposed of the slaughtered prisoners by burning them in massive ovens. *Holocaust studies* refers to scholarly research into the historical details of the Holocaust, the search for political causes for such inhumanity, and the understanding that would prevent any similar events in the future.

If your city was to become a mecca for bird-watchers, would you have many visitors?

Yes   No   because _____

3. ecumenical [ek yoo MEN ih kul]: of the whole church, not only of separate sects.

From the Greek *oikoumene*, meaning the "whole world," ecumenical means seeking to benefit a wide range of groups, not merely one. The ecumenical movement seeks common values among all Christian churches.

If your city sponsored an ecumenical conference, would Methodists likely be excluded?

Yes   No   because _____

4. karma [KAR muh]: self-created fate or destiny.

From the Sanskrit *kri* meaning "deed" or "work," karma is the structure of your life caused by your previous actions. In Hinduism and Buddhism, karma is the force you generate from your actions in a previous life that shapes your destiny in the next life.

If someone says, "As you sow, so shall you reap," are they talking about your karma?

Yes   No   because _____

5. holocaust [HOHL oh kawst]: large-scale destruction by fire.

When capitalized, Holocaust refers to the Nazis' murder of six million Jews (see "Have You Heard?").

Could you describe an apartment fire in which many people died as a holocaust?

Yes   No   because _____

6. pariah [pu RYE uh]: outcast.

From the Tamil word *paraiyan,* meaning "drummer," the lowest caste in southern India and Burma. The drummers are outcast because they handle the skin of calves, sacred animals for the Hindi. A pariah is anyone outcast or scorned by society. Lepers, the mentally ill, the hearing impaired, and even cancer and AIDS patients have been pariahs for some groups.

If you had a disease that made friends and family abandon you, would you be a pariah?

Yes   No   because _____

7. blasphemy [BLASS fuh mee]: irreverent talk about God or sacred things.

Blaspheme and *blame* have the same Greek root. Blasphemy, then, means to blame or insult God. The word *blasphemy* now also refers to statements of disrespect toward things highly valued in society. "Senator Simony uttered blasphemy when he said the progressive tax structure should be eliminated."

If a blasphemer utters blasphemes, is he being blasphemous?

Yes   No   because _____

8. secular [SEK yoo lir]: concerned with wordly affairs rather than spiritual ones.

A secular life means one divorced from the influence of religion. From the Latin *saecularis* ("the times," "the age," "the world"), the secular stands in contrast to the sacred.

Would secular people be likely to spend most of their time worshipping in a cathedral?

Yes   No   because _____

9. iconoclast [eye KON uh klast]: a person who attacks cherished beliefs.

Icon is Greek for "image." Iconoclast literally means "breaker of images." The first iconoclasts in the eighth century were members of the Easter Orthodox Church (Constantinople) who objected to pictures and statues of Jesus, Mary, and the saints. In 726, they destroyed works of art and persecuted icon worshippers as idolaters. Icon veneration was restored in 787.

Would an iconoclast be a welcome guest at a Buddhist temple?

Yes   No   because _____

Fill in the Blank: Complete the sentence with the vocabulary word that best suits the context.

A. Martin is so _____, he holds each tradition strictly.

B. All the soccer enthusiasts flocked to their _____ in Rome.

C. Kelly's _____ attitude makes her care about the whole world.

D. Patrick has been so unethical in his life, his _____ must be troubled.

E. Will is always acting irreverently in church and uttering _____.

F. Lee's interests are _____, not religious.

G. When diagnosed with AIDS, Kim became a _____ at work.

H. The blazing fire at the hotel nearly turned into a _____.

I. Paul is an _____ who always attacks sacred beliefs.

(a) karma

(b) mecca

(c) orthodox

(d) blasphemy

(e) iconoclast

(f) pariah

(g) holocaust

(h) secular

(i) ecumenical

Matching: Match the religious meaning, history, or usage with the word.

J. ___ Conflict in Greek Orthodox Church over pictures and statues of saints.

K. ___ The opposite of the sacred.

L. ___ To blame God.

M. ___ A low caste in India known as "the drummers."

N. ___ Greek word meaning "to burn whole."

O. ___ Sanskrit word meaning "deed" or "work" that determines your fate.

P. ___ A movement to forge agreements among all Christian churches.

Q. ___ Birthplace of Mohammed, holy city of Islam.

R. ___ Strict observers of Jewish laws and customs.

(a) karma

(b) Mecca

(c) orthodox

(d) blaspheme

(e) iconoclasm

(f) pariah

(g) holocaust

(h) secular

(i) ecumenism

For Your Critical Reflection: Creative people are sometimes known as "unorthodox." In what ways are you orthodox and in what ways unorthodox?

_____

_____

II. Words from the Philosophers

10. Platonic [pluh TON ik]: favoring intuition and cultivation of ideals to discover truth.

The ancient Greek philosopher Plato wrote dialogues featuring wise, old Socrates. When young nobles tried to ask Socrates "What is the most virtuous career?" he would ask them "First, what is virtue?" thus tapping their own knowledge. Platonic love, familiar to many who want to remain "just friends," is ideal and spiritual rather than carnal.

Would a Platonist say, "I believe in no ideals—I like only the here and now"?

Yes   No   because _____

11. Aristotelian [AIR is to TEEL ee un]: favoring reason and experiment to discover truth.

The ancient Greek philosopher Aristotle used formal logic to arrive at conclusions about science, ethics, law, and the nature of reality. He favored deduction, which is reasoning from known principles. Aristotle classified fields of study, types of knowledge, and beliefs. Samuel Taylor Coleridge, an English poet, once commented that all people seemed to be either Aristotelian or Platonic by nature. Platonic people use intuition in a quest for ideals; Aristotelians favor logic and the physical world. The first and most influential commentator on Aristotle was the Arab scientist abu-Ali-Husayn ibn-sina (*Avicenna*).

If you love to daydream more than anything, would you be an Aristotelian?

Yes   No   because _____

12. cynic [SIHN ik]: one who mistrusts the motives of others, seeing them as selfish at root.

The Cynics also lived in ancient Athens. One member of that school supposedly carried a lantern through the marketplace in broad daylight, unsuccessfully searching for someone who was honest. Cynical people distrust others and sometimes convey a sneering attitude.

If you said, ''People only donate to a charity in order to make themselves feel good,'' would you be cynical?

Yes   No   because _____

13. stoic [STOH ik]: one who endures life's misfortunes with calm acceptance, even indifference.

Ancient Athenian Stoics believed that virtuous people should rise above passions and longings, whether of joy or of grief. The term has narrowed a bit in modern usage, which sees stoicism mostly in the ability to suffer without complaint or resistance.

If you burst into tears after discovering your cynical friend betrayed you, would you be a stoic?

Yes   No   because _____

14. hedonist [HEED un ist]: a person who believes pleasure is the chief good in life.

From the Greek *hedone* meaning ''delight, enjoyment, pleasure,'' hedonists explain all behavior, including their own, by the desire to increase pleasure and avoid pain.

If you believed chocolate cream pie was good for the soul, would you be a hedonist?

Yes   No   because _____

15. Pascal's wager [Pass KALZ WAY jir]: believing (in God or a premise) because there is nothing to lose but everything to gain.

The seventeenth-century French mathematician Blaise Pascal decided to believe in God after concluding that the evidence could point in either direction. Addressing his secular friends, many of whom were gamblers, Pascal argued that if you believe God exists and He does, the reward is eternal bliss; if you believe God exists and He does not, you have nothing to lose. Pascal's wager can be extended to other choices.

Could Pascal's wager be used to persuade you to follow the advice of a fortune-teller?

Yes   No   because _____

16. existentialism [eg zis TEN shull izm]: philosophy emphasizing human situations, freedom, and responsibility.

"Existence precedes essence," says the existentialist Jean-Paul Sartre. This means that your daily existence guides your actions more than your essence as "good person," "friend," "courageous person," "patriot," and so on. You must prove your "charity," for instance, each time a beggar approaches you. Existence requires you to be aware of your absolute freedom to choose. To choose authentically means taking responsibility. The apology "Sorry, I was not myself last night" is absurdity to existentialism.

Would you be true to existentialism if you said, "I will never betray you, my friend, never"?

Yes   No   because _____

17. epistemology [i PIST uh MOL o jee]: philosophy that questions how we know that we know.

From the Greek *episteme* ("knowledge" or "science") and *logos* ("knowledge"). Epistemology is the branch of philosophy concerned with knowledge about knowledge. A classic epistemological question is Berkeley's: "If a tree falls in the forest and no one hears it, does it make a sound?"

Would studying epistemology help you understand why you know that you do not know epistemology?

Yes   No   because _____

Matching: Match each statement with the philosopher that best fits.

S. ___ "Never trust the ingrateful biped, human."

T. ___ "To know the ideal good is to do the good."

U. ___ "The key to knowledge lies in categorizing the world."

V. ___ "It is better never to be born, but if so, endure."

W. ___ "I have nothing to lose by believing in God."

X. ___ "Life is a cabaret, old chum."

Y. ___ "Talk to me of patriotism *after* the enemy knocks."

Z. ___ "How do we know what we know?"

(a) follower of Pascal's wager

(b) stoic

(c) Platonist

(d) Aristotelian

(e) cynic

(f) existentialist

(g) hedonist

(h) epistemologist

True-False: Mark "T" for true and "F" for false.

a. ___ Your Platonic friend might enjoy contemplating the ideal society.

b. ___ Pascal believed in God because even if he were wrong, he would not lose much by believing.

c. ___ Your friend who says that people marry for convenience, not for true love, might be a cynic.

d. ___ Someone who becomes weepy at the sight of a kitten with a hurt paw might be a stoic.

e. ___ Your Aristotelian friend might enjoy categorizing the various parts of a real society.

f. ___ A hedonist would believe that self-sacrifice is the key to wisdom.

g. ___ Epistemology explains why you know that you know that you do not know.

h. ___ An existentialist could predict how she would act under torture.

Using Context: Fill in each blank with the vocabulary word that best suits the context.

Armchair Philosophy

My friends and I were sitting around the house one rainy day. We somehow got onto the topic of religion. I suggested that we might as well believe in God, because we had little to lose by being wrong. But Carole told me that my playing _____ was only the first step in logical analysis of the problem. "Let us take as our major premise that all things seek perfection," Carole began, but Jose interrupted her. He said, "Let us not use such _____ logic to examine this issue. Let's have a dialogue along _____ lines instead." No one felt quite wise enough to play Socrates, though. "Even if we knew God existed, how would we know that we knew?" added Charles, the student of _____. "Let us say we had absolute knowledge of God," said the _____ Jean, donning her beret, "we would still be free to make our own choices, even in terrible situations and dark nights of the soul." "If God is so loving, how come people are all so selfish?" asked Steve, our token _____. Maria laughed and said, "Steve, I think you're just going to have to accept the fact that we're never going to agree with you. We all must accept our misfortunes." On that _____ note, we decided to return to homework. Just then Salome arrived in a ski suit with her arms full of pizzas, sodas, ice cream, and cookies, and said, like a true _____, "Pleasure is the ever and only good, and thank God for it."

For Your Critical Reflection: If forced to choose, can you use Pascal's wager (that it is a safe bet to believe in something when there is nothing to lose by being wrong) to select the safest bet among the philosophies?

_____

_____

III. Words from Politics—The Art of the Possible

18. enfranchise [en FRAN chize]: to admit to citizenship, especially the right to vote; to free.

From the French *franc* meaning "free," to enfranchise is to bring to freedom. Enfranchised people enjoy full rights of citizens; disenfranchised people have lost these rights. The Eighteenth Amendment to the Constitution enfranchised African-American males; the Twenty-first enfranchised American females; and the Twenty-third, eighteen-year-olds.

If you lost your right to vote, would you be enfranchised?

Yes   No   because _____

19. egalitarian [ee GAL i TAIR ee uhn]: holding the principle of equal rights for all persons.

The slogan of the French Revolution was *liberté, egalité, fraternité. Egalité* means "equality." An egalitarian person or act tries to further human equality.

Is the phrase "All American men are created equal" an egalitarian statement?

Yes   No   because _____

20. hegemony [hi JEM o nee]: dominance of leadership or influence.

Hegemony is the influence people have in the world. The Greek *hegemon* was chief ruler. A stronger nation may exercise its hegemony over a weaker one. Within countries, people with cultural hegemony will dominate other people's ideas about politics, religion, and even hobbies and fashion.

If the United States could command a country not to go to war, would it have political hegemony?

Yes   No   because _____

21. coup d'état [KOOH day TAH]: the sudden overthrow of a government by a small group.

From the French, *coup d'état* means "stroke of state." A coup d'état differs from a revolution in that revolution is effected by the people, whereas a "coup" involves one small group of leaders wresting control from another.

If the president of the country was overthrown by several trusted advisors, would that be a coup d'état?

Yes   No   because _____

22. anarchy [AN ark ee]: absence of government.

Anarchism is the belief that government is intrinsically evil. Anarchy usually refers to lawlessness and chaos, but an anarchist would find anarchy to be a perfect society (see "Who Rules?" following).

Would an anarchist be likely to support enormous military budgets?

Yes   No   because _____

True-False: Write "T" for true and "F" for false.

i.   ____ To enfranchise means to make someone free.

j.   ____ Egalitarianists like elitists.

k.   ____ Hegemony is the influence or power you have to make the world run your way.

l.   ____ A coup d'état is the same as a revolution.

m. ____ Anarchy is the belief that all governments are inherently evil.

Practice with Word Forms: Fill in each blank with the proper form of the word.

n. **enfranchise, enfranchised, disenfranchised, enfranchisement:**

Bringing people the legal right to vote is one way to

_____ them. In the United States

_____ is nearly complete, even though many of the

officially _____ people never vote or participate ac-

tively in politics. Thus even legal citizens, by their lack of power and

commitment, can be virtually _____ from public life.

o. **hegemony, hegemonic:** The ability of one nation to assert its influ-

ence or _____ over another is determined by

the _____ power it can wield.

• • • • • • • •

Guess What! Who Rules?

Arch means "ruler" in Greek. Governments get their names from who is the ruler. *Anarchy* means "no ruler or government." A monarchy, which has a king or queen, derives its name from the Greek *mono,* meaning "one." An oligarchy is ruled by a small group (*olig* means "the few"). A patriarchy is ruled by the father or more generally by males (*patri,* from the Latin "father"). Matriarchy is ruled by the mother or females. Invent your own. A polymath is a person who knows a great deal. If these people ruled? A polymatharchy, of course.

Kratia is the Greek root translated as "cracy." An aristocracy is rule by the *aristos,* Greek for "the best"—the aristocrats. In aristocracy, the best are determined by blood lines, not necessarily by talent. Thomas Jefferson, in contrast, imagined a society in which the intellectually talented would rise to power through education: a meritocracy, ruled by the meritorious. Although we usually think of democracy to mean freedom for individual people, democracy actually means rule by the *demos,* "the people." Plutocracy is the name used to describe a society ruled by the wealthy, because *pluto* comes from the Greek *ploutus,* "wealth." A theocracy is a rule by religious leaders (*theos* means "God.") The root *ocracy* is as flexible as *arch*. You can invent your own words to describe the new ruling powers. If vocabulary students govern, it is a lexocracy. When taxes rule, it is a taxocracy. When the hip rule, it is a "hipocracy." And if television fans governed?

p. **anarchy, anarchic, anarchist:** Whenever chaos strikes in the public streets, people declare that _____ is rampant. However, a true _____, one who believes that people are good but government is always evil, can envision an _____ society without chaos and lawlessness.

For Your Critical Reflection: Do you know any people or groups whose hegemony influences you?

_____

_____

IV. Words from Politics—Where Do You Stand?

23. status quo [STAY tus KWOH]: the existing state of affairs.

Status quo refers to social and political order as it now stands or as it stood before recent changes. Moderate politicians maintain the status quo or adjust it only slightly; more extreme politicians want to change it drastically. The terms *the left, leftist, left wing* and *the right, rightist, right wing* refer to political attitudes toward the status quo.

Would people who support the status quo want radical change in society?

Yes   No   because _____

24. left wing (left, leftist): dedicated to increasing power for the underclass.

The word *left* originated in the habit of the democratic and the liberal side of the French Assembly to sit to the left of the president's chair. Leftists want to increase power and resources for people traditionally disenfranchised, such as workers, women, people of color, the poor. When left-wing movements use force, the means are usually guerrilla warfare, sabotage, and revolution.

Would a left-wing party be likely to use tax money to support a royal family?

Yes   No   because _____

25. right wing (right, rightist): dedicated to increasing power for the ruling class.

The term *rightist* originated in the French Estates General of 1789, in which the nobility sat on the king's right. Rightists seek to increase power and resources for those who have historically ruled societies, which includes the military, the wealthy, the highborn. When right-wing movements use force, the means are typically martial law (the use of military as police) and states of emergency that suspend rights of speech, assembly, and due process, and coups d'état.

Would a right-wing party support increased taxes to educate the poor?

Yes   No   because _____

"In all fairness, I demand that you toss out an extreme right-winger as well."
Drawing by J. Mirachi; © 1973 The New Yorker Magazine, Inc.

26. reactionary [ree ACK shun air ee]: ultraconservative; opposed
to progress or reform.

Reactionary is usually a negative word used to describe people whose ideas or actions seek to stop or reverse the achievements of revolution or reform. From a leftist perspective, reactionaries are rightists who disagree with them. Reactionaries seek to change the status quo to the way it was before reforms.

Would an attempt to disenfranchise eighteen-year-olds be seen as a reactionary idea?

Yes   No   because _____

27. conservative [con SIRV uh tihv]: disliking or opposed to great
or sudden change.

In all countries conservatives seek to maintain (or "conserve") the status quo. In the United States conservatives favor free enterprise and private business, oppose government regulation, and vote for laws that retain or establish traditional morals and state's rights. Outside of politics, conservative can mean moderate and careful—"a conservative suit."

Would a conservative be likely to vote for deregulation of the airlines?

Yes   No   because _____

28. liberal [LIB ir uhl]: favoring democratic reform and individual liberty.

From the Latin *liberalis* meaning "suitable for the free," liberal has a long history. In all countries, liberals favor reforming the status quo. In the United States liberals favor public institutions, seek government action to redress grievances among businesses and individuals, and vote for laws that retain or establish individual liberties. Outside of politics, liberal can mean generous and open-minded—"a liberal attitude."

Would a liberal be likely to vote for restrictions on freedom of the press or speech?

Yes   No   because _____

29. radical [RAD ih kul]: tending to extreme change in the status quo.

From Latin *radix* meaning "root," radicals seek to change society from the ground up, sometimes through open revolt. When radicals attack the status quo, they do so from the left or the right (see "status quo"). Both might demand sweeping changes in the Constitution: the leftist because it gives too little power to the people, the rightist because it gives too much. Mostly, the term *radical* describes people who seek to dramatically change the power structure to reflect the needs of the most oppressed groups.

Would a radical be opposed to a Constitutional Convention to rewrite the Bill of Rights?

Yes   No   because _____

Left Wing	Moderate . . . Centrist	Right Wing
←————————————————————————————————————→		
←Radical ←Liberal ←*Status Quo*→ Conservative→ Reactionary→		

Multiple Choice: Enter your choice in the blank on the left.

q. ＿＿ Desires to change the status quo to benefit traditional ruling
powers: (a) leftist (b) rightist.

r. ＿＿ Desires to change the status quo to benefit traditionally dis-
empowered: (a) leftist (b) rightist.

s. ＿＿ In extreme cases, will resort to sabotage and guerrilla warfare: (a) leftist (b) rightist.

t. ＿＿ In extreme cases, will resort to martial law and suspending of
rights: (a) leftist (b) rightist.

u. ＿＿ Seeks to give more power to the wealthy, highborn, or military: (a) leftist (b) rightist.

v. ＿＿ Seeks to give more power to workers, women, people of
color, the poor: (a) leftist (b) rightist.

w. ＿＿ Considers a moderate too far on the right: (a) leftist
(b) rightist.

x. ＿＿ Considers a moderate too far on the left: (a) leftist
(b) rightist.

Matching: Match the political action with the vocabulary word. Use one
word twice.

y. ＿＿ Favors moving the status quo back to where it
was many years ago.

z. ＿＿ Favors gradual reform in the status quo.

A. ＿＿ Favors maintenance of the status quo.

B. ＿＿ Favors extreme change in the status quo.

C. ＿＿ Favors major changes in power structure to aid
the underclass.

(a) radical

(b) reactionary

(c) liberal

(d) conservative

True-False: Write "T" for true and "F" for false.

D. ＿＿ A radical would likely support student rights over teacher
rights.

E. ＿＿ A conservative would likely support traditional religion over
"cosmic consciousness."

F. ＿＿ A liberal would likely support more federal money to prevent job discrimination.

G. ____ A reactionary would likely support heavy taxes for the wealthy.

H. ____ A radical in a communist country would probably support capitalism.

I. ____ A conservative in a communist country would probably support rapid change to democracy.

For Your Critical Reflection: On what issues are you a liberal or radical? On what issues are you a conservative or reactionary?

_____

_____

Chapter Review

I. Yes-No Questions

1. Would an anarchist be orthodox?

   Yes   No   because _____

2. Would an Aristotelian agree with a Platonist?

   Yes   No   because _____

3. Would a conservative praise blasphemy?

   Yes   No   because _____

4. Would a coup d'état benefit ecumenism?

   Yes   No   because _____

5. Would a cynic believe Platonic ideals?

   Yes   No   because _____

6. Would a rightist like a reactionary?

   Yes   No   because _____

7. Would a radical egalitarian work for the enfranchisement of pariahs?

   Yes   No   because _____

8. Would a stoic react to a coup d'état more calmly than a liberal?

   Yes   No   because _____

9. Would an existentialist believe epistemology can tell you what is the best religion?

   Yes   No   because _____

10. Would a temple be a mecca for iconoclasts?

   Yes   No   because _____

11. Would iconoclasts like the orthodox?

   Yes   No   because _____

12. Would liberals wish anarchists well?

   Yes   No   because _____

13. Would a pariah seem to have good karma?

   Yes   No   because _____

14. Would Pascal's wager be useful to convince someone to support a coup d'état?

   Yes   No   because _____

15. Would epistemology help you understand why Pascal made his wager?

   Yes   No   because _____

16. Would a liberal have much hegemony in a right-wing government?

   Yes   No   because _____

17. Would an Aristotelian likely know the difference between radical and liberal?

   Yes   No   because _____

18. Would a Platonist be an existentialist?

   Yes   No   because _____

19. Would a Stoic find hedonism a blasphemy?

   Yes   No   because _____

20. Would a reactionary see leftists as friends?

   Yes   No   because _____

II. Using Context: Use the word list at the beginning of the chapter to fill in the blanks. You might not use all the words, or you might use one word more than once.

Hollywood on Trial

The House Un-American Activities Committee (HUAC) was founded in
1938. Its purpose was to investigate fascist, communist, and other groups
considered un-American. After World War II, many _____
and strict believers in free enterprise and democracy became increasingly
threatened by the growing communist _____ in Europe
and Asia. In 1947, HUAC began to investigate Hollywood on the grounds
that some movies, such as the *Grapes of Wrath,* seemed to be espousing
communist propaganda. Ten famous writers, actors, and agents, called the
Hollywood Ten, refused to testify about their political affiliations, arguing
from the _____ perspective that the ideal American soci-
ety should not infringe on an _____ person's right to
speech, privacy, and assembly. They considered these trials sinful, a
_____ against their sacred constitutional rights. They
were all imprisoned for contempt. The movie industry reacted quickly to
the investigations. Hundreds of people suspected of communism were fired
and despised as _____. Creative and bold artists, especially the _____ who attacked the sacred cows of the
industry, were silenced. Some writers produced screenplays under the
names of other people; others left the country. Indeed, Paris became a
_____ for Americans who were unemployed by the investigations. The expatriates were well received, especially by the French
_____ philosophers, who respected their courageous
choice not to succumb to the House Committee. Although the bounty
of French food, art, and culture provided pleasure for the
_____ among the exiles, most families of the Hollywood
Ten were _____ who stayed in the United States
and endured. Historians have continued to question why a
_____ and constitutional government would adopt the
religious procedures of an inquisition or witch-hunt. Some believe it was
caused by excessive patriotism, fueled by American pride in its victory over
the Nazis and Japanese in World War II. Unfortunately, few people re-

membered that many communists and subversives, along with Jews, were victims of Hitler's _____. However, _____ doubt such high-minded rationalization; they claim that the investigations were a strategy to allow Hollywood studios to fire people who desired powerful unions. The final judgment of the Holly- wood trials depends on where you sit on the political spectrum: leftists, political _____, and even _____ mourned the day, for they saw the trials as an attack on individual liberties of free speech. _____ and other people on the right wing claimed a victory over communist influence in American films. Clearly, the members of HUAC did not question the basis of their knowledge, or _____; that is, they did not ask "How can we really know if someone is a subversive?" Instead they borrowed a form of _____, reasoning that it was better to be safe than sorry. The HUAC probably needed an _____ thinker, who could carefully categorize the difference between leftists, radicals, commu- nists, subversives, and traitors; instead, all these types of people were un- critically tarred with the same red brush.

Reading for Chapter 9

THOMAS JEFFERSON

The Declaration of Independence

On July 4, 1776, the Congress adopted a draft of the Declaration of Independence, written by a committee of John Adams, Benjamin Franklin, Thomas Jefferson, Robert R. Livingston, and Roger Sherman. Before approving the resolution, the Congress struck out a passage con- demning slavery. The intention of the Declaration, Jefferson wrote later, was not to say something new, but ''to place before mankind the com- mon sense of the subject, in terms so plain and firm as to command their assent.'' People today might not find the language of the Decla- ration ''plain and firm'' but rather overwritten and complex. Never- theless, the Declaration remains a solid introduction to political vo- cabulary. Following is the introduction to the Declaration.

Words to Notice

Prepare for the reading by reviewing the following key words:

dissolve: to melt
entitle: grant
impel: force
self-evident: true without needing evidence
endowed: granted
unalienable: unable to be removed

deriving: receiving
alter: change
prudence: wisdom
transient: quickly passing
usurpations: seizures
despotism: tyranny

THE UNANIMOUS DECLARATION OF THE THIRTEEN
UNITED STATES OF AMERICA

1   When in the Course of human events, it becomes necessary for one people to dissolve the political bands, which have connected them with another, and to assume among the powers of the earth, the separate and equal station to which the Laws of Nature and of Nature's God entitle them, a decent respect to the opinions of mankind requires that they should declare the causes which impel them to the separation.—We hold these truths to be self–evident, that all men are created equal, that they are endowed by their Creator with certain unalienable Rights, that among these are Life, Liberty and the pursuit of Happiness.—That to secure these rights, Governments are instituted among Men, deriving their just powers from the consent of the governed,—That whenever any Form of Government becomes destructive of these ends, it is the Right of the People to alter or to abolish it, and to institute new Government, laying its foundation on such principles and organizing its powers in such form, as to them shall seem most likely to effect their Safety and Happiness. Prudence, indeed, will dictate that Governments long established should not be changed for light and transient causes; and accordingly all experience hath shewn, that mankind are more disposed to suffer, while evils are sufferable, than to right themselves by abolishing the forms to which they are accustomed. But when a long train of abuses and usurpations, pursuing invariably the same Object evinces a design to reduce them under absolute Despotism, it is their right, it is their duty, to throw off such Government, and to provide new Guards for their future security.—Such has been the patient sufferance of these Colonies; and such is now the necessity which constrains them to alter their former Systems of Government. The history of the present King of Great Britain is a history of repeated injuries and usurpations, all having in direct object the establishment of an absolute Tyranny over these States. To prove this, let Facts be submitted to a candid world.

Questions for Class Discussion

1. Have you ever heard or read the Declaration of Independence? On what occasions?
2. What does Jefferson mean when he says that "mankind are more disposed to suffer, while evils are sufferable, than to right themselves by abolishing the forms to which they are accustomed"? Is this true?
3. Does it change your attitude toward the Declaration to know that an earlier draft contained criticisms of the slave trade, which were removed before the final draft? How?

Making a New World

For Class Discussion

1. Which of the philosophies in section II seem old-fashioned or out of date? Which seem relevant today?
2. Who are some people whom our society considers pariahs? Are the reasons just?
3. What has had the most influence on human history—religion, philosophy, or politics? Which now has the most influence in your life or in society?

Collaborative Learning

1. Who Rules?
   Purpose: To learn to use the roots *arch* and *cracy* to label political systems.
   A. Your group has been assigned to use the roots *arch* (as in monarch, matriarch) and *cracy* (as in democracy, plutocracy) to make a list of possible forms of rule that can exist if different kinds of people governed a society (see the box "Who Rules?").
   B. Share your list with the class.
2. Who Has Hegemony?
   Purpose: To weigh the benefits and losses of different political positions.
   A. Your teacher will assign your group the task of making a list of the advantages and disadvantages of one or more of the following political positions: (1) maintaining the status quo, (2) reforming the status quo, (3) radically changing the status quo, (4) moving society to the left, (5) moving society to the right.
   B. Share your list with the class.

Ideas for Writing

1. In a paragraph, describe which three of the following philosophies make the most sense: Aristotelian, egalitarianism, existentialism, hedonism, Pascal's wager, Platonism, or stoicism.
2. In a page, describe a person religiously, philosophically, and politically using at least five words from the chapter.
3. At home, write a letter to the president describing what you admire and question about your society's religion, philosophy, or politics. Use at least ten words from the chapter.

More Words for Chapter 9

agnostic: a person who suspends belief, from the Greek *a* ("not") and *gignoskein* ("to know")

bicameral government: a system of government having two houses, such as Senate and House

checks and balances: Thomas Jefferson's reason to separate government into three branches: executive (President), legislative (House and Senate), and judicial (Courts), which prevents power and tyranny in only one branch

decalogue: the Ten Commandments or any similar list of ten rules or principles

devout: earnestly religious or sincere, a "devout believer"

dualism: beliefs that split the world into two things: mind/body; good/evil; earth/heaven; capitalist/communist

ex cathedra: literally "from the cathedral," speaking dogmatically, as if you have the power of a bishop

fascism: a system of extreme right-wing dictatorial government; nationalism, hostility to democracy

glasnost: Russian word for "openness," suggesting liberties of speech, assembly, and religion

imperialism: the extension of power through conquest or the pursuit of empire; aggression against smaller states

kismet: Arabic word meaning "fate"

koan: a problem designed to baffle one's ordinary intellect: "What is the sound of one hand clapping?"

mantra: Sanskrit for "instrument of thought"; holy syllables or sacred sounds in Mantra Yoga or Buddhism

monasticism: from the Greek *monazein* ("to be alone"), a life of withdrawal, meditation, and self-denial

perestroika: Russian word for "restructuring," suggesting evolution toward free-market economics

pontificate: to speak as if you are the "pontiff" or Pope and your statements are without error

progressive tax structure: taxing the wealthy a larger percentage of income than the poor

proselytize: to try to convert people to your beliefs or opinions; a proselyte is a converted person

republic: a political system run by consent of the people instead of obedience; a separate independent state

regressive tax structure: taxing the poor with a larger percentage of income than the rich; flat taxes

satori: term for "enlightenment" or sudden illumination, which is the goal of the religious quest in Zen Buddhism

sophistry: clever and subtle but perhaps deceptive reasoning, from Greek *sophist*, "city teacher"

tabula rasa: Latin for "blank tablet," the concept that the mind begins without innate knowledge, gaining all knowledge from experience

utopia: any ideal or unrealizable society or social structure, from Greek *ou* + *topos* ("no place")

Answer Key to Chapter 9

I. WORDS FROM THE WORLD RELIGIONS

Yes-No Questions

1. No; orthodox people follow tradition closely.
2. Yes; meccas attract visitors.
3. No; ecumenical does not separate groups.
4. Yes; good actions create good karma.
5. Yes; any large-scale destruction is a holocaust.
6. Yes; pariahs are outcast.
7. Yes; blasphemers blaspheme blasphemously.
8. No; secular people are not religious.
9. No; Buddhist temples are full of icons.

Fill in the Blank

A. (c) B. (b) C. (i) D. (a) E. (d)
F. (h) G. (f) H. (g) I. (e)

Matching

J. (e) K. (h) L. (d) M. (f) N. (g)
O. (a) P. (i) Q. (b) R. (c)

II. WORDS FROM THE PHILOSOPHERS

Yes-No Questions

10. No; Platonists seek to know ideals.
11. No; Aristotelians have their feet on the ground.
12. Yes; cynics deny good intentions to people.
13. No; stoics take trouble calmly.
14. Yes; eating is a pleasure.
15. Yes; if you have nothing to lose.
16. No; situations must be taken into account.
17. Yes; epistemology studies how we know.

Matching

S. (e) T. (c) U. (d) V. (b)
W. (a) X. (g) Y. (f) Z. (h)

True-False

a. T b. T c. T d. F e. T f. F
g. T h. F

Using Context: Armchair Philosophy

Pascal's wager, Aristotelian, Platonic, epistemology, existentialist, cynic, stoic, hedonist

III. WORDS FROM POLITICS—THE ART OF THE POSSIBLE

Yes-No Questions

18. No; a key citizen right would be gone.
19. No; it excludes women and other nations.
20. Yes; hegemony *is* political influence.
21. Yes; a few leaders on top, not the people.
22. No; anarchists want no government at all.

True-False

i. T j. F k. T l. F m. T

Practice with Word Forms

n. enfranchise, enfranchisement, enfranchised, disenfranchised
o. hegemony, hegemonic
p. anarchy, anarchist, anarchic

IV. WORDS FROM POLITICS—WHERE DO YOU STAND?

Yes-No Questions

23. No; they would want things to stay as they are.
24. No; they do not promote traditional rule.
25. No; they would not tax traditional rulers.
26. Yes; the suffrage has already been granted.

27. Yes; it would increase business freedom.
28. No; liberals support individual freedoms.
29. No; change is good regardless of left or right.

Multiple Choice

q. (b) r. (a) s. (a) t. (b) u. (b)
v. (a) w. (a) x. (b)

Matching

y. (b) z. (c) A. (d) B. (a) C. (a)

True-False

D. T E. T F. T G. F H. T I. F

CHAPTER REVIEW

I. Yes-No Questions

1. No; anarchists challenge tradition.
2. No; realists disagree with idealists.
3. No; conservatives support tradition.
4. No; it would not support everyone.
5. No; cynics suspect high ideals.
6. Yes; they both support traditional rulers.
7. Yes; all people should be equal.
8. Yes; stoics react to everything calmly.
9. No; experience means more than knowledge.
10. No; iconoclasts do not respect temples.
11. No; iconoclasts do not respect the religious.
12. No; liberals believe in good government.
13. No; a pariah seems to have bad fate.
14. Yes; you could calculate the advantage.
15. Yes; it would help you see contingent truth.
16. No; liberals would have no influence.
17. Yes; she would be good at categorizing.
18. No; existence precedes essence (ideal).
19. Yes; Stoics believe in controlling pleasure.
20. No; their ideals are completely opposite.

II. Using Context: Hollywood on Trial

orthodox, hegemony, liberal, enfranchised, blasphemy, pariahs, iconoclasts (radicals), mecca, existentialist, hedonist(s), stoics, secular, holocaust, cynics, liberals (radicals), conservatives, reactionaries, epistemology, Pascal's wager, Aristotelian

MYTH, FICTION, LEGEND, AND POETRY

Quick Reference Word List

Achilles' heel	haiku	metaphor/simile	quixotic
allusion	iambic pentameter	nemesis	Sappho
aphrodisiac	labyrinth	odyssey	sonnet
apostrophe	lilliputian	pander	sphinx
Dionysian/bacchanalian	Luddite	personification	tantalize
epic	malapropism	protean	utopia
Frankenstein monster			

Introduction: The Power of Myth

Although many people think of "myth" as a religion we no longer believe, myth can be any story that helps people understand the universe. How was the earth created? Why are there seasons? What is our link to the planets? What is the purpose of life? These are the questions that myths answer. A myth helps us feel the truth of human existence, even if we know it is only fiction. Any story that is imagined or created and not historically true is a fiction, such as novels and short stories. Some stories, passed down through generations, become legends. Legends tell of the heroic deeds of a nation or individual heroes. Poetry comes from the Greek *poesis*, meaning "to make." Poets are makers of reality. Thus all myths, fictions, and legends are shaped by the same poetic instinct. "There's more in heaven and earth," says Hamlet to Horatio, "than is dreamed of in your philosophy." We find some of this "more" in myth, fiction, legend, and poetry.

I. Going on a Journey?

1. utopia [yoo TOPE ee uh]: an imaginary place or society where everything is perfect.

Thomas More (1478–1535) was a statesman in the court of Henry VIII. To show what kind of advice Henry could expect, More wrote *Utopia*, Greek for "no place," a story of a journey to an ideal state that enjoyed religious tolerance, equal distribution of wealth, a six-hour working day, an enlightened education system, and rule by the wisest leaders. Not only a dream, *Utopia* criticized the existing state. Later, More was accused of treason and executed for not recognizing Henry (instead of the Pope) as the head of the Church of England. He was canonized in 1935. Utopia now refers to any story of a perfect society; a dystopia, such as Orwell's *Nineteen Eighty-four*, shows a perfectly horrible society.

. . . .

Have You Heard?
Hermes

Hermes was a Greek god who has given names to many modern things. On the day he was born, Hermes crept from his cradle and stole Apollo's cattle. The angered Apollo was appeased when Hermes played him a song on a lyre, which he invented from a tortoise shell (which he also stole). Hermes was worshipped by the ancient Greeks as the god of luck and wealth, the patron of merchants and thieves; he was also the god of roads and the messenger or herald of the gods. He is typically drawn with wings on his sandals for swift journeying with messages and a broad-rimmed hat. This is the symbol of the FTD Florist. He carries a staff on which serpents are twined—the *caduceus*, the symbol of the American Medical Association. *Hermeneutics* [her men OO tiks] is a method for interpreting the Bible and other literature. The Romans also worshipped Hermes, but they called him Mercury. From him we get the name for the planet, the quicksilver element, the fluid in thermometers, and the word *mercurial*, meaning someone whose mood changes quickly.

Would a place where pumpkins baked themselves into pies be a utopia?

Yes   No   because _____

2. quixotic [kwik SOT ik]: chivalrous or unselfish engagement in a hopeless cause.

Don Quixote [kee HOH tay] is the hero of the Spanish story by Cervantes (1547–1616). This visionary "knight errant" traveled around trying to hold to his ideals in the face of grim realities. Quixotic now describes any admirable fool who struggles for noble deeds and high ideals against impossible odds.

If people called you quixotic, would they imply that your ideals are too much for reality?

Yes   No   because _____

3. odyssey [ODD ih see]: a long journey or eventful adventure.

The *Odyssey* was the Greek epic poem by Homer. It tells of the wandering of the hero Odysseus as he tried to return home from the Trojan War to his wife,

Penelope. An odyssey is a journey to amazing places, characterized by a longing for home and by problems that need to be solved by cunning and wit.

Would a trip in which you were lost, robbed, arrested, freed, and mistaken for the mayor be an odyssey?

Yes   No   because _____

4. sphinx [SFEENKS]: a person who does not reveal thoughts or feelings.

Sphinx (meaning "strangler") is the mythical monster of the ancient Middle East, portrayed in statues as a lion with a female head. In the story of Oedipus, the Sphinx posed a riddle to travelers on the road to Thebes: "What walks on four legs in the morning, on two at noon, and three in the evening?" The answer was "man," who as an infant crawls on all fours and in old age walks leaning on a stick. When Oedipus answered right, the Sphinx threw herself from her rocky perch, and Oedipus was declared king.

If your teacher answered all of your questions with questions, could you call her a sphinx?

Yes   No   because _____

5. labyrinth [LAB ih rinth]: a complicated network of paths in which one gets lost; a maze.

King Minos, legendary king of Crete, had Daedalus build a huge maze to hold the minotaur. The minotaur was a beast with the head of a bull and the body of a man who devoured young maidens and youths sent from Athens to be sacrificed. Labyrinth and labyrinthine describe places or procedures (such as college registration) that make it difficult to find your way and dangerous if you get lost.

Could you describe a many-leveled, complicated office building as a labyrinth?

Yes   No   because _____

6. lilliputian [lill uh PYOO shun]: very small.

The Lilliputians were the inhabitants of Lilliput, a country in Jonathan Swift's *Gulliver's Travels*. Lilliputians were only six inches tall. More than a children's fantasy, Lilliput was meant as a satire on contemporary England, ridiculing "small" or "petty" behaviors and attitudes.

Would a ten-cent tip for a hundred dollar meal be lilliputian?

Yes   No   because _____

Matching: Match the statement with the vocabulary word.

A. ____ "It's incredibly small!"

B. ____ "The poor guy always expects the world to conform to his ideals."

C. ____ "She never reveals her thoughts or feelings!"

D. ____ "It's so complicated to find things here without getting lost."

E. ____ "Everyone here is kind, just, and happy!"

F. ____ "I didn't think I'd ever get home from this eventful trip."

(a) utopia

(b) quixotic

(c) odyssey

(d) sphinx-like

(e) labyrinth

(f) lilliputian

Practice with Word Forms: Fill in each blank with the proper form of the word.

G. **utopia, utopian:** Although people will probably never live in a

_____, the world would be intolerable if we cynically

decided to rid ourselves of all _____ fantasies.

H. **labyrinth, labyrinthine:** The registrar sent me back through a

_____ series of offices and hallways, but I wouldn't

leave the bureaucratic _____ until I got my grade

change slip.

Using Context: Fill in each blank with the vocabulary word or form that best suits the context.

Academic Journeying

All my friends told me that my first heroic task would be to survive the

long _____ of registration, wandering helplessly from

one building to another through a _____ of hallways and

offices. After this trial, I knew that the classroom would seem like a perfect

_____. Armed with high ideals, I boldly carried my pencil like a lance and committed myself to a _____ battle against the cynics. The first day was fine. I was taken aback for a moment when the _____ -like professor walked in and said, "What is the sound of one hand clapping?" After an uncomfortable silence, during which we all felt shrunken, like _____ intellects in the face of a giant wizard, he said, "Brilliant, people! Your silence is precisely correct. Now, reward yourself. What is the sound of two hands clapping?" The applause echoed down the hallways.

For Your Critical Reflection: If Don Quixote, Odysseus, and Lilliput never really existed, why do people continue to learn about them?

_____

_____

II. The Desires and Downfalls of Gods, Heroes, and Monsters

7. protean [PRO tee uhn]: taking many forms; variable, unstable, slippery.

In the *Odyssey*, Proteus is the ancient prophet of the sea who herds the seals and knows all things. To avoid being questioned, he has the power to assume different shapes. To benefit from his advice, a hero must hold tightly to him as he shifts from one shape to another. Protean now describes people who are "hard to pin down" or question because of their instability or shifting alliances.

Would you describe a public relations expert who never gives a straight answer to a question as protean?

Yes   No   because _____

8. tantalize [TANT uh lyze]: to tease someone by the sight of something desired but out of reach.

Inviting the gods to a banquet, the legendary King Tantalus served them the flesh of Pelops, his son. Angered, the gods brought Pelops back to life and condemned Tantalus to stand in Hades surrounded by water and fruit that magically receded when he tried to quench his hunger or thirst.

If you left your money at home and were hungry, might you be tantalized by a bakery window?

Yes   No   because _____

9. aphrodisiac [aff roh DEEZ ee ack]: something that stimulates or intensifies sexual desire.

Aphrodite, the Greek goddess of love, fertility, and beauty, sprang from the foam ("aphros") of the sea near Cyprus, though she has kinship to the Asian goddess Astarte. She inspired romance. The Romans called her Venus, from which we get the word *venereal*. Her son, Eros, is remembered in the word *erotic*. The Romans knew this winged archer who mischievously shoots arrows of love as Cupid, from which we get *cupidity*, meaning avarice or greed for gain. The myth of "aphrodisiac foods" developed because of their high protein, rarity, and texture (oysters, for instance). Chemical aphrodisiacs are in reality nerve irritants that can lead to paralysis and death.

Can a romantic dinner at a darkly lighted restaurant and a night of dancing be an aphrodisiac?

Yes   No   because _____

10. Dionysian/bacchanalian [die oh NEEZ ee uhn/bahk uh NAYL ee uhn]: ecstatic, orgiastic, riotous, irrational.

Dionysus was the Greek god of vegetation and wine. Legend has it that he roamed the countryside followed by female votaries who would fall into violent frenzies and tear to pieces with their teeth a goat, stray animal, or anyone who did not honor their god. These crazed revelries were the foundation of modern drama. *Dionysian* describes riotous celebrations, such as football pep rallies, and also tremendous creative energy, the opposite of the critical-rational power embodied by Apollo. The Romans renamed Dionysus "Bacchus," the god of wine. A bacchanal is thus any drunken party.

Would you describe a meeting of Quaker deacons as Dionysian?

Yes   No   because _____

Doonesbury © 1989 G. B. Trudeau. Reprinted with permission of Universal Press Syndicate. All rights reserved.

11. pander [PAN dir]: to appeal to or gratify a person's base nature or vulgar tastes.

Pandarus is a character in the works of Boccaccio, Chaucer, and Shakespeare who destroyed the innocence of his cousin, the Greek maid Cressida, to satisfy the lust of the Trojan prince Troilus. A panderer is someone who procures carnal pleasure or acts as a go-between in illicit acts. To pander is to arouse and then satisfy people's vulgar tastes in sex, violence, or fear in order to win their support.

Can you describe a tabloid newspaper that promises you nude photos of a senator as pandering?

Yes   No   because _____

12. Achilles' heel [uh KILL eez HEEL]: weak or vulnerable point.

Achilles was a Greek hero in the Trojan War who was invincible except for his heel. To make him invulnerable, his mother, Thetis, dipped him into the underworld river Styx. But she neglected the spot where she held him. His enemy Paris did not. He killed Achilles by shooting an arrow into his heel.

If you earned perfect grades in all classes but failed math, could math be your Achilles' heel?

Yes   No   because _____

13. nemesis [NEM eh sis]: any source of disaster, misfortune, or woe, especially well-deserved.

Nemesis is the Greek goddess who punishes humans for excess pride. The legendary cause of the fall of empires, a nemesis brings a well-deserved disaster or revenge. Drink is the nemesis of the alcoholic; chocolate is the nemesis of the dieter; Paris was the nemesis of Achilles.

Could a stock-market crash be the nemesis of a hasty investor?

Yes   No   because _____

14. Frankenstein monster [FRANK en STINE MON stir]: something dangerous to its creator.

The title character of Mary Shelley's 1818 novel about the danger of the self-obsessed imagination, Frankenstein was a doctor who, in an attempt to re-create life, created a hideous monster who eventually killed him. To "create a Frankenstein monster" is to start something that gets dangerously out of control.

If you trained a new worker who then wanted to take away your job, would you have created a Frankenstein monster?

Yes   No   because _____

15. Luddite [LUDD ite]: person who opposes or destroys labor-saving technology.

To protest the unemployment and the shoddy merchandise produced by labor-saving textile machinery, bands of English weavers—led by "General" Ludd—traveled through the Midlands smashing the new looms. The weavers were brutally repressed by 1816 and several leaders were hanged. Luddism came to mean opposition to any new technology.

Can you call someone who refuses to use the new office computer a Luddite?

Yes   No   because _____

Matching: Match the description with the vocabulary word.

I. ____ The rebellious republic that brings the empire to its knees.	(a) protean
J. ____ A violent execution in front of a crowd screaming "We want blood!"	(b) tantalizing
K. ____ The window of the delicious-smelling but overpriced French pastry shop.	(c) aphrodisiac
L. ____ The office worker who switches loyalties before you know it.	(d) Dionysian/ bacchanalian
M. ____ The victory celebration that turns into a drunken, crazy party.	(e) pandering
N. ____ The clumsy right-fielder on your otherwise strong baseball team.	(f) Achilles' heel
O. ____ The meal, song, or movie that arouses romantic interest.	(g) nemesis
P. ____ The people who jam wrenches into the assembly line to slow it down.	(h) Frankenstein monster
Q. ____ The garden you planted that swallows the whole house.	(i) Luddites
	(j) cupidity

True-False: Write "T" for true and "F" for false.

R. ____ Your Frankenstein monster could eventually become your nemesis.

S. ____ A Luddite would be tantalized by the window of a new computer store.

T. ____ A person might employ aphrodisiacs in the act of pandering.

U. ____ Stability is probably the Achilles' heel of a protean person.

V. ____ A party can be both Dionysian and bacchanalian.

Practice with Word Forms: Fill in the blank with the best form.

W. **nemesis, nemeses** (plural): Having lived an impeccable life, I knew I

was free from _____, but inconstant fortune cast a

_____ before me that brought me to ruin—my perfect pride.

    X. **Luddite, Luddism:** When it comes to using automatic teller machines instead of tellers, I am a real _____, but in general I think that _____ keeps a country in the Dark Ages.

    Y. **bacchanalian, bacchanals:** Beta Tappa Keg was infamous for its _____ after football games, yet the party I attended was only as _____ as a tea party—the Boston Tea Party!

    Z. **panders, pandering:** I can't stand the student politician who always _____ to the students by promising them more parking spaces and cheaper books. More effective _____ can be done if she promises a winning basketball team, 4.0s for everyone, and pizza delivery to the library!

For Your Critical Reflection: Do you know people who are Luddites? Are you a Luddite when it comes to some technology? Can Luddism ever be justified?

_____

_____

III. Poetic Devices and Figures of Speech

    16. malapropism [MAL uh PROHP izm]: a comical confusion of words that sound alike.

A character in R. B. Sheridan's play *The Rivals,* Mrs. Malaprop (from *mal,* "bad" + *propre,* "ownership") often confused words that sounded alike: "as headstrong as an allegory [alligator] on the banks of the Nile," "illiterate [obliterate] him, I say, from your memory."

If you say, "Blast the Infernal Revenue Service," have you uttered a malapropism?

Yes   No   because _____

. . . .

Guess What!
Sappho's Poetry

One of the greatest poets of all time, Sappho wrote nine books in a variety of meters. Sadly, only a few fragments of her work survive. The sapphic stanza bears her name. It consists of three lines followed by one shorter line, composed to be sung to the lyre. The name Sappho has been associated with sharp observations of complicated and ambivalent emotions and an acute awareness of inner and outer selves. The following poem, translated by the authors, is one of her most famous works.

Like a god ablaze is he who
sits near you, hears every word,
knows your soft voice. How sweetly to
mumble love,

wax giddy, for him alone. Yet my soul
sinks, my heart shakes my breasts.
Let me see you coming, my tongue is stone,
my voice drops,

lips shut. Flames dance under
my skin, my eyes see nothing
but dazzle, and ah me! my ears
pound like thunder.

Sweat beads run down my sides, I shiver
with fever, turn white as dry grass;
changed utterly, just this
side of death.

17. Sappho [SAF oh]: a great woman poet; or a lesbian.

Sappho's poetry was famous among Greeks for its beauty and romantic ardor. *Sapphic* refers to the four-line verse form Sappho made famous. The writer Mary Wortley Montagu was named "The English Sappho" by Alexander Pope. On Lesbos, a Greek island in the Aegean Sea, Sappho taught poetry to a select group of young women in the seventh and sixth centuries B.C. A legend developed that Sappho and her followers engaged in homosexual love, from which we get the word lesbian, resident of Lesbos.

Can you call Robert Frost a Sappho?

Yes   No   because _____

18. haiku [HIE koo]: Japanese poetic form.

Haiku means "beginning verse." It is a three-line poem of seventeen syllables that provides a sudden glimpse into the nature of a season. "Haiku," said Basho, a great haiku writer, "is simply what is happening in this place at this moment." One of Basho's famous haiku, translated into compressed English, is the following: "In the old stone pool a frog leaps. Kerplunk."

Haiku has / seventeen syllables, / hasn't it?

Yes   No   because _____

19. sonnet [SAHN it]: A fourteen-line poem of rhyming iambic pentameter.

The most popular form in English poetry, the sonnet was devised in thirteenth-century Italy and perfected by Petrarch, who wrote a series of sonnets about his loved one, Laura. Shakespeare further developed the sonnet in English, creating the English sonnet form: three four-line quatrains rhyming *abab cdcd efef* and a stinging couplet to close. The Petrarchan sonnet, which does not rely on a strong witty conclusion, requires two quatrains rhyming *abba* (an octave) and a sestet with a variety of endings. William Wordsworth, who published more sonnets than any other English poet, uses a sestet rhyming *cdcdcd* in the sonnet below.

The World Is Too Much with Us

The world is too much with us; late and soon,	1	a	Octave
Getting and spending, we lay waste our powers:	2	b	|
Little we see in Nature that is ours;	3	b	|
We have given our hearts away, a sordid boon!	4	a	|
This Sea that bares her bosom to the moon;	5	a	|
The winds that will be howling at all hours,	6	b	|
And are up-gathered now like sleeping flowers;	7	b	|
For this, for everything, we are out of tune;	8	a	|
It moves us not.—Great God! I'd rather be	9	c	Sestet
A Pagan suckled in a creed outworn;	10	d	|
So might I, standing on this pleasant lea,	11	c	|
Have glimpses that would make me less forlorn;	12	d	|
Have sight of Proteus rising from the sea;	13	c	|
Or hear old Triton blow his wreathèd horn.	14	d	|

Explanatory Notes: 2 *Getting and spending:* making a living. **4** *a sordid boon:* an undignified exchange or gift. **10** *Pagan suckled:* though their myths are gone, the pagan at least had a link with nature. **11** *lea:* a grassland. **12** *forlorn:* alone and unhappy. **13** *Proteus:* see "protean" on preceding pages. **14** *Triton:* a merman, fish-shaped from bottom down, depicted as blowing a conch shell.

Would a pocket full of sonnets be an appropriate Valentine's Day present?

Yes   No   because _____

20. iambic pentameter [eye AM bik pen TAM uh tir]: line of poetry with ten syllables and five stresses.

An iamb is a poetic foot of two syllables, the second one stressed (te TUM). Pentameter is a line of poetry that has five of these feet in each line. Sonnets must be written in iambic pentameter. Notice the pattern in Wordsworth's sonnet. Line 1: "The **world** | is too | much **with** | us; **late** | and **soon.**" Or line 14: "Or **hear** | old Tri- | ton **blow** | his **wreath-** | ed **horn.**" Ten syllables; five stresses.

Could you write in iambic pentameter if you could not count?

Yes   No   because _____

21. personification [per SON ih fi KAY shun]: poetic device that gives human qualities to inanimate things.

To personify something is to grant it human qualities. Liberty is personified as a woman holding a torch. Some scholars say that personifications replace mythical figures when myths are no longer believed. In the poem here, Wordsworth, hungry to see something in "Nature that is ours," personifies in several spots: the sea has a bosom (line 5); the wind can howl (line 6); and flowers can sleep (line 7). Some modern poets consider personification absurd, like a cartoon. Yet we all say "table leg."

Is saying "My pen sings over the page" a personification?

Yes   No   because _____

22. apostrophe [uh POS troh fee]: turning to address a thing or an absent person as if alive and present.

Apostrophe in Greek means "to turn away." "Oh car, don't break down now" is an apostrophe, as is "Grandmother Jones, what can I do with this child?"

when grandmother is absent or dead. Wordworth's poem (line 9) includes one of the most famous apostrophes in English: "Great God!"

Can you use an apostrophe to address a person in your presence?

Yes   No   because _____

23. **metaphor/simile** [MET uh for/SIM ih lee]: figures of speech that compare unlike subjects.

Metaphors compare one thing to another: "Pat is a dead duck." Similes make the comparison explicit by using *like* or *as:* "Linda is pretty as a picture." "My house is like yours" is not a simile, but "My house leaks like a sieve" is. Aristotle thought that the ability to use metaphors was a sign of genius, the ability to see similarities that others miss. Wordsworth uses metaphor in his sonnet. To say "we are out of tune," implies that a "harmony" exists between humans and nature that we have lost.

Is the statement "He sits there nightly, regular as sin and Walter Cronkite" a simile?

Yes   No   because _____

24. **allusion** [uh LOO zhin]: a brief and casual reference to historical or literary characters or places.

Allusions are indirect references. The speaker or writer taps your knowledge and memory. Biblical allusions are frequent in English literature. Wordsworth makes classical allusions to Proteus and Triton. Some people say all writing is by nature "allusive." Do not confuse allusion with illusion (false picture).

Is the phrase "Happy as two new folks in the garden" an allusion to Eden?

Yes   No   because _____

25. **epic** [EP ik]: a long narrative poem that records heroic deeds.

Noble in conception and style, epic poems include the *Iliad* and the *Odyssey* by Homer, the *Aeneid* by Virgil, the *Divine Comedy* by Dante, *Paradise Lost* by Milton, the Old English *Beowulf,* the Eastern Indian *Mahabarata,* the Spanish *Cid,* and the Finnish *Kalevala.* Some American epics are Longfellow's *Hiawatha,* Whitman's *Leaves of Grass,* Pound's *Cantos,* and Berryman's *Dream Songs.*

Can a haiku be an epic?

Yes   No   because _____

Matching: Match the definition with the vocabulary word.

a. ____ A long narrative poem, such as the *Odyssey*, that focuses on a hero.

b. ____ A writer's indirect reference to the Bible or the classics.

c. ____ A poetic comparison, such as "That car is a lemon."

d. ____ A fourteen-line rhyming poem of iambic pentameter.

e. ____ A line of poetry that goes te-TUM te-TUM te-TUM te-TUM te-TUM.

f. ____ To give inanimate things human qualities: "The sky cries."

g. ____ To turn to address someone absent or inanimate: "Great Heavens!"

h. ____ Famous Greek female poet.

i. ____ A comparison using *like* or *as*: "He stood like a gull in the water."

j. ____ A comic misuse of words that sound alike: "Please percussion my fall."

k. ____ A brief Japanese poem.

(a) malapropism

(b) Sappho

(c) haiku

(d) sonnet

(e) simile

(f) Kabuki

(g) epic

(h) metaphor

(i) iambic pentameter

(j) personification

(k) apostrophe

(l) allusion

Context Cues: Match lines from Wordsworth's poem to the prominent poetic device. Use one word twice.

l. ____ The *world* is *too* much *with* us; *late* and *soon,*

m. ____ The Sea that bares *her bosom* to the moon;

n. ____ For this, for everything, *we are out of tune;*

o. ____ It moves us not.—*Great God!* I'd rather be

p. ____ Have sight of *Proteus rising* from the sea;

q. ____ Or hear *old Triton* blow his wreathèd horn.

r. ____ The form of Wordsworth's fourteen-line poem.

(a) allusion

(b) metaphor

(c) personification

(d) sonnet

(e) iambic pentameter line

(f) apostrophe

True-False: Write "T" for true and "F" for false.

s. _____ An iambic pentameter line has ten syllables and five stresses.

t. _____ Biblical and classical allusions are the two most popular allusions in English poetry.

u. _____ Metaphor and simile are both forms of comparisons.

v. _____ Haiku means "heroic poem."

w. _____ Some people say that personification replaces mythical figures when belief dies away.

x. _____ Dante's *Divine Comedy* is an example of a sonnet.

y. _____ Sappho's poetry was famous for its romantic ardor.

z. _____ Malapropisms confuse two words that sound alike to comic effect.

For Your Critical Reflection: Poetry has always been one of the most important forms of education. How much poetry did you study in high school? What is your attitude toward poetry? Why do you think you like it or do not like it?

_____

_____

Chapter Review

I. Yes-No Questions

1. Could poetry class be your Achilles' heel?

   Yes   No   because _____

2. Could you make an allusion to the *Odyssey?*

   Yes   No   because _____

3. Could a tantalizing sight be an aphrodisiac?

   Yes   No   because _____

4. Could a Dionysian festival pander to people?

   Yes   No   because _____

5. Is the word *quixotic* an allusion?

   Yes   No   because _____

6. Is "Praise General Ludd!" an apostrophe?

   Yes   No   because _____

7. Could you write an epic about Frankenstein in iambic pentameter?

   Yes   No   because _____

8. Could your Frankenstein be your nemesis?

   Yes   No   because _____

9. Would a Luddite's utopia have computers?

   Yes   No   because _____

10. Would you be on an odyssey if you came to a village of Lilliputians?

   Yes   No   because _____

11. Would long and many-syllable words be the nemesis of Mrs. Malaprop?

   Yes   No   because _____

12. Would people be tantalized in utopia?

   Yes   No   because _____

13. If you call a person sphinx-like, are you using a simile?

   Yes   No   because _____

14. Could modern Sapphos write sonnets?

   Yes   No   because _____

15. Would a quixotic person pander?

   Yes   No   because _____

16. Would a protean sphinx be easy to talk to?

   Yes   No   because _____

17. Is "semaphore" a possible malapropism for metaphor?

   Yes   No   because _____

18. Would a quixotic person fear a labyrinth?

   Yes   No   because _____

19. Would a lilliputian labyrinth be hard to escape?

   Yes   No   because _____

20. Would an epic poem about an odyssey to discover a utopia of aphrodisiacal sonnets tantalize and pander to a Dionysian?

   Yes   No   because _____

II. Using Context: Use the word list at the beginning of the chapter to fill in the blanks. You might not use all the words, or you might use one word more than once. *Clue:* all lines are iambic pentameter.

Epic Vocabulary

O Muses, ruling the heroic sky,

hear and bless my verse before I die!

Help me to write an _____ poem, or two,

but nothing short, like Japanese _____.

No _____ poems for tiny minds;

I want my poems to be ten thousand lines.

Nor will a pocket full of _____ do—

just fourteen lines of iambs, then I'm through!

No, I prefer a _____ of rhyme,

With minotaurs and corridors that wind.

Nobly I strive, _____, high-idealed;

I've never cared to feed the pigs that squealed.

Or turn to swine myself, mysteriously,

like Homer's sailors in the _____.

Don't get me wrong; I'm not afraid of dirt;

I once slid home, got grass stains on my shirt,

and cleaned the shirt by hand, which is my way;

I hate machines! A _____, you might say.

            * * *

_____ might be the *perfect* place,

but malls and trinkets charm our human race,

along with ads that _____ the eye:

"A brand new gadget or machine to buy!"

            * * *

How sadly dazzled! Though we work so hard,

our _____ becomes the credit card.

Revenge for _____, god of wine?

Meet ATM, our newest _____.

_____ to the classics now abound,

to show what truth the Greeks and Romans found.

_____ 's a weak or vulnerable spot;

The _____ will pose a riddle, like as not.

_____ 's lyrics make a romance sweet;

_____ _____ means five feet.

''O Zeus!'' _____ sound just like that.

_____, like weeping rain, falls flat.

Yet here's a problem for this _____ life,

which changes daily for husband or wife.

Can poetry be _____,

and charm our Valentines to heaven and back?

''Charm'' here, you know, is just a _____.

A prudent choice of phrase we're better for!

Reading for Chapter 10

MARY SHELLEY

Frankenstein

Mary Shelley wrote most of Frankenstein *when she was only eigh-teen. This stunning novel has been translated into many languages, including translations in Japanese, Russian, Urdu, Arabic, and Ma-layalam. Most people have seen one of the many movie versions. When-ever you hear someone say, ''I've created a monster,'' they probably have Shelley's work in the back of their minds. The germ of the story is to be found in Shelley's wide-ranging interests in ghosts, haunted houses, and scientific theories of galvanism (electricity). Yet she was also inspired by the myth of Prometheus, to which she alludes in her title page,* Frankenstein, or the Modern Prometheus. *Prometheus was the Greek god who brought fire from the sun to help humankind. Zeus punished him for his efforts by chaining him to a rock, with an eagle that would nightly feed on his liver. A Roman myth about another Prometheus, who was said to have re-created humankind by animating a figure of clay, was also relevant. Shelley was perhaps also inspired by the dangerous consequences of creative power that she witnessed in herself, her husband (the poet Percy Bysshe Shelley), and their friend Lord Byron. Whatever the origin, the story of Dr. Frankenstein contin-*

*ues to teach readers about the destructive sides of self-obsessive imagi-
nation. The following passage is from Chapter V, originally the book's
first page.*

Words to Notice

Prepare for the reading by reviewing the following key words:

infuse: fill
convulsive: violently heaving
agitate: to shake
delineate: describe
wretch: a miserable person
inarticulate: mumbled
detain: hold

demoniacal: like a demon
lustrous: shiny
inanimate: having no life
traversing: pacing back and forth
lassitude: tiredness
tumult: uproar

1   It was on a dreary night of November, that I beheld the accomplishment of
my toils. With an anxiety that almost amounted to agony, I collected the instruments of life around me, that I might infuse a spark of being into the lifeless
thing that lay at my feet. It was already one in the morning; the rain pattered
dismally against the panes, and my candle was nearly burnt out, when, by the
glimmer of the half-extinguished light, I saw the dull yellow eye of the creature
open; it breathed hard, and a convulsive motion agitated its limbs.

2   How can I describe my emotions at this catastrophe, or how delineate the
wretch whom with such infinite pains and care I had endeavoured to form?
His limbs were in proportion, and I had selected his features as beautiful. Beautiful!—Great God! His yellow skin scarcely covered the work of muscles and
arteries beneath; his hair was of a lustrous black, and flowing; his teeth of a
pearly whiteness; but these luxuriances only formed a more horrid contrast
with his watery eyes, that seemed almost of the same colour as the dun white
sockets in which they were set, his shrivelled complexion and straight black
lips.

3   The different accidents of life are not so changeable as the feelings of human
nature. I had worked hard for nearly two years, for the sole purpose of infusing
life into an inanimate body. For this I had deprived myself of rest and health.
I had desired it with an ardour that far exceeded moderation; but now that I
had finished, the beauty of the dream vanished, and breathless horror and
disgust filled my heart. Unable to endure the aspect of the being I had created,
I rushed out of the room, and continued a long time traversing my bedchamber,
unable to compose my mind to sleep. At length lassitude succeeded to the
tumult I had before endured; and I threw myself on the bed in my clothes,
endeavouring to seek a few moments of forgetfulness. But it was in vain: I slept,
indeed, but I was disturbed by the wildest dreams. I thought I saw Elizabeth,
in the bloom of health, walking in the streets of Ingolstadt. Delighted and surprised, I embraced her; but as I imprinted the first kiss on her lips, they became

livid with the hue of death; her features appeared to change, and I thought that I held the corpse of my dead mother in my arms; a shroud enveloped her form, and I saw the graveworms crawling in the folds of the flannel. I started from my sleep with horror; a cold dew covered my forehead, my teeth chattered, and every limb became convulsed: when, by the dim and yellow light of the moon, as it forced its way through the window shutters, I beheld the wretch— the miserable monster whom I had created. He held up the curtain of the bed; and his eyes, if eyes they may be called, were fixed on me. His jaws opened, and he muttered some inarticulate sounds, while a grin wrinkled his cheeks. He might have spoken, but I did not hear; one hand was stretched out, seemingly to detain me, but I escaped, and rushed down stairs. I took refuge in the courtyard belonging to the house which I inhabited; where I remained during the rest of the night, walking up and down in the greatest agitation, listening attentively, catching and fearing each sound as if it were to announce the approach of the demoniacal corpse to which I had so miserably given life.

Questions for Class Discussion

1. What words show you that Dr. Frankenstein is disgusted with his creation?
2. Is there anything in this brief passage to suggest why Frankenstein's monster eventually turns to destroy him?
3. Have you ever created a Frankenstein monster?

Making a New World

For Class Discussion

1. Do you know any people you might call Luddites? Why would you call them that?
2. Do you know any people you might call quixotic? Why would you call them that?
3. What creations of the modern world might you call Frankenstein monsters?

Collaborative Learning

1. Utopia/Dystopia
   Purpose: To understand what makes a society utopian or dystopian.
   A. Utopia is a perfect place. Dystopia is a perfectly *horrible* place. Your group must decide which words, events, or types of people from this chapter would be in your utopia. Which ones would you put in your dystopia?

    B. Justify your choices.
    C. Report to the class.
2. Sappho/Wordsworth
    Purpose: To develop language for judging poetry.
    A. Your group is assigned to decide which is the better poem, Sappho's
      or Wordsworth's.
    B. First, note the things they have in common. Use at least three words
      from the chapter.
    C. Second, note the things that make them different. Use at least two
      words from the chapter.
    D. Finally, decide which poem is the best. Use any standards you want.
    E. Report to the group.

Ideas for Writing

1. Write a haiku. The rules are discussed in the chapter.
2. In a page, describe a time you thought you were on an odyssey.
3. At home, write a letter to a school president who wants to eliminate literature classes because myths, fictions, legend, and poetry are not practical. Supply reasons for keeping or not keeping the courses. Use five words from the chapter.

More Words for Chapter 10

Adamic: acting like Adam, the first man; trying to name all things anew without care for tradition

aegis [EE jes]: protection, sponsorship; from the name of the shield of Zeus, head of Olympian gods

Cassandra: a person who prophesies disaster (but is often ignored); named after a prophetess in Greek legend who foretold evil events but was doomed never to be believed

chautauqua: popular education combined with entertainment often presented outdoors or in a tent

chimera: an imaginary monster, illusion, fabrication of the mind that unnecessarily terrifies

creed: a formal statement of religious belief or confession of faith; from Latin *credo* ("I believe")

epicure: a person with sensitive tastes; from the legend that the philosopher Epicurus was a hedonist

Gaea [JEE uh]: the Greek earth goddess and mother of the Titans, root of geology

gargantuan: gigantic; from the name of the monster in François Rabelais's novels *Gargantua* and *Pantagruel*

Golden Bough, The: Sir James Frazer's famous study of myths, cults, and religions throughout the world

gradgrindian: a person who rigidly demands facts, without regard for values or imagination; after Thomas Gradgrind, the rigid schoolmaster, in Dickens's *Hard Times:* "Teach these children nothing but facts, Sir!"

Harlem Renaissance: literary movement of the 1920s among black writers, led by poets Claude McKay, Jean Toomer, Langston Hughes, and Countee Cullen, which declared a break from tradition and the foregrounding of individual voices and experience

Horatio Alger story: a story about a person moving from rags to riches through honesty and hard work

mentor: a trusted advisor; named after Mentor to whom Odysseus gave charge of his home while away

mercurial: a person who is liable to have sudden changes of mood or personality; after Mercury

Olympian: majestic and imposing; from the Olympians, Greek gods

paen [PAY on]: a song of praise or triumph; from an ancient Greek hymn to Apollo

pagan: a person who is not a Christian, Moslem, or Jew; one who has no religion or who worships nature

procrustean: a person who seeks to enforce conformity with a theory by violence (such as ignoring all contradictory evidence); named after Procrustes, a robber in Greek legend, who fitted victims to his bed by stretching them or lopping bits off

Pyrrhic victory: a victory gained at too great a cost, such as that of Pyrrhus over the Romans in 279 B.C.

Quetzalcoatl: the plumed serpent; ancient Mexican god identified with the morning and evening star

thespian: an actor or actress; things of the theater; from Thespis, the ancient Greek founder of drama

Answer Key to Chapter 10

I. GOING ON A JOURNEY?

Yes-No Questions

1. Yes; unless you hate pumpkins.
2. Yes; quixotic people stick to ideals.
3. Yes, it is adventurous and re-quires cunning.
4. Yes; her riddling might disem-power.
5. Yes; especially if you could get lost in it.
6. Yes; it is very small, considering the price.

Matching

A. (f) B. (b) C. (d) D. (e) E. (a)
F. (c)

Practice with Word Forms

G. utopia, utopian H. labyrinthine, labyrinth

Using Context: Academic Journeying

odyssey, labyrinth, utopia, quixotic, sphinx, lilliputian

II. THE DESIRES AND DOWNFALLS OF GODS, HEROES, AND MONSTERS

Yes-No Questions

7. Yes; protean people are hard to pin down.

8. Yes; it would be desirable but out of reach.
9. Yes; probably, though some might say no.
10. No; it would probably not be a drunken riot.
11. Yes; pandering appeals to illicit knowledge.
12. Yes; it could be your downfall, despite strengths.
13. Yes; nemeses bring disaster, even unjustly.
14. Yes; it could lead to your de-struction.
15. Yes; a Luddite opposes new tech-nology.

Matching

I. (g) or (f) J. (e) K. (b) L. (a)
M. (d) N. (f) O. (c) P. (i) Q. (h)

True-False

R. T S. F T. T U. T V. T

Practice with Word Forms

W. nemeses, nemesis X. Luddite, Luddism Y. bacchanals, bacchanalian Z. panders, pandering.

III. POETIC DEVICES AND FIGURES OF SPEECH

Yes-No Questions

16. Yes; it should be internal.
17. No; Sappho is a great woman poet.

18. Yes; and this question is a haiku.
19. Yes; the sonnets of Petrarch are about love.
20. No; ten syllables, five stresses.
21. Yes; pens do not sing, though they might fly.
22. No; apostrophe addresses something absent.
23. Yes; the comparison uses *as.*
24. Yes; though some people might not get it.
25. No; an epic is a long narrative poem.

Matching

a. (g) b. (l) c. (h) d. (d) e. (i)
f. (j) g. (k) h. (b) i. (e) j. (a)
k. (c)

Matching

l. (e) m. (c) n. (b) o. (f) p. (a)
q. (a) r. (d) or (e)

True-False

s. T t. T u. T v. F w. T x. F
y. T z. T

CHAPTER REVIEW

I. Yes-No Questions

1. Yes; if it were a weak point in your schedule.
2. Yes; in fact, most allusions are to Homer.
3. Yes; if it were out of reach and inspired desire.
4. Yes; it could appeal to the baser instincts.
5. Yes; to Cervantes' Quixote, or *Man of La Mancha.*
6. Yes; Ludd is imaginary, or at least dead by 1816.
7. Yes; a long poem in lines of ten syllables.
8. Yes; your creation could bring you disaster.
9. No; Luddites do not like high technology.
10. Yes; Lilliputians are six-inch tall people!
11. Yes; they would give her contusions, eh, confusion.
12. No; their desires would all be within reach.
13. Yes; you are comparing using *like* or *as.*
14. Yes; a great female poet could write in any form.
15. No; quixotic people stick to ideals, not base desires.
16. No; impossible; all riddles, no straight answers.
17. Yes; sounds enough alike to cause confusion.
18. No; excessive (stupid?) chivalry would win out.
19. No; it would be small. Yes; on Lilliput.
20. Yes; without a doubt.

II. Using Context: Epic Vocabulary

epic, haiku, lilliputian, sonnets, labyrinth, quixotic, *Odyssey,* Luddite, utopia, tantalize, nemesis, Dionysus, Frankenstein, allusions, Achilles' heel, sphinx, Sappho, iambic pentameter, apostrophe(s), personification, protean, aphrodisiac, metaphor

Chapter 11

THE SCIENCES

Quick Reference Word List

acculturation	cybernetics	homeostasis	osmosis
aerobic	demographics	id	pH
autism	ecosystem	inertia	plate tectonics
behaviorism	ego	kinetic	psychosis
calculus	entropy	libido	schizophrenia
catalyst	ethnography	metabolism	superego
chromosome	greenhouse	neurosis	uncertainty
critical mass	effect	Oedipus complex	principle

Introduction: The Language of Science

"Language is a virus." So says the American poet William S. Burroughs. Burroughs means that language acts like a virus—it grows only in living cells, depends on them for sustenance, and, sadly, potentially can destroy its host. On the other hand, anyone who tries to understand AIDS (acquired *immunodeficiency syndrome*) quickly discovers that a virus can also be a "language." To speak about viruses, as well as diseases and other human phenomena, you often need a whole new vocabulary. Medicine is, of course, only one of the sciences with a specialized vocabulary. Some sciences are known as "hard" sciences, such as biology, chemistry, physics, and earth sciences. Others are called social or "soft" sciences. Social sciences study human behavior, such as anthropology, economics, psychology, and sociology. The difference between the two is controversial, but this disagreement can be settled if we remember that science originally meant "knowledge." This chapter includes some of the most important vocabulary words from science. And because vocabulary is such an important part of scientific study, we have included a hefty "More Words" supplement, organized according to kinds of sciences.

I. Keeping the Body in Balance

This section includes words that explain how the body keeps itself in order.

1. **homeostasis** [HOHM ee oh STAY sis]: the tendency of the body to keep a balanced internal state.

Feeling cold? You shiver. Feeling hot? You sweat. Blood sugar too high after cookies? Insulin brings it back down. Too much salt from eating potato chips? Thirst tells you to drink water. Homeostasis is the delicate balance that the body must maintain to protect your internal environment.

• • • • • • • • •

Have You Heard?
Eureka! I Found It!

"Eureka!" ("I have found it!") is what you shout when you discover something valuable. Although most people think of the gold rush when they hear "Eureka," the word comes from Archimedes, an ancient Greek scientist and inventor. Archimedes shouted "Eureka" when he sat in his bath and the water rose. Thus he realized that one could tell the volume of an object by measuring how much water it displaced. This knowledge came in handy, because there was a local debate about the gold content of a royal crown. After measuring the crown's weight and volume, he could determine its mass density, proving that it was not dense enough to be real gold. Popular legend holds that Eureka was actually the name of Archimedes' wife, and he shouted it at his discovery and ran through the town in his towel to share the news with her.

If you shiver at the bus stop on a cold morning, is it a sign that your body seeks homeostasis?

Yes   No   because _____

2. metabolism [meh TAB uh lizm]: the sum of biochemical reactions that keep organisms alive.

"If I could just increase my metabolism, I'd lose weight in no time." Metabolism refers to all the processes that change food into living material and energy. Digestion and respiration are part of metabolism. All living things, including the tiniest cell, engage in metabolism.

If metabolism stopped for very long, would an organism live?

Yes   No   because _____

3. osmosis [oss MOH sis]: the spreading of a fluid through a permeable membrane.

Osmosis is important for homeostasis. A cell with too much salt will attract water to keep balance; and a cell with too much water will diffuse it. Informally, osmosis is a process by which knowledge comes to a person "naturally," without conscious effort.

If you place raisins in water, will osmosis cause them to puff like grapes?

Yes   No   because _____

4. aerobic [ah ROHB ik]: something that requires or uses oxygen.

In biology, aerobic describes any organism that requires oxygen to live. Aerobic exercise, such as jogging or swimming, requires the body to use oxygen. Anaerobic exercise, such as sprinting or weight lifting, relies on the oxygen in the blood, not in the lungs. Anaerobic processes—such as fermentation—take place without oxygen, and anaerobic organisms—such as bacteria—can exist without oxygen.

Could you perform aerobic exercise by holding your breath?

Yes   No   because _____

5. chromosomes [CHROHM uh zohmz]: the threadlike structures in the nucleus of a cell that carry genes.

Chromosomes are made of strands of DNA, the molecule that carries all the genetic information. Humans have forty-six chromosomes. Sex is determined in humans by two chromosomes, an X chromosome, which is female, and a Y, which is male.

Would experts in genetic engineering be experts on chromosomes?

Yes   No   because _____

6. pH [PEE AYCH]: a measure of the strength of an acid or base.

Chemists use pH to measure the acidity or alkalinity of a solution. The pH scale runs from 0 to 14. A solution with neutral pH, such as pure water, is measured as 7. Below 7, you have various degrees of acid; and above 7, various degrees of base. Litmus paper can be used to measure an acid or base.

If a solution had a pH of 3, would it be acidic?

Yes   No   because _____

7. catalyst [CAT uhl ist]: a substance that aids a chemical reaction while remaining unchanged itself.

Enzymes, for example, speed up chemical reactions without being changed. The word *catalyst* often refers to anyone or anything that serves as a force for change: "The stock report was a catalyst that galvanized us into action."

Would a catalyst be destroyed in a chemical reaction?

Yes   No   because _____

Matching: Match the definition with the vocabulary word.

A. ____ All the biochemical reactions that keep an
organism alive.

B. ____ The structures in the nucleus of the cell that
carry genes.

C. ____ The measure of the strength of an acid or base.

D. ____ The tendency of the body to maintain a
constant internal state.

E. ____ Something that requires or uses oxygen.

F. ____ A substance that aids a chemical reaction
without changing itself.

G. ____ The spreading of a fluid through a permeable
membrane.

(a) homeostasis

(b) metabolism

(c) osmosis

(d) aerobic

(e) chromosomes

(f) pH

(g) catalyst

(h) litmus

True-False: Write "T" for true and "F" for false.

H. ____ Shivering is a sign that your body is seeking homeostasis.

I. ____ All living things, including the tiniest cells, engage in metabolism.

J. ____ Cells keep a balance between salt and water solutions
through osmosis.

K. ____ Any exercise that you can perform holding your breath is
aerobic.

L. ____ Sex is determined in human beings by two chromosomes.

M. ____ Litmus paper is used to determine the pH of a solution.

N. ____ Catalysts, such as enzymes, are crucial to metabolism.

For Your Critical Reflection: How many of the body's self-regulating mecha-
nisms do you have conscious control over?

_____

_____

II. Keeping the World Moving

This section deals with vocabulary from physics and the physical world.

8. inertia [ih NIR shuh]: the property of matter that makes a resting object stay there or a moving object keep going unless it is interrupted.

Inertia was one of Newton's three laws of motion: (1) All objects move in a straight line unless acted on by an external force. (2) The speed at which an object accelerates is in direct proportion to the net force exerted. (3) For every action, there is an equal and opposite reaction. Inertia can also describe such human qualities as the tendency to rest or keep moving unless motivated or inspired.

Could inertia be one reason why it is hard to get out of bed in the morning?

Yes   No   because _____

9. kinetic [kih NET ik]: having to do with motion.

Kinetics is the branch of science that deals with the effect of forces on material objects. Kinetic theories are based on the fact that the minute particles of an object are in constant motion even though that object appears at rest. Kinetic energy is the energy an object has because of its motion. An object at rest has potential energy.

Does a baseball in the pitcher's hand have kinetic energy?

Yes   No   because _____

10. critical mass [KRIT uh kul MASS]: the minimum amount of something needed.

In physics, a critical mass is the amount of material needed before a chain reaction can sustain itself. The term *critical mass* is used in other situations as well: an organization needs a critical mass of good workers to survive; a nation may need a critical mass of dissenters before any political change occurs.

If you felt that you were part of a critical mass, would your group have influence?

Yes   No   because _____

11. **entropy** [ENT ruh pee]: a measure of the disorder and energy loss in systems.

One law of thermodynamics states that heat will not flow from a cold to a hot object spontaneously. Because heat energy is constantly lost, the overall entropy or disorder of an isolated system must increase. Once people discovered that entropy was a principle of the universe, they feared that the universe would gradually run out of energy and stop. Such fears are unwarranted. *Entropy* is often used, nevertheless, to refer to the breakdown, disorder, or loss of energy in a system or society.

If your studying is gradually losing focus, substance, and energy, are you experiencing entropy?

Yes   No   because _____

12. **uncertainty principle** [un CIRT en tee PRIN sip ul]: the theory that it is impossible to measure the speed of an electron (or other subatomic particle) while being precise about its location.

In 1934 Werner Heisenberg formulated the uncertainty principle (also called the Heisenberg principle) to explain how hard it is to study subatomic particles: the principle states that you cannot specify the location of an electron and its speed at the same time. Some people extend the meaning of the uncertainty principle to assert the absolute unknowability of all things.

Does the uncertainty principle suggest why studying subatomic particles is so difficult?

Yes   No   because _____

True-False: Write "T" for true and "F" for false.

O. ____ The laws of inertia suggest that without atmosphere a baseball would never curve.

P. ____ A book on a table has kinetic energy.

Q. ____ A critical mass is a group of people who complain about everything.

R. ____ According to entropy, the universe is gradually losing energy and order.

S. ____ The uncertainty principle explains why people are insecure in physics classes.

Using Context: Fill in each blank with the vocabulary word that best suits the context.

Back to the Drawing Board

No one was moving at the physics laboratory; _____ had set in. The energy level was low. No one was inspired. The whole place suffered from _____. A few years ago, the place was constantly moving, the most _____ lab in the country. That energy came from a _____ of young physicists who suddenly felt confident about studying subatomic particles. The new super atomic microscope they had designed promised them astonishing insights. Although Heisenberg had said that one cannot identify the location of an electron and its location at the same time, these scientists were now uncertain about the _____. Just at the height of their hopes, however, uncertainty returned. The federal government cut grants from the National Science Foundation.

For Your Critical Reflection: What is more mysterious and therefore more interesting to study—the inner universe of the human body or the outer universe of the cosmos? Why?

_____

_____

_____

III. Earthlings and Earth Things

13. cybernetics [SY ber NET iks]: the science of communication and control in humans and machines.

Cybernetics comes from the Greek word *kybernetes,* meaning "pilot" or "governor." Cybernetics studies the similarities between the automatic control systems in humans, such as the nervous system, and mechanical and electronic devices. A cyborg is a human being linked to one or more machines for survival.

If you wanted to see how humans are like machines, would you ask an expert in cybernetics?

Yes   No   because _____

14. calculus [KALK yoo lus]: a branch of advanced mathematics.

Calculus gives you a method for describing the rates at which things change. Calculus is usually studied after algebra. The word *calculus* is Greek for "pebble" and Latin for "reckoning stone."

Might calculus be useful in determining the changes in the shape of an airplane wing in cold weather?

Yes   No   because _____

15. plate tectonics [PLATE tek TAHN iks]: a branch of geology concerned with the movement of earth plates.

Earthquake faults and volcanoes are the interests of plate tectonics. There are a dozen or so plates that make up the structure of the earth. Geologists study their motion, faulting, and overlapping. The plates, about thirty miles thick, are roughly the same as the continents but not identical.

If you wanted to know what causes earthquakes or volcanoes, would you study plate tectonics?

Yes   No   because _____

16. ecosystem [EEK oh SIS tum]: all the organisms living together in a place in mutual interdependence.

An ecosystem includes all the living things and their environment. An ecosystem can be very small, such as a pond, or very large, such as the Brazilian rain forest. A pond ecosystem, for instance, might include the muskrats, the fish on which they feed, and the algae on which the fish feed.

Would you change the ecosystem of an ocean if you killed all the sharks?

Yes   No   because _____

17. greenhouse effect [GREEN ows uh FEKT]: the gradual heating of the earth's atmosphere.

In a greenhouse the sun heats the air, but the heat does not escape into the air (in the form of infrared radiation). Instead, the glass traps the radiation, thereby warming the air. The greenhouse on the earth's atmosphere works the same way. When carbon dioxide and other gases from the burning of fossil fuels fill the atmosphere, they trap the infrared radiation. Thus, the earth is gradually warmed.

Could the greenhouse effect have a permanent influence on weather patterns in the world?

Yes   No   because _____

Matching: Match the definition or situation with the vocabulary word.

T. ___ Concerned with earth movement that causes earthquakes.

U. ___ The gradual heating of the earth's atmosphere.

V. ___ All the organisms living together in one place.

W. ___ The science of communications in humans and machines.

X. ___ Advanced mathematics dealing with measuring change.

(a) cybernetics

(b) agronomy

(c) plate tectonics

(d) ecosystem

(e) greenhouse effect

(f) calculus

True-False: Write "T" for true and "F" for false.

Y. ___ A cyborg is a human being linked to one or more machines for survival.

Z. ___ Calculus is studied after algebra.

a. ___ Plate tectonics is a branch of geology dealing with weather prediction.

b. ___ Ponds, deserts, rain forests are all ecosystems.

c. ___ The greenhouse effect is caused by the increased burning of fossil fuels.

For Your Critical Reflection: What kinds of scientists are needed to understand the greenhouse effect? Is solving the greenhouse effect a scientific or political problem?

_____

_____

IV. Freudian Psychology

Sigmund Freud was a physician in Vienna, Austria, in the late nineteenth and early twentieth centuries. He believed that psychological problems could be traced to experiences in early childhood, especially those repressed desires for pleasure or independence. To help these people, he founded psychoanalysis, known as the "talking cure." In psychoanalysis people recollect the circumstances of childhood that repressed or traumatized them, thus leading to understanding. Freud also believed that dreams supply a map of the unconscious conflicts and desires. In this section, you will learn some of the most important vocabulary of psychology, including some from Freud.

18. id [ID]: the part of the psyche that seeks pleasure, power, and death.

Freud believed that the unconscious mind greatly influenced the conscious mind. He also identified different parts of the unconscious. The id is associated with the primitive or instinctual desires of pleasure or aggression, which we see in young children, regardless of social or practical barriers. The id also desires death, because death represents a resting place, an oceanic floating, as in the womb. We are born with an id.

If you desired to consume an entire carton of ice cream, could you blame it on your id?

Yes   No   because _____

19. ego [EEG oh]: the part of the psyche that rationally negotiates the world's demands.

Ego is Latin for "I." The ego is the unconscious negotiator, the adult voice that mediates among the needs of the id, the constraints of the superego, and the realities of the outside world. Your *ego ideal* is your ideal picture of your best self. Ego can also refer to pride, as in "sensitive male ego."

Is your ego the first part of your psyche to develop?

Yes   No   because _____

20. superego [SOUP ir EEG oh]: the part of the psyche that checks behavior and desires according to the rules of parents or community values.

The superego is the unconscious version of parents, ministers, bosses, and rulers of all sorts. The superego controls the desires of the id and sometimes oppresses the rational arguments of the ego. The anxiety or fear that results in neuroses is often caused by an overpowering superego, which threatens grave punishment for any misstep.

Would your superego be different depending on your family, religion, and culture?

Yes   No   because ――――――――――――――――――――――――

21. **libido** [luhb EE do]: psychic or emotional energy, associated with desire for sex or power.

Libido is the goal-oriented energy that comes from the id. *Libido* is Latin for "desire" or "lust." A libidinal desire is, therefore, usually sexual. Some people shift or sublimate their libidos into other activities, such as work, politics, or art. A failed libido refers to a decreased sexual appetite.

Would a person with a raging libido be likely to have little energy?

Yes   No   because ――――――――――――――――――――――――

22. **neurosis** [nurh ROH sis]: a mental disorder producing anxiety, depression, or abnormal behavior.

Neurosis is usually marked by anxiety and fear or neurotic behavior, including excessive worry. Neurotic behavior, although dysfunctional, does not keep a person from leading a life in the real world. Nervousness, compulsive hand washing or cleaning, and fear of crowds, heights, public spaces, and other phobias are forms of neuroses. Psychoanalysis is only good for neuroses.

Would a person terrified of elevators be likely to have a neurosis?

Yes   No   because ――――――――――――――――――――――――

23. **psychosis** [sy KOH sis]: a fundamental mental derangement manifested as a loss of contact with reality.

Psychosis is more serious than neurosis. Psychotic symptoms include hallucinations, manic behavior, and severe withdrawal. An example of a psychosis is schizophrenia. New treatment for psychosis suggests that psychotic individuals actually maintain some contact with reality.

Would a psychotic individual be likely to keep a job as a bank teller?

Yes   No   because ――――――――――――――――――――――――

24. Oedipus complex [ED ih puss COM pleks]: feeling like the parent of your own sex and competing for the love of the other parent.

Freud named this complex after the Oedipus of Greek legend, who unknowingly slew his father and married his mother. Freud believed that all children experience sexual feelings for the parent of the opposite sex. These feelings lead to wanting to be like the other parent but wanting to be better than the other parent, as well. The complex emerges when these are unresolved or lead to shame or guilt.

Might the competition of a boy and his father be a sign of the Oedipus complex?

Yes   No   because _____

Matching: Match the definition or syndrome with the vocabulary word.

d. ____ A severe mental disorder disturbing a person's whole personality.

e. ____ Competing for the love of your parent of the opposite sex.

f. ____ The part of the unconscious that negotiates the world's demands.

g. ____ The part of the psyche that seeks pleasure, power, and death.

h. ____ The part of the psyche that checks behavior according to rules.

i. ____ A mental disorder producing depression or abnormal behavior.

j. ____ Psychic or emotional energy associated with the desire for sex or power.

(a) id

(b) ego

(c) superego

(d) Freudian slip

(e) neurosis

(f) psychosis

(g) Oedipus complex

(h) libido

Using Context: Fill in each blank with the vocabulary word that best suits the context.

The Talking Cure

Freud is credited with the discovery of the unconscious. People had always understood that desires influence behavior, but Freud formulated and acted on the theory that much of what is important in mental life is outside consciousness. The unconscious is not more real or important than the conscious surface but actively present in daily life. Some people sublimate—or shift—their _____ into other socially acceptable activities, such as work, politics, or art. People who suffer from _____, such as obsessive behavior, are disabled in their daily life, unable to work or love fully. Some psychologists believe that the unconscious involves a conflict among three different "voices"—the child's, the adult's, and the parent's. The _____ is the part of the psyche which, like a child, seeks pleasure and power. The _____ is the part of the psyche which, like an adult, takes itself less seriously than its responsibilities. The last part of the unconscious to form is the _____, because it represents the interests of parents or society. Freud believed that some psychic disturbance was normal. All children, he said, experience sexual feelings for the opposite sex, but when these feelings become unresolved, the _____ results. All of these conflicts can be partially resolved by psychoanalysis, which allows people to bring unconscious desires to a conscious level. Some people cannot be helped by the talking cure, however. People with neuroses have mild conflicts. People with a _____, however, are seriously disturbed, suffering from paranoia, delusions, and depressions so severe that daily life is nearly impossible.

For Your Critical Reflection: Besides the reality of the unconscious, how else can you explain "slips of the tongue," memory gaps about things you want to remember, or dreams and nightmares?

_____

_____

V. Human Behavior

25. autism [AUT izm]: a mental illness of the nervous system causing a person to withdraw into a world of fantasy.

Autistics are pathologically self-absorbed. They suffer from a communication disorder and refuse to communicate with others. Autism usually manifests itself from infancy.

Might a baby that offered no response to cuddling or touching be autistic?

Yes   No   because _____

26. schizophrenia [skitz oh FREEN ee uh]: a psychotic mental disorder causing a person to disassociate from reality.

Schizophrenia is not actually a "split personality," although schizophrenics do not seem in control of their own personalities. Many schizophrenics can be cured by drug therapy. Sometimes people loosely use the word *schizophrenic* to describe a pressure from conflicting desires or demands.

Is feeling "schizophrenic" the same thing as having the disorder schizophrenia?

Yes   No   because _____

Stimulus-response behavior in dogs.

The Far Side cartoon by Gary Larson is reprinted by permission of Chronicle Features, San Francisco, CA.

27. behaviorism [bee HAYV yir izm]: a form of psychology focusing on human behavior instead of introspection.

Behaviorists believe human behavior can be changed without reference to a person's unconscious desires or social situations. They focus on changing the stimulation in the immediate environment in order to get a response. Behaviorists study those aspects of behavior that humans share with animals.

Would a behaviorist be likely to experiment with how white rats respond to loud noise?

Yes   No   because _____

28. acculturation [uh CULT yir ay shun]: adapting to the behavior, ideas, or values of a culture.

All babies are born without culture. They become part of their culture through acculturation, a process that anthropologists study. Joining a new culture requires a secondary acculturation, whereby you learn new rules and new ideas. Some students require an extended secondary acculturation when they go to school.

If your career required you to live in another country, would you experience acculturation?

Yes   No   because _____

29. demographics [dem oh GRAF iks]: the statistical characteristics of a human population.

To speak of demographics is to acknowledge social, ethnic, or class groups in society. Demography is the scientific study of different groups in society. Demographics studies the characteristics of different groups, gathering statistical information for marketing or government.

If you requested a study of the demographics in your neighborhood, would you be reading statistics?

Yes   No   because _____

30. ethnography [eth NOG ruh fee]: the study of a group in terms of how its members see themselves.

The prefix *ethno* (as in ethnic) means "cultural group." *Graphy* means "to write." So an *ethnography* is a written study of a cultural group. Your ethnicity is your identification with a racial, national, or cultural group. To be ethnocentric is to hold your own culture as superior to all others.

Would a professional ethnography likely be ethnocentric?

Yes   No   because _____

Matching: Match the definition with the vocabulary word.

    k. ____ The study of a group of people in terms of how they see themselves.

    l. ____ A mental illness causing a person to withdraw into a world of fantasy.

    m. ____ The study of a group in terms of statistical information.

    n. ____ The study of humans focusing on behavior instead of the unconscious.

    o. ____ A mental illness causing a person to disassociate from reality.

    p. ____ Adapting to the behavior, ideas, or values of a culture.

(a) autism

(b) schizophrenia

(c) ethnocentric

(d) acculturation

(e) demographics

(f) ethnography

(g) behaviorism

True-False: Write "T" for true and "F" for false.

    q. ____ Withdrawing from reality through alcohol or drugs is a form of autism.

    r. ____ Schizophrenics experience a split from reality, not a split personality.

    s. ____ Behaviorists study those aspects of behavior that humans share with animals.

    t. ____ Every person experiences acculturation.

    u. ____ The word *demographics* acknowledges differences in social, ethnic, or class groups in society.

    v. ____ To be ethnocentric is to hold your own culture as superior to all others.

For Your Critical Reflection: Why did the behaviorist order a demographic and ethnographic study of schizophrenics?

_____

_____

Chapter Review

I. Yes-No Questions

1. Would a healthy ego help you acculturate?

   Yes   No   because _____

2. Can the greenhouse effect interfere with aerobic production?

   Yes   No   because _____

3. Can autism be discovered in chromosomes?

   Yes   No   because _____

4. Would behaviorists study the Oedipus complex?

   Yes   No   because _____

5. Would calculus be useful in measuring the subtle changes in plate tectonics?

   Yes   No   because _____

6. Can a critical mass of kinetic people be the catalyst for an office suffering from inertia?

   Yes   No   because _____

7. Would experts in cybernetics be interested in metabolism?

   Yes   No   because _____

8. Would demographers study id and ego?

   Yes   No   because _____

9. Can pH measure a damaged ecosystem?

   Yes   No   because _____

10. Is the principle of entropy contradicted by the greenhouse effect?

    Yes   No   because _____

11. Might autistic persons seem ruled by inertia?

    Yes   No   because _____

12. Do the kinetic properties of an object contradict the principles of inertia?

    Yes   No   because _____

13. Can one's libido make one kinetic?

    Yes   No   because _____

14. Might a person neurotically obsessed with earthquakes study plate tectonics?

   Yes   No   because _____

15. Is psychosis acquired through osmosis?

   Yes   No   because _____

16. Might osmosis be interesting to a person studying an ecosystem?

   Yes   No   because _____

17. Might a psychotic person be suffering from schizophrenia?

   Yes   No   because _____

18. Is feeling "schizophrenic" the same as having the psychosis, schizophrenia?

   Yes   No   because _____

19. Can advanced technology diminish the truth of the uncertainty principle?

   Yes   No   because _____

20. Could ethnography tell us about the formation of the superego?

   Yes   No   because _____

II. Using Context: Use the word list at the beginning of the chapter to fill in the blanks. You might not use all the words, or you might use one word more than once.

Science, Knowledge, and Common Sense

Today the word *science* calls to mind lab coats, specimens, and electron microscopes, but originally the word *science* meant "knowledge." Science began with human wonder about how the universe works. Science and myth thus answer the same questions, although science usually conflicts with superstition. For example, people once believed that volcanoes and earthquakes were punishments from a god. But now students of

_____ can offer other reasons. People also once thought that demonic possession or sinful indulgence explained why people withdraw from reality (what we now call _____), why people have hallucinations (sufferers of _____ or

_____), or why people repeat obsessive behaviors or

seem unnaturally afraid (_____ behaviors). By providing

medical reasons for these problems, victims are helped instead of punished.

Science also challenges common sense. Common sense tells us, for in-

stance, that the earth is flat, that the sun revolves around the earth, and

that air is a vacuum. By designing new and precise measuring instruments,

scientists show that invisible things, such as atoms, exist. Litmus paper is a

simple measure of the _____ of a solution, and it can

prevent someone from being burned by an invisible acid. Although a rock

on a hillside seems perfectly still, electron microscopes show us the

_____ activity of molecules. Science seeks to establish

processes, patterns, and stages. Studying enzymes shows how a

_____ can alter a chemical reaction without changing

itself. A _____ would be interested in how humans

and animals both respond to stimuli. And the science of

_____ looks for the similarities between humans and

machines. Even a single-celled organism can be fascinating. How does

a cell "know" how to regulate its water and salt content through

_____? Scientists also like to see how processes work to-

gether to form systems. Many processes work together in the living orga-

nism to provide energy, but _____ is only one of the

complex processes to maintain the body's internal harmony, or

_____. More complex is an _____, in

which many organisms work together to maintain harmony and balance.

When science moves from studying automatic processes to human deci-

sions, it becomes social. Statistics from _____ can provide

information about how many Vietnamese immigrants live in Houston, and

how many are rich or poor or have large families. Further, a sociologist

might try to study the rules of _____, which explain

how these immigrants become accustomed to American culture. However,

a scholar of _____ might complicate these general rules

by interviewing Vietnamese-American families to understand how they feel about this process. Nevertheless, scientists still try to posit rules and laws. Newton's law of thermodynamics, including the principle of _____, which governs objects at rest, is still important to scientists. Having studied many different people, Freud tried to account for conflicts in families through positing an _____ complex which all children experience. Yet the importance of systems can also be seen when they break down. Freud was one of the first scientists to show that what is abnormal can be useful to show us what is normal. So the excessive heating of the atmosphere—called the _____ effect—fascinates a variety of people. Problems can become as interesting as answers. Perhaps this is why Heisenberg, faced with the impossibility of identifying the speed and location of subatomic particles at the same time, still posited a law: the _____.

Reading for Chapter 11

JOHN E. WILLIAMS, ET AL.
Energy and Matter

Energy is the capacity for doing work. Although we may define energy, it is difficult to study because it can only be measured when it is being changed, shifted, released, or absorbed. The study of energy is the unifying concept of physics. Pure physics is concerned with the laws that describe energy transformations. The following passage, from Modern Physics, *an introductory textbook, discusses potential energy, kinetic energy, and the relation between matter and energy—including Einstein's theory of relativity.*

Words to Notice

Optional Exercise: Answer the questions about the following vocabulary words from the reading:

   A. **Designated** means labeled. Would something **designated** have a name?

B. **Arbitrary** means randomly selected. Would you pick your spouse **arbitrarily**?

C. **Inseparably related** means always together. Would things **inseparably related** separate easily?

D. **Associated** means connected in the mind. If you **associated** tuna with nausea, could you eat it?

E. **Verifying** means testing for truth. Would **verifying** an experiment require more work?

F. **Interpreted** means understood. Would all the people who **interpreted** an experiment's results agree?

G. **Imparting energy** means giving energy. If a reaction **imparts energy**, is it useful to humans?

H. **Conserved** means saved. If you **conserved** your energy all the time, would you be an active person?

I. **Continually** means happening repeatedly. If a faucet dripped **continually**, would you have it repaired?

J. **Deviations** are changes. If your experiment had **deviations** every time, could you verify the truth?[1]

1   If a book is pushed off a desk top it falls to the floor. While it is falling it may strike some other object and exert a force on it. In the process, energy is transferred from the book to the other object. Tracing this energy backward, we see that it must have been contained in the book while it was lying on the desk. The book acquired this energy when someone did the work of lifting it to the desk top. *Stored energy in a substance is called potential energy.*

. . .

2   Every moving object has kinetic energy. This statement is the same thing as saying that everything has kinetic energy, because scientists believe that everything in the universe is moving in some way or other. Since the description of the motion of an object depends on another object in the universe designated as being "motionless," we are again faced with the necessity of choosing an arbitrary zero level or, in this case, an arbitrary stationary point. In ordinary, earthbound physics the surface of the earth is considered stationary, and an object resting on the earth's surface is said to have zero kinetic energy even though the object is rotating and revolving with the earth and is undergoing still other motions in and among the galaxies.

. . .

3   There is a constant interplay between potential energy and kinetic energy in physics. Consider the pendulum. When the bob is at the top of its swing, it is

[1] *Answers:* A. Yes B. No C. No D. No E. Yes F. No G. Yes H. No I. Yes J. No

momentarily stationary. At that point all the energy of the bob is gravitational potential except for internal energy (which is also potential). As the bob begins its downward swing, some of the gravitational potential energy changes into kinetic energy. At the bottom of the swing, which we will consider as the zero level for gravitational potential energy, the bob's kinetic energy is at a maximum because it is moving at its maximum rate. As the bob swings up the other side of its arc, the energy interchange is reversed. In an ideal situation, where no friction is involved, the total amount of energy is the same—it is merely changing from one kind to an other. This constancy of total amount of all kinds of energy in a system is called *conservation of energy*.

4   So far we have been discussing matter and energy as though they were two entirely different forms of reality. Yet the two are usually inseparably related. Every object contains some kind of energy. Usually, the idea of energy is associated with some substance like a hot gas or an electrified object. In some cases it may even be necessary to associate energy with the empty space surrounding an electrified object.

5   In 1905, Einstein expressed the relationship between mass and energy with the following equation:

$$E = mc^2$$

in which E stands for units of energy (work units), m stands for mass, and c is the speed of light. Einstein developed this formula entirely from theoretical considerations, and there was no way of verifying it in the laboratory at that time. Recent experiments, however, have shown that such a relationship does exist.

6   Einstein's formula states that mass and energy are proportional to each other, that is, when one increases the other increases also; and when one decreases the other also decreases. The equation may also be interpreted to mean that a given amount of mass is equivalent to a certain amount of energy. Thus, using 3×10^8 m/sec as the speed of light, a mass of one kilogram is equivalent to 1 kg $(3 \times 10^8$ m/sec$)^2$, or 9×10^{16} units of energy.

7   The mass of an object varies with the speed at which it is moving. When the object is at rest with respect to the observer and his measuring instruments, the mass of the object is said to be the *rest mass*. When the object is moving, its mass increases. This new mass, which increases rapidly as the object approaches the speed of light, is called the *relativistic mass* because it is in keeping with Einstein's *theory of relativity*. In the mass-energy equation, m is the relativistic mass.

8   A simple example will serve to illustrate the idea of relativistic mass and its relation to energy. When you throw a ball, you are imparting energy to it. Energy is transferred from you to the ball. The mass-energy equation says that while the ball is moving, its mass will be greater than it was while the ball was at rest. Both the energy and the mass of the ball have increased. The extra mass and energy of the ball both come from you. When the ball stops moving, its mass returns to the original rest-mass value, and its kinetic energy is transformed mostly to heat energy.

9   Throughout this event, the total of mass plus energy was conserved. This fact is expressed in the **_law of conservation of matter and energy:_** _the total amount of matter and energy in the universe remains constant._ According to Einstein's equivalence equation, mass may be converted into energy and energy may be converted into mass. Both processes are going on continually in the universe, but the total of all mass and energy remains constant. This is one of the most important laws of contemporary physics. It should not be assumed, however, that Einstein's mass-energy equation is a proof of the conservation law. Einstein's equation would work even though the matter and energy of the universe were constantly changing. The conservation laws rest on repeated measurements in the laboratory which show that mass and energy are not lost in chemical and physical reactions. Some scientists think that the law of conservation does not hold for large energies and masses in outer space, but this belief has not been verified. The deviations predicted by these scientists are too small for direct measurement with present instruments.

10   The relationship between matter and energy will become evident in the study of physics in still another way. We usually think of light energy in terms of waves and of matter in terms of particles. Actually, there are times when light acts as though it has granular properties. In other words, there are aspects of light that can be explained only by assuming that it is made up of discrete particles. Similarly, particles of matter exhibit wave properties. This wave-particle duality of nature is a key as well as a puzzle in physics, and scientists freely admit that we are far from understanding it completely. Perhaps you will play a role in unlocking this fundamental secret of nature.

Questions for Class Discussion

1. What are some things you have heard about either relativity or Einstein?
2. "Give me a place to stand, and I shall move the world," said Archimedes. Is this possible, according to the modern study of energy?
3. How can the meanings of potential and kinetic energy be extended to describe human activity?

Making a New World

For Class Discussion

1. Some people say the hardest part of learning a science is learning the vocabulary. Is this true? Consider your own experience in science. How did you learn the vocabulary?
2. Heisenberg's uncertainty principle can be extended to assert the absolute unknowability of things. Do you believe this is true? Why would scientists want to posit uncertainty?

3. What has had the most influence on the history of society—biology, physics, chemistry, geology, ecology, psychology, sociology, or anthropology? Which courses in these fields have had the most impact on your thinking?

Collaborative Learning

1. Making the Unconscious Speak
   Purpose: To distinguish the influences of id, ego, and superego.
   A. Make a list of all the things that your unconscious might tell you. Organize these suggestions based on the id, ego, and superego. For instance: id—"Eat the ice cream"; ego—"Too much ice cream will clog your arteries, but at least wait till after dinner"; superego—"Don't eat ice cream, because it's bad."
   B. Share your list with the class.
2. Solving the Greenhouse Effect
   Purpose: To distinguish the interests of different scientific disciplines.
   A. Select three to five of the following experts and make recommendations about how they could help understand and solve the greenhouse effect: (1) experts on plate tectonics, (2) experts on ecosystems, (3) experts on metabolism, (4) experts on psychology, (5) experts on behaviorism, (6) experts in demographics, (7) experts in ethnography, (8) experts in calculus, (9) experts in cybernetics.
   B. Share your recommendations with the class.

Ideas for Writing

1. In a paragraph, describe people who are catalysts.
2. In a page, write a letter to inspire a friend who seems to suffer from inertia and entropy.
3. At home, write an essay about the five scientific concepts, problems, or syndromes that you would like to study.

More Words for Chapter 12

Life Sciences

adaptation: the way an organism adjusts to its environment, usually by evolutionary change

agronomy: the management of farmland

amoeba: a one-celled animal of unfixed shape

anatomy: the structure of an animal or plant

asexual: without sex; reproducing itself without sexual union

biology: the study of life

botany: the study of plants

Brownian movement: the erratic movement of microscopic particles in solutions, mistaken for life, caused by molecule collisions

cardiac: pertaining to the heart

carnivore: a living thing that eats meat

cell: the basic unit of most living things

chlorophyll: the chemical that allows plants to perform photosynthesis

clone: a living being genetically identical to another

congenital: existing from birth

DNA: the molecule that stores genetic information and forms the chromosomes (*d*eoxyribo*n*ucleic *a*cid)

dominant: in genetics, a hereditary character that dominates a recessive character

double helix: the shape taken by DNA

ecology: the study of living things and their environment

endorphins: hormones released in the blood to relieve pain; the cause of the "runner's high"

evolution: the processes by which species are formed and changed through millennia

gene: the part of the DNA that controls heredity

genetic engineering: the alteration of heredity by manipulating DNA

genetics: the study of heredity

herbivore: a living thing that eats plants

heredity: the passing of characteristics to offspring through reproduction

hominids: the biological family that includes humans

horticulture: the science of gardening

hybrid: the offspring of two plants or animals of different varieties

immunology: the study of immunity from disease

in vivo: "in life," that is, in natural form

lipids: fats, oils, waxes

maturation: completion of growth, attaining maturity

metamorphosis: a major change in form
molecule: two or more atoms held together as one unit
morphology: the study of the structure of living things
mutation: changes in chromosomes as genes that affect offspring

omnivore: a living thing that eats both plants and animals
ovum: egg

RNA: a molecule that, with DNA, helps direct cellular activity (*ribonucleic acid*)

sociobiology: the study of heredity's role in shaping social behavior

taxonomy: the classification of living things into groups united by structured similarities based on heredity

vivisection: the cutting up of living animals

zoology: the study of animals

Social Sciences

alienation: a feeling of separateness from society or other people
anthropology: the study of humanity, particularly of human societies
archeology: the study of cultures done by examining physical objects of those cultures
archetype: original or shared patterns, often symbolic
assimilation: becoming part of a new culture by blending with it

blacklist: placing people's names on secret lists to keep those individuals from jobs, housing, and so on

caste: one of four hereditary social classes in Hindu society; a strict class system
Chicana/Chicano: Mexican-American female or male
class: a group of people who share the same social or economic status
culture: the beliefs and customs that distinguish one society from another

ethnocentrism: thinking one's own culture or ethnic group is the ideal norm
eurocentric: thinking European culture is the ideal norm or viewing history from a European perspective
extrovert: someone who is outgoing

gender roles: learned male or female behavior not based on biology

inhibition: something that makes a person afraid to perform an action or hold a belief

introvert: a person who is withdrawn or quiet, occupied with own thoughts and activities

IQ (*intelligence quotient*): a number that is thought to represent intelligence, 100 being average

kangaroo court: a court that violates sound principles of judgment through corruption or incompetence

kinship: family ties though blood or marriage

malpractice: serious incompetence or neglect by a professional, especially a doctor

meritocracy: a society in which superior status is achieved through work and accomplishments, not birth

mores: the values and customs of a society

narcissism: a neurotic state in which the person's emotional energy revolves around one's self

neuro-linguistic programming: the study of how linguistic habits influence the mind

parapsychology: the scientific study of mental phenomena often regarded as supernatural

Peter Principle: the theory that people at work will keep getting promoted until they prove incompetent

prejudice: a hostile and unfair judgment of a race, ethnic group, or individual

regression: childlike behavior exhibited by a mature person

sexism: the belief that one sex is superior to the other

status: the position a person holds in society

taboo: forbidden ideas or actions in a society

xenophobia: fear of strangers, foreigners, or people different from one's group

Physical Sciences

alchemy: a medieval form of chemistry used to convert cheap metal into gold

asteroid: a very small planet

atom: the smallest unit of an element that has all the properties of the element

atomic number: the number of protons or electrons found in an atom

Baconian method: the system of observation and experiment devised by Francis Bacon

buoyancy: the force that causes objects to float

calorie: the amount of heat required to raise one gram of water one degree Celsius

carbon 14: a form of carbon used to date fossils and other ancient objects

combustion: burning

cosmology: the study of the origin and development of the universe

decibel: the unit by which loudness is measured

dehydration: the removal of water

diffusion: the spreading of one substance though another

electrolytes: passing electricity through a substance to cause a chemical reaction

electron: parts of an atom that orbit around its nucleus

equilibrium: a balance of inertia

ion: an atom that has gained or lost one or more electrons

kinematics: the study of motion

light year: the distance light travels in one year (@5,878,000,000,000 miles)

mass: the resistance of an object to acceleration

matter: a substance that has mass

neutron: part of the nucleus of an atom

nova: a new star

nucleus: the center of an atom

optics: the study of light

periodic table: a chart of the chemical elements

proton: a part of the nucleus of an atom

quantum mechanics: the branch of physics that deals with matter at the atomic and subatomic levels

quarks: the smallest particle of matter; quarks have such qualities as "charm"

quasars: the most distant galaxies that can be seen from earth

radiation: energy emitted as waves or particles

relativity: Einstein's theory of light, time, space, and motion

solstice: one of the two days in the year when the sun's distance from earth's equator is greatest (June 22, December 22), causing a shift in seasons

theory: an explanation that has been confirmed by observation or experiment

vacuum: the absence of matter

zodiac: a part of the sky through which the sun, moon, and planets appear to move and in which the twelve constellations of astrology appear

Earth Sciences

acid rain: a type of pollution in which smog chemicals combine with rain
Air Quality Index: the measure of harmful particles in the air
aquifer: an underground river
aurora borealis: a display of light naturally occurring in northern skies

barometer: an instrument that measures the pressure in the atmosphere

continental divide: an imaginary line that cuts a continent in half
core: the central region of the earth
crust: the surface of the earth
cyclone: a storm characterized by circular winds

erosion: the wearing away of soil because of wind or water

fault: places where sections of the earth can shift
fossil: the impression of an ancient organism left in rock
fossil fuels: petroleum, coal, and natural gas

geology: the study of the earth

hydrology: the study of water

mantle: the part of the earth between its core and its crust

ozone layer: the layer of atmosphere composed of a type of oxygen, which absorbs harmful radiation of the sun

paleontology: the study of ancient life forms

renewable resource: any resource (wood, sunshine, etc.) that can replace itself, unlike fossil fuels

solar energy: the light and heat of the sun

water table: the place where someone digging in the ground will hit water

Answer Key to Chapter 11

I. KEEPING THE BODY IN BALANCE

Yes-No Questions

1. Yes; it is shaking the muscles for heat.
2. No; it is crucial to all life.
3. Yes; they are drier than the solution.
4. No; you need air supply for aerobics.
5. Yes; genetics studies chromosomes.
6. Yes; it is below 7.
7. No; catalysts are unaffected by reactions.

Matching

A. (b) B. (e) C. (f) D. (a) E. (d)
F. (g) G. (c)

True-False

H. T I. T J. T K. F L. T M. T
N. T

II. KEEPING THE WORLD MOVING

Yes-No Questions

8. Yes; the body has mass.

9. No; it has potential energy until thrown.
10. Yes; it is an energy source for change.
11. Yes; metaphorically, if not scientifically.
12. Yes; it shows how hard it is to observe them.

True-False

O. T P. F Q. F R. T S. F

Using Context: Back to the Drawing Board

inertia, entropy, kinetic, critical mass, uncertainty principle

III. EARTHLINGS AND EARTH THINGS

Yes-No Questions

13. Yes; she studies the similarities.
14. Yes; calculus measures change.
15. Yes; earthquakes are caused by shifting plates.
16. Yes; they are part of the food chain.
17. Yes; it could warm every region.

Matching

T. (c) U. (e) V. (d) W. (a) X. (f)

True-False

Y. T Z. T a. F b. T c. T

IV. FREUDIAN PSYCHOLOGY

Yes-No Questions

18. Yes; the id comprises childhood desires.
19. No; the id is developed first.
20. Yes; it is socially developed.
21. No; the libido is emotional energy.
22. Yes; it is an unreasonable fear or phobia.
23. No; the job would require mental health.
24. Yes; sons compete for mother's attention.

Matching

d. (f) e. (g) f. (b) g. (a) h. (c)
i. (e) j. (h)

Using Context: The Talking Cure

libido, neurosis, id, ego, superego, Oedipus complex, psychosis

V. HUMAN BEHAVIOR

Yes-No Questions

25. Yes; it seems totally unresponsive.
26. No; the common usage is imprecise.

27. Yes; he would like to measure response.
28. Yes; you would adjust to some degree.
29. Yes; demographics studies the composition of groups.
30. No; ethnography is open to the view of all.

Matching

k. (f) l. (a) m. (e) n. (g) o. (b)
p. (d)

True-False

q. F r. T s. T t. T u. T v. T

CHAPTER REVIEW

I. Yes-No Questions

1. Yes; you could negotiate new roles better.
2. Yes; it traps carbon dioxide, limits oxygen.
3. Yes; it is genetic.
4. No; they are not interested in one's past.
5. Yes; calculus measures all kinds of change.
6. Yes; they would add energy and movement.
7. No; machines do not metabolize, though they use energy.
8. No; these are personal qualities.
9. Yes; the water might be too acidic, say.
10. Yes; we are adding heat energy.
11. Yes; they seem stuck in one place.
12. No; it may be moving at a molecular level.
13. Yes; it can excite or stimulate.
14. Yes; the person is afraid.

15. No; it is inherited, not communicable.
16. Yes; osmosis keeps balance.
17. Yes; schizophrenia is a form of psychosis.
18. No; they are connected only very roughly.
19. Yes; we might be able to observe better.
20. Yes; the superego comes from society.

II. Using Context: Science, Knowledge, and Common Sense

plate tectonics, autism, psychosis or schizophrenia, neurotic, pH, kinetic, catalyst, behaviorist, cybernetics, osmosis, metabolism, homeostasis, ecosystem, demographics, acculturation, ethnography, inertia, Oedipus, greenhouse, uncertainty principle

Chapter
12

COMPUTERS IN THE INFORMATION AGE

Quick Reference Word List

artificial intelligence
(AI)
central processing unit
(CPU)
clock speed/MHz
compatibility
computer
computer literate
data
data-base management
disk drive
graphics
hacker

hardware
hypermedia
interface
I/O device
K and MB
keyboard
memory capacity
menu-driven/window-
driven programs
microcomputer/personal
computer (PC)
modem
monitor

mouse
network
printer
programmer
RAM
ROM
software
spreadsheet program
telecommunications
user friendly
word processing
program

Introduction: Do You Talk Computer?

"I'd really like to get into computers." Many people express this wish. Every day computers touch our lives, from the bar codes on grocery products and the automatic teller at the bank to our personal records at the IRS. Experts predict that by the year 2000, over half of all working hours will be spent on keyboards in front of computer screens. Car mechanics, for example, now spend as much time in front of computers as under hoods. The information age has brought along its own technical vocabulary, or jargon, called *computerese*. This chapter is designed to enhance your familiarity with the most important computer vocabulary and to increase your computer literacy. Studying this chapter should make it easier for you to take computer classes, buy a computer, or get a running start in a high-tech world.

I. Welcome to the Information Age

Living in the information age means that information becomes the most valued product. People who have information and can manipulate it powerfully become the most important "workers" in society. Begin your mastery of the information age with these words.

. . . .

Have You Heard?
What Are Sick Computers?

Computers, like people, can get sick. But they get sick in different ways. When humans have a virus, such as the cold or flu, we sometimes say, "He caught a bug." But in the world of computers a bug and a virus are drastically different. A *computer bug* is an error or defect in the program, usually caused by an accidental mistake by a programmer. To repair a bug, or to debug, you need to rewrite the program until all the bugs are out. Bugs are limited to one program and usually to one crucial step in it.

Viruses are a wholly different matter. Viruses are small programs—so small that you cannot easily detect them—that someone, usually a hacker, purposely writes to interfere with your computer. Viruses are designed to upset operations and to cause damage. A virus can get into the computer's memory and copy itself, spreading its menace to other programs. At a time set by the hacker, the virus goes off and begins to destroy.

Viruses can change information, destroy data on disks, disable programs, or send up unexpected messages, such as I LOVE YOU, KISS OFF, or WE SAID DON'T COPY: NOW YOU'VE HAD IT! In their worst form, viruses can destroy computer equipment. To counteract viruses, computer programmers design programs that can track down viruses, called vaccines. Viruses are designed to spread, so careful computer owners avoid sharing software.

1. **computer literate** [com PYOOT ir LIT ir uht]: to understand and use computer terms easily and correctly.

To be computer literate means that you understand much of the shoptalk (or jargon) of the computer world. This is no small task: a recent dictionary of computer terms has over forty-five hundred terms. To get computer literate, talk to people who use computers; browse computer stores, books, and magazines; or start using a computer yourself.

If you learn the meaning of all the words in this chapter, will you be on your way to computer literacy?

Yes   No   because _____

2. artificial intelligence (AI) [ART eh FISH uhl in TELL ih jens]: programs designed to make computers imitate human thought.

People who work in artificial intelligence, or AI, try to make computers "think" like humans. Some AI programs teach computers to play chess and even learn by their mistakes!

If you learned everything you know from computers, would you have artificial intelligence?

Yes   No   because _____

3. hardware [HARD WEAR]: the physical devices that make up a computer system.

Hardware refers to all the parts of the machine that compute information.

Would you be computer literate if you thought hardware referred to the screwdrivers used to repair computers?

Yes   No   because _____

4. software [SOFT WEAR]: the programs or instructions that tell a computer what to do.

Software programs are the mind of the computer. Designing computer software means writing instructions to make computers process information in a certain way. These instructions are known as *routines*.

If you designed routines to make a computer calculate your grades, would you be writing software?

Yes   No   because _____

5. programmer [PROH gram ir]: a person whose job is to design, write, and test software.

Programmers rewrite problems into a language that computers can understand and obey.

Might a programmer design software to create artificial intelligence in a computer?

Yes   No   because _____

6. hacker [HACK ir]: someone who enjoys breaking into secret computer systems.

Hackers are extremely talented computer users. Partly by deep study and partly by trial and error, hackers learn to get information from secret and complicated computer files. Hacking is illegal.

If you accessed your school computer and changed all your grades to A+, would you be a hacker?

Yes   No   because _____

7. K and MB (kilobytes and megabytes) [KAY and EM BEE]: ways to measure the quantity of information a computer (or other digital technology) can measure or hold in memory.

Bit stands for binary digit. A digit (1 or 0) is how numbers appear in binary notation. "Digital technology" is another way of saying computerized.

A *byte* is roughly equivalent to one character (word or number) entered into the computer.

Kilo means one thousand, but a kilobyte, abbreviated *K*, is actually 1,024 bytes. *Mega* means a million, but a megabyte, abbreviated *MB* or *meg*, represents 1,048,576 bytes. K and MB are typically used to measure memory and storage capacity. Thus, a desktop computer may have from "4K to 128K in ROM" or "64K to 2MB in RAM." Users talk about personal computers with "20-meg," "40-meg," or "80-meg" hard disks when they discuss storage capacity.

If your word processing program had 6K of data, and your computer had 4K capacity, would the program be usable?

Yes   No   because _____

8. data [DAY tuh or DAT uh]: raw pieces of information entered into and received from a computer.

Shoe prices, customer addresses, or your birthdate—all these are data. In formal usage, data is a plural noun; datum is singular, but most computer users ignore the difference.

If you felt overwhelmed by the number of data on your job, might you enter them into a computer?

Yes   No   because _____

Matching: Match the definition with the vocabulary word.

A. ___ Information processed by a computer.

B. ___ Expert at breaking into systems.

C. ___ Ways of measuring storage capacity and memory.

D. ___ Instructions to make a computer work.

E. ___ Physical equipment of computing.

F. ___ Making machines think and learn.

G. ___ Person who writes software.

H. ___ Familiar with computer technology.

(a) computer literate

(b) artificial intelligence

(c) hardware

(d) programmer

(e) software

(f) hacker

(g) K and MB

(h) data

(i) access

Using Context: Fill in each blank with the vocabulary word that best suits the context.

The Sales Pitch

Have I got a system for you! Don't be shy. You don't have to be a professional _____ to learn to compute on my machines. Now, let's start with _____, that is, the computer, monitor, keyboard, and printer. This DATAMASTER is a fine machine. Designed by experts in the field of _____, it's so friendly that it thinks like a human. Do you have problems with numbers, information, and other kinds of _____? Don't worry. The DATA-MASTER has a huge amount of memory capacity, so you can run almost any _____ on it. You can start with 640 _____ and advance up to 2 _____. Can you imagine how many _____ and _____ we are talking here? Maybe you know very little about computers; maybe you are not the most _____ person on the block. But I promise that with this little system, you'll be processing and programming like a happy _____ in no time flat.

For Your Critical Reflection: Can you remember situations where you wish you were more computer literate? Can you imagine situations in which being computer illiterate might cause someone problems?

_____

_____

II. Computer Hardware

9. **computer** [com PYOOT ir]: a machine for solving problems or manipulating data.

Computers come in three types: *microcomputers,* for home and desk use; *minicomputers*, about the size of washing machines, for use in small offices; and *mainframes*, large-scale computers for large businesses and institutions.

If you want to modernize your accounting system, would a minicomputer be faster than a microcomputer?

Yes   No   because _____

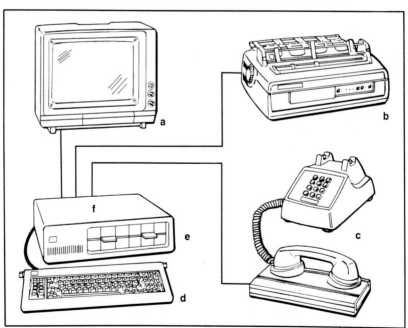

A typical PC system: (a) monitor (b) printer (c) modem (d) keyboard (e) disk drive (f) central processing unit

10. ROM [ROMM]: factory-programmed memory that starts a computer running; acronym for read-only memory.

ROM is a computer program designed by the factory. It cannot usually be re-programmed. Read-only memory means that it can be read from, but cannot be "written onto," that is, changed. ROM (and anything saved on it) is not lost when the computer is turned off.

If I turned off the computer for a week, would I lose the program on the ROM chip?

Yes   No   because _____

11. RAM [RAMM]: the "working memory" of the computer; acronym for random access memory.

RAM is the memory used for programs and data when the computer is in use. RAM can be read from and written to. The content of RAM changes often; if the contents are not stored or saved, they are lost when the computer is turned off.

Would a limited RAM allow you to use a large, complicated program on your computer?

Yes   No   because _____

12. central processing unit (CPU) [SEN truhl PRAH sess ing YOO nit]: the "brain" of the computer that controls the basic operations of a computer.

The CPU is a complicated integrated circuit (IC) chip. Also known as the microprocessor, the CPU rests on the main circuit board of the computer (called the "motherboard").

If someone offered you a discount computer system without a CPU, should you buy it?

Yes   No   because _____

13. I/O device [EYE OH dehv ice]: the name for any of the input/output devices connected to a computer.

I/O devices are used to get data into and out of a computer. Your keyboard is an input device. Your monitor and printer are output devices. Your disk drive is both an input and an output device. I/O devices, sometimes called *peripherals,* are connected to computers through special plugs called *ports*. There are *serial ports* and *parallel ports*.

If you bought a computer without any I/O ports, could you use your keyboard?

Yes   No   because _____

14. monitor [MON iht or]: the TV-like screen for displaying information.

The monitor displays the data you input with your keyboard. Data that appears on the screen is called *soft copy*, in contrast to *hard copy*, which is printed on paper.

If your eyes got tired using a computer, would watching the monitor probably be the cause?

Yes   No   because _____

15. keyboard [KEE BORHD]: an input device that looks like a typewriter, but has more keys.

The keyboard inputs or writes data into the computer's RAM. The keyboard includes all typewriter keys, plus such other keys as Escape, Control, Alternate, and so on.

If you are already familiar with typewriters, would a computer keyboard be strange to you?

Yes   No   because _____

16. mouse [MOWS]: a device for moving the cursor around a computer's display screen.

The cursor is the flashing mark that shows where the next character will be typed on the display screen of a computer's monitor. A mouse lets you move the cursor without using keys. A typical mouse has one small button and sits on a flat surface or in the palm of your hand.

If your computer came with a bug and a mouse, would you exterminate them both?

Yes   No   because _____

17. disk drive: the data reader or "tape player" of the computer.

The disk drive reads data from a disk and copies it into the computer's RAM to be used. A hard disk drive is an internal drive that holds an aluminum disk. The floppy disk drive reads from plastic or floppy disks, sometimes called *diskettes*. The program that manages the disk is called DOS (disk operating system).

If you wanted to save your brilliant ideas, would you put a diskette in the disk drive and command the computer to save them?

Yes   No   because ——————————————————————————————

18. printer: an output device that produces hard (paper) copy of computer information or graphic images.

Printers put data and images on paper. A dot-matrix printer uses small dots, called pins, to make its mark, much like a typewriter. A laser printer works like a copy machine. When a printer is *on line*, it is communicating with the CPU and is ready to run.

Before you make a hard copy of a document, should you check to see if the printer is on line?

Yes   No   because ——————————————————————————————

19. modem [moh DEM or MOH dem]: a device that allows computers to talk to one another over telephone lines.

A modem allows you to receive electronic mail (or E-MAIL), to reach (or access) data from other computers, and to partake in electronic conversation.

If you wanted to communicate with people through the computer, should you ask them if they have a modem?

Yes   No   because ——————————————————————————————

True-False: Mark "T" for true and "F" for false.

I.   ____ Without a mouse, you could not move the cursor around the screen.

J.   ____ Monitor, video monitor, and computer screen generally refer to the same I/O device.

K.   ____ The keyboard looks like a typewriter but has more keys.

L. ____ When you want a hard (paper) copy of your data, you send it through a disk drive.

M. ____ A computer without I/O devices would be completely useless.

N. ____ All computers must have CPUs.

O. ____ *Floppy* and *hard* are both terms used to describe kinds of disk drives.

P. ____ All computers are basically the same size.

Q. ____ ROM stands for write-on memory.

R. ____ RAM is a memory programmed by the factory so that it cannot be erased.

S. ____ A modem allows you to have a computer conversation over telephone lines.

Using Context: Fill in each blank with the vocabulary word that best suits the context.

Mother Gets a Computer

As soon as I unpacked the hardware for the new _____ that my family gave me for Christmas, I began to assemble it. Now I finally had the technology to keep my home business (and my home!) in order. First I connected the computer to the numerous _____ that came along with it. Then, I turned it on. I could just imagine the central brain of the computer, the _____, awaking from slumber. The factory-programmed _____ went though its routines quickly, and I was soon ready to input data. The instructions said I had 640K in _____, so I knew I had plenty of room to write. I inserted the disk with *WordSoul*, my word processing program, into the _____ and copied it onto the computer's hard disk. I dropped both hands on the _____ (I had long been an experienced typist) and began writing a warm and loving thank you letter to my family. They insisted I thank Santa, but I knew they had saved their pennies. To move the cursor around, I had the choice of using the keyboard keys or the cute little _____. After composing a beautiful letter, I decided to store the document for later. This was one collection of bytes I did not want to lose. One of my children suggested that I send a soft copy of the letter to Uncle Kim in Los Angeles via electronic mail. So I plugged the computer to the telephone lines, using my _____ , dialed his access number, and sent a copy to his data base. My family was impressed with my writing, but they all wanted a copy of the letter. To make a hard copy for each one, I connected the dot-matrix _____ by plugging the cable into the _____ port designed for that purpose, made sure the printer was on line, and produced twenty-five copies for each of the children who live with me in the shoe.

For Your Critical Reflection: For the vast majority of people, computers are tools to help them do what they normally do better. Which of the pieces of hardware is most familiar to you now? Which would you like to become familiar with?

_____

_____

III. Software and Computer Applications

Computer applications are all the tasks a computer can perform for you. Here are some of the mainstream applications.

20. **word processing program** [werd PRAH sess ng PROH gram]: a software system that allows you to write, revise, manipulate, format, and print documents.

Word processing makes writing much easier. Some word processing programs include spell checkers, grammar checkers, and thesauruses. Word processing programs are constantly redesigned to make them faster and easier.

Might a word processing program help you to write the "great American novel"?

Yes   No   because _____

21. spreadsheet program [SPRED sheet PROH gram]: a software system that uses the memory of the computer as a large worksheet for numbers and formulas.

Spreadsheet programs are especially designed for bookkeeping, accounting, and business planning. A spreadsheet allows you to make any calculations you normally make with a pencil and paper.

If you were a high-tech tax consultant, might you use a spreadsheet program?

Yes   No   because _____

22. data-base management [DAYT uh BASE MAN ij mehnt]: a software program that allows you to systematically store, update, and retrieve data.

A data base is organized to make particular items of information easy to locate and reach (or access). Data is typically arranged in rows (records) and columns (fields).

Can a standard dictionary, a list of good restaurants, or the batting averages of your favorite team be put on a data base?

Yes   No   because _____

23. graphics [GRAF iks]: computer-generated pictures produced on screen, paper, or film.

Graphics can range from a single bar graph to studio-quality artwork. Business graphics include bar graphs and pie charts that visually explain data from sales, inventory, and profits.

If you wanted to illustrate your comparative GPA for the last six semesters on a bar graph, might you use a graphics program?

Yes   No   because _____

24. telecommunications [TELL uh cuh MYOON ih KAY shuns]: the transfer of data from one place to another over communication lines.

Telecommunications provide an alternative to travel and face-to-face communication. A teleconference is an "electronic meeting" conducted among people at distant locations through telecommunications.

If you shared data with another computer user through a modem and telephone lines, would you be telecommunicating?

Yes   No   because _____

25. network [NET wirk]: a system for linking microcomputers.

A network allows microcomputers to communicate with one another and to share I/O devices, software, and data bases. A network is not the same as a mainframe computer connected to different stations, or *terminals*. That is why network users sometimes call their system a LAN (limited access network). An example of a LAN might be twenty-four computers, five printers, and one large computer that holds all the data (sometimes called a *server*).

If your computer was on a network, would you probably share either software or an I/O device with another computer?

Yes   No   because _____

26. hypermedia [HIGH per MEED ee uh]: a technology that combines film, video, computer graphics, sound, music, and text in a unified system, all from a personal computer.

Hypermedia is a system for organizing and using different types of audiovisual and textual information. You can "call up" a definition of the word *mitosis* from a dictionary, then call up a series of slides demonstrating the splitting of cells, and finally call up a video of a professor explaining the concept to a lab of students (see reading selection in this chapter).

Would hypermedia allow you to study from texts, pictures, and videos in the same sitting?

Yes   No   because _____

Matching: Match the function with the technology.

T. ____ Provides a master list of your happiest customers.

U. ____ Helps you design art for the cover of a report.

V. ____ Helps you write letters, proposals, and reports.

W. ____ Allows you to hold a sales meeting without traveling.

X. ____ Combines audiovisual and textual types of data.

Y. ____ Calculates your profits and losses automatically.

Z. ____ Allows all the computers in your office to share a printer.

(a) word processing program

(b) spreadsheet program

(c) data-base management

(d) graphics

(e) telecommunications

(f) server

(g) hypermedia

(h) network

Using Context: Fill in each blank with the vocabulary word that best suits the context.

The English Department Goes High Tech

Mr. Seeger was the most modern English teacher I ever had. We took our class in the computer lab and wrote all of our essays using a

_____ program. The textbook, called *Writing the Nutty Way,* was placed onto a disk, and we all could access it through the limited access _____, or LAN system. Quick and entertaining explanations, lectures, and even videos on how to get ideas, organize, or write with style were available through a _____ system. But writing was still not easy, because Mr. Seeger wanted information, not just opinions. We had to back up our statements with facts from a _____ of world statistics. It was more entertaining to use the _____ package to illustrate our papers with charts, graphs, or even humorous cartoon figures. Also, Mr. Seeger asked us to calculate and graph our most common grammar mistakes, and the

_____ program came in handy for that. One more thing

made this a modern class. I never learned what Mr. Seeger looked like. He

stayed at his beautiful mountain home the whole semester, yet his guid-

ance was always available, because we communicated using a modem and

a _____ program.

For Your Critical Reflection: If you could invent a computer software program to do anything possible, what would it do and what would you call it?

_____

_____

IV. Choosing Hardware and Software

Here are some key terms you will need to know when you are in the market
to buy a personal computer (PC) or software for yourself.

27. microcomputer/personal computer (PC) [MIKE roh cum PYOOT ir]: a
complete computer system designed to fit on the top of a desk.

Also called a home computer or desktop, a microcomputer includes a CPU,
I/O devices, and storage devices (disk drives), usually in one box or package.

When people talk about PCs, desktops, home computers, and microcomputers,
are they usually talking about different things?

Yes   No   because _____

28. memory capacity [MEM ir ee kuh PASS eh tee]: the amount of data that
can be kept in a computer's RAM.

Memory is expressed in terms of computer bytes (kilobytes or megabytes). Storage capacity, which is measured the same way, refers to the number of data
that can be stored in hard or floppy disks. Buffer capacity refers to how much
a program or printer can hold in waiting while the computer is active with
another process.

If a software program required 840K of RAM and your computer only had 640K
capacity, would you be able to use the software?

Yes   No   because _____

"I'd like a Jaron 1000 PC with an 80486 CPU running at a 33-MHz clock speed; 2 megs RAM expandable to 16 megs; 8 expansion slots composed of 2 8-bit, 5 16-bit, and 1 32-bit; a 1.2-meg floppy drive; a 40-meg hard disk; a socket for an 80387 math co-processor; MS-DOS, OS/2, and XENIX ready; and a Super VGA CRT."

Drawing by Cheney; © 1990 The New Yorker Magazine, Inc.

29. clock speed/MHz (megahertz) [klok speed/MEG uh hurtz]: the way to measure how fast a computer can process data.

The clock speed is a measure of the processing power of a machine. Megahertz (MHz) stands for one million cycles per second. The higher the megahertz, the faster the clock speed, and the more powerful the machine.

If you needed a computer to process data and commands very fast, would you ask the computer salesperson about MHz?

Yes   No   because _____

30. compatibility [cum PAT uh bill uh tee]: the quality of some software to run on machines other than the one it was designed for.

Computers, software, and I/O devices must be compatible. An IBM or DOS-compatible machine should run software designed for IBMs. Apple-compatible printers should work well with Apple computers.

If a certain software program is not compatible with your computer, should you buy it?

Yes   No   because _____

31. interface: the way that people, computers, and I/O devices come together.

As a noun, *interface* refers to the connection between the face of a person and the computer screen. A typical interface is the keyboard and the monitor. The mouse is another kind of interface. Advanced technology now allows a *voice-activated interface,* meaning the computer can take oral commands. When used as a verb, *to interface* means to connect smoothly.

Is a voice-activated interface easier to use than a mouse-driven interface?

Yes   No   because _____

32. menu-driven/window-driven programs: software that presents your options in a window on the screen; easy to use.

Some software programs show your choices (or menu) right on the screen. Sometimes a menu appears in a "window" (or small box) at the bottom of the screen. A menu-driven program keeps you from having to use a manual all the time.

Would a menu-driven program with windows be good for a beginning computer user to purchase?

Yes   No   because _____

33. user friendly: a computer or program that is easy to use.

As computers get more user friendly, almost everyone can use them.

Can you use the phrase *user friendly* to describe a window-driven software program?

Yes   No   because _____

True-False: Write "T" for true and "F" for false.

a. ____ If a printer was compatible with an Apple computer, it would be too powerful for it.

b. ＿＿ Microprocessors, PCs, personal computers, and desktop computers are the same.

c. ＿＿ If Alphabyte provides 16MHz clock speed and Betabyte 8MHz, Alphabyte would be faster.

d. ＿＿ User-friendly equipment means that a person must be computer literate to use it.

e. ＿＿ A computer with a 2-megabyte RAM has more memory capacity than one with a 2-kilobyte RAM.

f. ＿＿ *Menu-driven* refers to a computer hacker who cannot stop munching between programs.

g. ＿＿ If a computer and printer are not compatible, they will not interface.

h. ＿＿ For most users, the memory capacity of the ROM is not as important as that of the RAM.

i. ＿＿ If someone said your RAM was too small, you might want to feed it more often.

j. ＿＿ *To interface* is to meet with other computer users and share chips and bytes.

Using Context: Fill in each blank with the vocabulary word that best suits the context.

Buying the Perfect Computer

My aunt asked me to purchase some hardware and software for her new international antique dealership. This was not an easy task, because we needed something that could process data fast, something with at least 16 MHz ＿＿＿＿＿＿＿＿＿＿, and something that would be ＿＿＿＿＿＿＿＿＿＿ with the IBM computer she already had. Further, because she had collected a large data base of antique dealers around the world, we needed something with a hefty storage capacity, at least 2MB in the RAM. My aunt was not an experienced computer user, however, so we needed hardware that was ＿＿＿＿＿＿＿＿＿＿. We purchased a ＿＿＿＿＿＿＿＿＿＿ for her desktop, and a cute little laptop portable for her trips to Tibet. The data-base management system we purchased was high-level, but comparatively friendly, because it was

_____. Once we made sure all the machines could
_____ without any difficulty, we were ready to go. Now,
where is that list of all the dealers in Paris who are interested in Chinese
scrolls?

For Your Critical Reflection: Some people say you should buy a computer
when you are sure you can use it. Other people say if you get a computer
you will find ways to use it. Which side is correct? Which do you think a
computer salesperson believes?

_____

_____

Chapter Review

I. Yes-No Questions

1. Can learning too many computer terms make you artificially
   intelligent?

   Yes   No   because _____

2. Do you measure how long it takes to become computer literate by
   clock speed?

   Yes   No   because _____

3. Is it more important for I/O devices to be compatible than to be user
   friendly?

   Yes   No   because _____

4. Is a computer and a CPU the same thing?

   Yes   No   because _____

5. Can you turn information or ideas into data by entering them into the
   computer?

   Yes   No   because _____

6. Would a data-base management program be useful for registration at
   college?

   Yes   No   because _____

7. Should a disk drive have memory capacity?

   Yes   No   because _____

8. Would an artist be more interested in a graphics program than a hacker would be?

   Yes   No   because _____

9. Can hardware and software interface if they are not compatible?

   Yes   No   because _____

10. Do I/O devices help you identify hackers?

   Yes   No   because _____

11. Do we measure clock speed by kilobytes?

   Yes   No   because _____

12. Is the keyboard an I/O device?

   Yes   No   because _____

13. Can modems be useful to companies with computers in different countries?

   Yes   No   because _____

14. Would a telecommunications program be useful if you lived two hundred miles from work?

   Yes   No   because _____

15. Does a monitor show you what characters you have inputed?

   Yes   No   because _____

16. Are bugs, viruses, and mice equally damaging to your computer?

   Yes   No   because _____

17. Is a menu-driven program more user friendly if it has windows?

   Yes   No   because _____

18. Does a network allow you to interface with other computer users?

   Yes   No   because _____

19. Would a hypermedia program allow you to coordinate texts and images?

   Yes   No   because _____

20. Is RAM capacity more important than ROM?

   Yes   No   because _____

II. Using Context: Use the word list at the beginning of the chapter to fill in the blanks. You might not use all the words, or you might use one word more than once.

Computers in Your Life

A recent dictionary of computer terms had over forty-five hundred entries, so becoming _____ is not easy. But how much literacy do you need? That depends on the size of the _____ you work around. Most desk people at stores, offices, and hospitals enter _____ such as your name, address, and phone number while complicated _____ programs organize them. On the other hand, if you want to be a _____ and write programs or a _____ and learn to break into them, you will need to know much more. If you work for a small business, you will probably use desktop computers; these _____, as they are called, are very powerful. In fact, their memory and storage capacity have become so mammoth that people measure them more in _____ than in _____. At a smaller business, the computer applications will probably include some kind of _____ program for writing letters, a _____ program for calculating sales and inventory, and a _____ package for creating charts, pies, and other visuals. In college you may work on a _____ that allows you to share software, peripherals, and ideas with other students. Other educational applications include the use of _____ to bring together ideas and information from texts, slides, videos, and music. If you buy a home computer for yourself, you might want to ask hard questions: ''Does it have _____ software so that I can use windows instead of flipping through the manuals for options? What is the _____, that is, how fast is the CPU? How many pins are in the dot-matrix _____? Does my _____ have all the keys I need? If I need to move the

cursor around the page fast, can I get a _____? Are the
software and hardware _____ so that the computer and
the I/O devices can _____ with one another?" Finally, if
you want to communicate with people from long distances via telephone
lines, ask "May I have a _____ program and a
_____ please?"

Reading for Chapter 12

RICHARD PASKE

Hypermedia: A Brief History and Progress Report

> Hypertext *and* hypermedia *are terms you will hear more and more
> on college campuses. They describe some of the most exciting computer
> applications to learning, thinking, and using the imagination. In the
> following essay, Richard Paske, an instructor in arts education, de-
> scribes some of the exciting options that hypermedia gives to students.
> Of course, hypermedia requires creative, innovative designers, too, and
> perhaps this article will inspire you to design presentations of your own.*

Words to Notice

Prepare for the reading by reviewing the following key words:

digital communications:
  communication that uses bits (or
  binary digits)
scenario: a possible scene
voice commands: a form of interface
hierarchical: from top to bottom, most
  important to least
scrolling: scanning several pages of text
  or instruction on the computer screen

animated graphic: a graphic
  that appears to be alive
video icon: a little picture on
  the computer screen
invigorated: filled with
  energy
antecedent: something that
  comes before
denote: refer

1   As a prelude to what the next phase of the digital communications revolution
has in store for us, consider the following scenario from the first half of the 21st
century. In this imaginary scene, you play the role of a pre-medical student
studying non-human physiology for a required course. Your assignment is to

familiarize yourself with the muscular structure of *C. Taurinus*, a member of the genus *Connochaetes*, more commonly known as a wildebeest or gnu. You address your computer in plain English (and Latin), "Get me information on *C. Taurinus*." Since your computer understands voice commands, the screen begins to fill with information in under a minute.

2   Because the computer "knows" you are a pre-med student it presents the results of its search in hierarchical fashion, graphically emphasizing the data most immediately appropriate for your needs. A window labeled "*C. Taurinus*" occupies the left third of the screen and contains a long listing of all current research papers dealing with wildebeest physiology. Buttons along one edge of this window allow you to arrange its contents by article title, publication, author, date or subject via mouse or verbal command. Below it is a smaller window labeled "Related Topics" containing titles of related articles. They cover subjects such as the geography, plant and animal ecology, cultural anthropology, and history of the Serengeti Plain where the wildebeest resides, the country Tanzania on which the plain lies, and the greater region of East Africa. This window also contains buttons to let you easily organize and navigate its contents.

3   Scrolling through the primary topic window you find an article assigned by your professor. Since you don't feel much like talking, you use the mouse instead to choose and open the article for reading, viewing and listening. In about 30 seconds two more windows appear. One contains a still from the video portion of the article; the other contains the text. Both windows have re-sizing controls so that either can take over the entire screen if you wish an expanded view.

4   Controls in the video window also let you play a clip of broadcast-quality color video showing a wildebeest running through the brush of its native habitat. Speed and direction buttons control viewing at regular, fast, or slow-motion speeds, both forwards and backwards. Another control exposes an animated graphic of the skeletal and/or muscular structure of the animal as it runs, for comparison with the external view.

5   While carefully studying the neck muscles of the video wildebeest as it runs forward, a fleeting image comes from your childhood. You remember a Saturday afternoon trip to a natural history museum with a magical collection of African masks. One image stands out clearly in your mind: a large wooden wildebeest head. You say to the computer, "Get information relating masks and wildebeests." In less than a minute a window labeled "Masks and Wildebeests" appears, overlaying most of the "Related Topics" window. Along with the titles of a number of scholarly print articles, this window contains titles of video documentaries on African arts and culture. You click on the video icon next to the title of one that catches your eye.

6   In a few seconds a second video window overlays the first and immediately begins playing a video of sculptors talking and singing about the creative process as they fashion masks with wood and paint. As soon as this segment stops playing, a flashing icon appears over the frozen image of the last frame. The icon is a small still of a related video clip and is labeled "Ritual." Clicking on it

displays a 5-minute film of a Tanzanian nighttime ritual complete with music from a 10-member percussion and vocal ensemble, a scene of masked dancers encircling a bonfire, and the sounds of the natural environment in the background. Invigorated by your contact with these creative cultural expressions of wildebeests, you return to your physiology lesson.

7   Sound fantastic? Admittedly our current level of digital communications technology is missing a number of the pieces required to build a system with sufficient capability to make this scenario a reality. But just as assuredly, current trends and developments in both the industrial and educational fields show that we are well on the way.

DEFINITIONS AND ORIGINS

8   First, let's define the word "hypermedia." Its historical antecedent is "hypertext," a term coined by Ted Nelson in the early 1960s to mean "...*non-sequential writing*, text that branches and allows choices to the reader, best read at an interactive screen."

9   While studying philosophy and sociology at Harvard, Nelson had been frustrated in his efforts to physically represent the linkages his mind was making between the material he was learning in one class with material from another. With no formal training in computers he nevertheless envisioned an electronic system by which these linkages could be physically represented and stored for future reference. Somewhat of a global anarchist, his vision is of a universal information utility that allows every person on the planet access to everything ever written. His Xanadu Project attempts to make this vision a reality and is, in fact, now being developed for commercial use by Autodesk, Inc., makers of AutoCAD.

10   Nelson coined the term "hypermedia" somewhat later to describe a higher bandwidth technology that combines film and video, computer graphics, sound, music and text in a unified information-delivery system centered upon the personal computer. The "hyper" part of the term means "beyond" or "over"; the "media" portion means "channel of communication." Together they denote a system of audio-visual and textual communication that allows users to interactively navigate through a multimedia information base using their intuition, memory, and interest as a guide.

Questions for Class Discussion

1. Would you be interested in studying via hypermedia?
2. Which courses do you think would be best suited for hypermedia? Which would be badly suited?
3. What would you say if the course you are now in were translated into a hypermedia program? What would be the advantages and disadvantages? Do you think you would study more, less, or about the same?

Making a New World

For Class Discussion

1. Do you use computers? In what applications?
2. What are the advantages and disadvantages of becoming computer literate?
3. Hackers can sometimes get access to secret information. What data bases should hackers never access? What data bases would you like to access? What impact does hacking have on our society?

Collaborative Learning

1. Choosing Hardware and Software
   Purpose: To match a computer user's needs with the hardware and software to meet the needs.
   A. Read the following advertisement:

   > POWER! How much do you need? It depends. Do you have massive data bases to manipulate? Or lengthy reports to write? Do you want bolder, gutsier graphics? Or more sharply displayed spreadsheets?

   B. Assuming the answer is "Yes" to each question, make a shopping list of hardware and software to meet the needs. Use at least ten words from the chapter.
   C. (Optional) Write a list of questions the buyer should ask before purchasing.
   D. Report to the class.
2. Designing the Ideal Computer Classroom
   Purpose: To apply specific computer applications to one's own life.
   A. Using at least ten terms from the chapter, design the hardware, software, and applications of your ideal computerized classroom.
   B. Report to the class.

Ideas for Writing

1. In a paragraph, write about the most useful computer application for your life today.
2. In a page, write about the most interesting computer application you would like to see.
3. Visit your college or university computer lab. At home, write a report on what you found.

More Words for Chapter 12

access: transfer of data to or from a location in the computer

ASCII: American Standard Code for Information Interchange

backup: pertaining to system, device, file, or facility to be used for emergencies

code: to translate data into a symbolic form that can be accepted by a computer; to write a routine

default: a value or option that runs automatically when none is specified

diagnostic: pertaining to the detection and isolation of a malfunction or mistake; written on ROM

directory: a table of references; a directory for a diskette that lists the names of files on it

DOS (disk operating system): software that controls the execution of programs

edit: to enter, modify, or delete data

execute: to run an instruction or a computer program

font: a family or assortment of characters of a particular size and style; pica and elite are fonts

joystick: a lever that can pivot in all directions and is used as a locator device

justify: to align characters in a straight horizontal or vertical line

pixel: a graphics point; a monitor screen is measured in the number of pixels (picture elements)—the more pixels, the higher the resolution and the better the picture

prompt: a question the computer asks when it needs you to supply information

resolution: in computer graphics, a measure of the sharpness of an image

routine: part of a program that may have some general or frequent use

string: a sequence of characters

syntax: the rules that govern the structure of a language

terminal: a device, usually equipped with a keyboard and display, capable of sending and receiving data

update: to modify, usually a master file, with current information

wordwrap a feature of word processing that permits you to continuously enter text without having to press RETURN

Answer Key to Chapter 12

I. WELCOME TO THE INFORMATION AGE

Yes-No Questions

1. Yes; they allow you to start studying.
2. No; only machines can have AI.
3. No; hardware is the machines themselves.
4. Yes; you are writing instructions.
5. Yes; the computer must follow a routine.
6. Yes; that information is secret.
7. No; the program is too large.
8. Yes; it could organize the data better.

Matching

A. (h) B. (f) C. (g) D. (e) E. (c)
F. (b) G. (d) H. (a)

Using Context: The Sales Pitch

programmer, hardware, artificial intelligence, data, software, K, MB, kilobytes, megabytes, computer literate, hacker

II. COMPUTER HARDWARE

Yes-No Questions

9. Yes; it is larger and more powerful.
10. No; ROM is programmed by the factory.

11. No; RAM is the working memory.
12. No; the computer now has no brain.
13. No; no place to hook it or other I/Os.
14. Yes; the monitor is where data appears.
15. No; the keyboard is like a typewriter.
16. No; the mouse improves the speed.
17. Yes; you would lose them if not saved.
18. Yes; that shows the printer is connected.
19. Yes; you need a modem to telecommunicate.

True-False

I. F J. T K. T L. F M. T N. T
O. T P. F Q. F R. F S. T

Using Context: Mother Gets a Computer

computer, I/O devices, CPU, ROM, RAM, disk drive, keyboard, mouse, modem, printer, I/O

III. SOFTWARE AND COMPUTER APPLICATIONS

Yes-No Questions

20. Yes; it makes writing easier.
21. Yes; it allows you to do accounting.

22. Yes; the information can be organized.
23. Yes; it is a computer-generated image.
24. Yes; you would be using telephone lines.
25. Yes; a network means you share things.
26. Yes; hypermedia links texts and images.

Matching

T. (c) U. (d) V. (a) W. (e)
X. (g) Y. (b) Z. (h)

Using Context: The English Department Goes High Tech

word processing, network, hypermedia, data base, graphics, spreadsheet, telecommunications

IV. CHOOSING HARDWARE AND SOFTWARE

Yes-No Questions

27. No; these are all terms for microcomputers.
28. No; the RAM could not hold the program.
29. Yes; it measures clock speed or processing time.
30. No; it will not work.
31. Yes; it requires no hand movement at all.
32. Yes; it gives you options on the screen.
33. Yes; it would present options on the screen.

True-False

a. F b. T c. T d. F e. T f. F
g. T h. T i. F j. F

Using Context: Buying the Perfect Computer

clock speed, compatible, user friendly (menu/window-driven), microcomputer, menu/window-driven, interface

CHAPTER REVIEW

I. Yes-No Questions

1. No; it makes you computer literate.
2. No; clock speed measures processing time.
3. Yes; they need to work together first.
4. No; the CPU is the brain of the computer.
5. Yes; that is the computer name for information.
6. Yes; it would organize the files.
7. Yes; it is used to store files.
8. Yes; it deals with images, not codes.
9. No; they will not work together.
10. No; they are input/output devices.
11. No; we measure it by MHz.
12. Yes; it allows you to input instructions.
13. Yes; it allows them to communicate.
14. Yes; you could work from home.
15. Yes; it displays on the screen.
16. No; a mouse is a useful device.
17. Yes; it keeps the options right on the screen.
18. Yes; you can share data or programs.
19. Yes; hypermedia links text and images.
20. Yes; RAM is the working memory.

II. Using Context: Computers in Your Life

computer literate, computer, data, data-base management, programmer, hacker, microcomputers, MB, K, word processing, spreadsheet, graphics, network, hypermedia, menu-driven (window-driven), clock speed, printer, keyboard, mouse, compatible, interface, telecommunications, modem

ACKNOWLEDGMENTS

From *The Prince and Selected Discourses: Machiavelli* by Daniel Donno, translated by Daniel Donno. Translation copyright © 1966 by Bantam, a division of Bantam Doubleday Dell Publishing Group, Inc. Used by permission of Bantam Books, a division of Bantam Doubleday Dell Publishing Group, Inc.

From "Vocabulary and Success" by Johnson O'Connor. Reprinted by permission of the Johnson O'Connor Research Foundation, Inc.

"Caught in the Web of Bytes" by Cullen Murphy. From *The Atlantic,* February 1989. Used by permission of *The Atlantic.*

From *Authority* by Richard Sennett. Copyright © 1980 by Richard Sennett. Reprinted by permission of Alfred A. Knopf, Inc.

"Anatomical Terminology" by John Boyle. Used by permission of John Boyle.

From "Aspects of Japanese Culture" by Daisetz T. Suzuki. Reprinted from *Zen and Japanese Culture,* Bollingen Series LXIV. Copyright © 1959, renewed 1987 by Princeton University Press. Reprinted by permission of Princeton University Press.

Excerpt from *The New Realities* by Peter Drucker. Copyright © 1989 by Peter F. Drucker. Reprinted by permission of HarperCollins Publishers.

From *Hunger of Memory* by Richard Rodriguez. Copyright © 1982 by Richard Rodriguez. Reprinted by permission of David R. Godine, Publisher.

Excerpts from *Modern Physics* by John E. Williams et al., copyright © 1972 by Saunders College Publishing, a division of Holt, Rinehart and Winston, Inc., reprinted by permission of the publisher.

"Hypermedia: A Brief History and Progress Report" by Richard Paske. Used by permission of Richard Paske.

INDEX

• • • •

The first number lists the page where the word is defined. The bold-faced number is the chapter in which the word is taught. Roots are listed as words.